INDISCRETION

RELIGION AND POSTMODERNISM

A SERIES EDITED BY MARK C. TAYLOR

INDISCRETION

*Finitude and the
Naming of God*

THOMAS A. CARLSON

THE UNIVERSITY OF CHICAGO PRESS
CHICAGO AND LONDON

Thomas A. Carlson is assistant professor in the Department of Religious Studies at the University of California, Santa Barbara. His translation of Jean-Luc Marion's *God Without Being* was published by the University of Chicago Press in 1991.

The University of Chicago Press, Chicago 60637
The University of Chicago Press, Ltd., London
© 1999 by The University of Chicago
All rights reserved. Published 1999
Printed in the United States of America
08 07 06 05 04 03 02 01 00 99   1 2 3 4 5
ISBN: 0-226-09293-3 (cloth)
ISBN: 0-226-09294-1 (paper)

Portions of chapters 4 and 5 and of the Conclusion also appear in "Apophatic Analogy: On the Language of Mystical Unknowing and Being-toward-Death," in *Rhetoric and Religion in Our Time*, edited by Walter Jost and Wendy Olmstead (New Haven: Yale University Press, 1999), and are reprinted with permission.

Library of Congress Cataloging-in-Publication Data

Carlson, Thomas A.
    Indiscretion : finitude and the naming of God / Thomas A. Carlson.
        p.   cm. — (Religion and postmodernism)
    Includes bibliographical references and index.
    ISBN 0-226-09293-3 (alk. paper). — ISBN 0-226-09294-1 (pbk. : alk. paper)
        1. Philosophical theology.   2. God—Knowableness.   3. Heidegger, Martin, 1889–1976.   4. Via negativa (Christian theology)   I. Title.
    II. Series.
    BT55.C37   1998
    211—dc21   98-19277
                                                                           CIP

♾ The paper used in this publication meets the minimum requirements of the American National Standard for Information Sciences—Permanence of Paper for Printed Library Materials, ANSI Z39.48-1992.

In loving memory of

Kerry Alice Batchelder

April 15, 1965–March 3, 1998

And the bold request which goes up the mountains of desire asks this: to enjoy the Beauty not in mirrors and reflections, but face to face. The divine voice granted what was requested in what was denied, showing in a few words an immeasurable depth of thought. The munificence of God assented to the fulfillment of Moses' desire, but did not promise any cessation or satiety of the desire.

God would not have shown himself to his servant if the sight were such as to bring the desire of the beholder to an end, since the true sight of God consists in this, that the one who looks up to God never ceases in that desire. For he says: *You cannot see my face, for man cannot see me and live.*

— GREGORY OF NYSSA

LIFE OF MOSES 2:232–33

CONTENTS

ACKNOWLEDGMENTS

The present work began before I knew it was beginning—with a gift. At the end of our freshman year in Williams College, my new dear friend Kerry Batchelder entered my dorm room unseen, left a book on my desk, and disappeared for the summer. Returning to the room from God-knows-where and finding the surprise of Annie Dillard's *Holy the Firm*, I opened the book to Kerry's inscription: "'So love is greater than knowledge. How could I have forgotten?' Amazing Grace." In the following days, I would discover that the inscription derived from *Holy the Firm*'s meditation on the angelic orders in Dionysius the Areopagite, whose name and thinking then appeared to me for the first time. Four years later, in Paris and Chicago, I began to study Dionysius in earnest, and so he appears now at the center of this work.

Kerry's inscription had another context: she and I had just struggled together, frightened and amazed, through one of the most difficult courses we would ever take: "Introduction to the Study of Religion," taught by Mark C. Taylor. In the subsequent years, Taylor's extraordinary teaching would prove decisive, guiding me as it did into the writings of Hegel and Kierkegaard, Nietzsche and Derrida. Through that teaching came friendship, and Taylor's support over the years has been unparalleled. Also at Williams, I had the great fortune to know the incomparable passion of H. Ganse Little, Jr., who cultivated in me, among other things, the obsession with language and desire that stands at the heart of what follows. Again, the teacher became a friend whose impact exceeds words.

Between Williams and the University of Chicago, I found in Paris an invaluable guide into the thinking of Dionysius—and of Heidegger—in the person of Jean-Luc Marion, whose teaching, writing, and friendship continue to be indispensable for me. My graduate years at Chicago were defined by several remarkable teachers and scholars, among whom I note especially my dissertation advisers, David Tracy and Bernard McGinn, whose rigorous demands were always matched by the heartiest encouragement and most trustworthy guidance.

In my move from the role of student to that of scholar, the support of several other individuals has been essential, and here I note above all John D. Caputo and Merold Westphal, whose generous readings of my work have challenged and improved it. Likewise, the move from student to teacher has been an inspiration and a joy, and for this I am indebted to all of my students and colleagues at the University of California, Santa Barbara. Among those students I recognize especially Patrick Clemens, Suzanne Garner, and Wendy Wiseman, and among those colleagues, my departmental chair, Richard Hecht, whose dedication to his junior faculty is utterly extraordinary. I also acknowledge the generosity of the Regents of the University of California, whose Junior Faculty Fellowship in the summer of 1996 aided much in the completion of this book. The path from completion to publication is itself a challenging one, and in this direction I thank the superb staff of the University of Chicago Press, with whom it has been again a pleasure to work.

Work, of course, invariably distracts one from family and friends, but only family and friends make the work worthwhile. Here I acknowledge especially my grandparents, Antonette and Thomas A. Lee, whose love is exemplary; my parents, Rosanne Lee Carlson and Joseph Carlson II, whose generosity knows no limits; David Carlson, Patty Ruprecht, and Jay Carlson, who have been teaching me from the beginning; Lisa Carlson, Francie Tidey, Pat Tidey, Linda Moore, Tim Grieve, and Quincey Tidey, who appreciate family both in and out of law; my irreplaceable friends Doug Johnson, Todd Alden, Cliff Ruprecht, and Jeff Kosky, who bring their insight and humor to the difficult and joyous times alike; Grégoire Tidey Carlson, who always remains herself; and finally, Ashley Tidey, my best friend day in and day out, who patiently reminds me not to forget that love is indeed greater than knowledge.

But I do forget, and in the very days that the present work was to end, I was reminded of this by the death of my dear old friend Kerry Batchelder, whose love I was graced to know—the friend whose gift began the work, herself a gift to whose loving memory I dedicate it.

May 1998
Bloomington, Indiana

ABBREVIATIONS

The following texts are cited parenthetically within the work. English page numbers precede the page numbers of the original language versions. I have often modified the established English translations.

Jacques Derrida

AP   *Aporias*, trans. Thomas Dutoit (Stanford, Calif.: Stanford University Press, 1993)

GT   *Given Time: I. Counterfeit Money*, trans. Peggy Kamuf (Chicago: University of Chicago Press, 1992)

HAS   "How to Avoid Speaking: Denials," trans. Ken Frieden, in *Derrida and Negative Theology*, ed. Harold Coward and Toby Foshay (Albany: State University of New York Press, 1992)

PS   "Post-Scriptum: Aporias, Ways, and Voices," trans. John P. Leavey, Jr., in *Derrida and Negative Theology*, ed. Harold Coward and Toby Foshay (Albany: State University of New York Press, 1992)

Dionysius the Areopagite (Pseudo-Dionysius)

All references to the Dionysian corpus will be given parenthetically according to the pagination of the J. P. Migne edition (*Patrologiae cursus completus. Series graeca*, vol. 3), but all citations are taken from the new critical edition edited by Beate Regina Suchla, Günter Heil, and Adolf Martin Ritter, *Corpus Dionysiacum*, vols. 1 and 2 (vols. 33 and 36 of *Patristische Texte und Studien*, ed. by K. Aland and E. Mühlenberg, Berlin: Walter de Gruyter, 1990, 1991). For English translations, I rely on the edition of *The Complete Works* (New York: Paulist Press, 1987) by Colm Luibheid and Paul Rorem.

CH   *Celestial Hierarchy*

DN   *Divine Names*

EH   *Ecclesiastical Hierarchy*

MT   *Mystical Theology*

G. W. F. Hegel

LPR   *Lectures on the Philosophy of Religion*, One-Volume Edition: *The Lectures of 1827*, ed. Peter Hodgson, trans. R. F. Brown, P. C. Hodgson, and J. M. Stewart, with the assistance of H. S. Harris (Berkeley: University of California Press, 1988); *Vorlesungen über die Philosophie der Religion*, ed. Walter Jaeschke, in *Vorlesungen: Ausgewählte Nachschriften und Manuskripte*, vols. 3–5 (Hamburg: Felix Meiner Verlag, 1983, 1984, 1985)

PhG   *Phenomenology of Spirit*, trans. A. V. Miller (Oxford: Oxford University Press, 1977), *Phänomenologie des Geistes*, ed. Wolfgang Bonsiepen and Reinhard Heede, in *Gesammelte Werke*, vol. 9 (Hamburg: Felix Meiner Verlag, 1980)

SL   *Hegel's Science of Logic*, trans. W. H. Johnston and L. G. Struthers, vol. 2 (London: George Allen and Unwin, 1966); *Wissenschaft der Logik*, Zweiter Band, Die Subjektive Logik, ed. Friedrich Hogemann and Walter Jaeschke, in *Gesammelte Werke*, vol. 12 (Hamburg: Felix Meiner Verlag, 1981)

Martin Heidegger

SZ   *Being and Time*, trans. John Macquarrie and Edward Robinson (Oxford: Basil Blackwell, 1962); *Sein und Zeit*, 16th edition (Tübingen: Max Niemeyer, 1986). German page numbers indicated parenthetically are preceded by H.

HCE   *Hegel's Concept of Experience* (New York: Harper and Row, 1970); "Hegels Begriff der Erfahrung," in *Holzwege* (Frankfurt am Main: Vittorio Klostermann, 1950)

HPS   *Hegel's Phenomenology of Spirit*, trans. Parvis Emad and Kenneth Maly (Bloomington: Indiana University Press, 1988); *Hegels Phänomenologie des Geistes*, in the *Gesamtausgabe*, vol. 32 (Frankfurt am Main: Vittorio Klostermann, 1980)

ID   "The Onto-theological Constitution of Metaphysics," in *Identity and Difference*, trans. Joan Stambaugh (New York: Harper and Row, 1969); *Identität und Differenz* (Pfullingen: Günther Neske, 1957)

Jean-Luc Marion

ED   *Etant donné: Essai d'une phénoménologie de la donation* (Paris: Presses Universitaires de France, 1997) [translations my own]

GWB   *God without Being*, trans. Thomas A. Carlson (Chicago: University of Chicago Press, 1991)

IED   *L'Idole et la distance* (Paris: Grasset, 1977) [translations my own]

INT   "L'Interloqué," in *Who Comes after the Subject?* ed. Eduardo Cadava, Peter Connor, and Jean-Luc Nancy (New York: Routledge, 1991)

MP   "Metaphysics and Phenomenology: A Relief for Theology," trans. Thomas A. Carlson, *Critical Inquiry*, vol. 20, no. 4, Summer 1994

RG   *Reduction and Givenness: Investigations of Husserl, Heidegger, and Phenome-*

nology, trans. Thomas A. Carlson (Evanston, Ill.: Northwestern University Press, 1998)

RMM *Revue de Métaphysique et de Morale*, 96/12, Janvier–Mars 1991 [translations my own]

SP "The Saturated Phenomenon," trans. Thomas A. Carlson, *Philosophy Today*, Spring 1996.

INDISCRETION

INTRODUCTION:

Finitude and the Naming of God

(the one who sees God dies: for "dying" is a
manner of seeing the invisible, a manner of saying
the unsayable—the indiscretion wherein God,
become somehow and necessarily a god without
truth, would give himself over to passivity)
— MAURICE BLANCHOT

To think through the death of God and, correlatively, the critique of modern subjectivity means, among other things, to confront a dynamic field of crises and questions that touch fundamentally on the functions of language and representation in the articulation of God and self. The difficulty, necessity, and fruitfulness of such confrontation are known acutely and in multiple ways by those many from the fields of religion and philosophy, critical and psychoanalytic theory, literary and cultural studies, who find themselves somehow in or near a "post-" age whose blurred and shifting borders are marked, however ambiguously, by a disappearance of God and by a dissolution of the human subject. After the death, or the deaths, of God in the modern mind, how do our time and culture unavoidably know a lack or absence of the divine (granting the genitive here all its ambiguity), and how might such lack or absence be articulated or imagined? After suffering its deepest critique, how does the human subject who had been rendered (or at least imagined) self-transparent and autonomous by the modern light of reason prove to be, in various ways, irreducibly passive and opaque to itself, and how might such passivity and opacity now shape or define the meaning of existence? In turn: how might the seeming absence and unknowability of God, however one figures them, be tied today to the seemingly incurable wounds of a once enlightened and autonomous subject?

This questioning of language and representation in the "post-" age arises precisely with their crisis: in what sense, one now asks, do the slips or failures of language and representation, their silences and blind spots, prove in fact internal and essential to their very operation? As provoked specifically by the death of God (from Hegel and Nietzsche to Altizer and Taylor) and by the critique of subjectivity (from Kierkegaard and Heidegger to Levinas and Derrida), such a questioning of language and representation can seem—and in many important ways is—relatively new; it is a questioning that defines—and is defined by—the modern and postmodern worlds. At the same time, however, as indicated by a significant body of scholarship that has been growing now for three decades (especially the last), the "negative" operations of language and representation regarding both God and the human subject, or the functioning of such language and representation only in and through their silences and failures, are in fact fundamental to the decidedly premodern

3

traditions of "apophatic" and "mystical" theology and spiritual practice. The present work maintains that these two spheres of questioning, at once so close and so distant, these premodern and postmodern reflections on language and its interstices, can and should be read in light of one another. In doing so, the work argues that the contemporary fascination with language and representation from the medieval traditions of apophatic and mystical theology is best understood in relation to the question of human finitude as approached, today, following the death of God and the critique of the modern subject.

Indeed, the forms of language and representation that define the classic traditions of "negative" or apophatic theology—and its twin, mystical theology—have recently attracted sustained and creative inquiry especially among scholars who are concerned with the finitude of the human subject and with the marks or conditions of such finitude— above all, the subject's insurmountable "thrownness" into language, its radically temporal dynamic, and its subjection to desire. Among post-Heideggerian thinkers in particular, the fascination with textual and discursive traditions deriving from the apophatic and mystical theology of Pseudo-Dionysius (ca. 500) almost always involves also a fascination with the finite, temporal, and desiring subject of language—to the point that one might suspect contemporary interest in negative theology to constitute at bottom a fascination with negative anthropology. Indeed, in light of the insistent conjunction between reflection on negative theological language and reflection on the finitude of human existence, one might rightly ask: do these contemporary approaches to the apophatic and mystical traditions simply mistake for an ever desired but unknowable God a desiring human subject that remains opaque to itself? Do they constitute a misguided effort to baptize the abysses of a fragmented but purely human, linguistic existence with the name of apophatic theology's mystically unknowable and thus unnameable God?[1] I argue here that this question can be answered—or, better, suspended and kept open—insofar as one can signal a point at which the negative logic of Being-toward-God within classic apophatic and mystical forms of language and representation reveals a strikingly forceful analogy to the negative logic of Being-toward-death in contemporary (Heideggerian and post-Heideggerian) discourse on human finitude. In and through the development of this "apophatic analogy," the work moves toward a point

---

1. As Jean-Luc Nancy suggests in *Des lieux divins* (Mauvezin: Trans-Europ-Repress, 1987), p. 5.

of "indiscretion" at which the negativity of the divine and of the human, of the theological and of the thanatological, can (and do) prove to be neither distinct nor identical—but bound in the radical indeterminacy that haunts the experience of all language and representation regarding an ineffable God and/or an impossible death.

In working toward that point of indiscretion, the book privileges the most recent and most forceful treatments of apophatic and mystical theology among post-Heideggerians: those of Jacques Derrida and Jean-Luc Marion. This focus, however, should not prevent us from recognizing the long-standing and multilayered connections between Heideggerian thought and inquiry into the apophatic and mystical traditions.

As early as 1967, in a theological and philosophical study on the "absence and unknowability of God" according to Dionysius the Areopagite (the Pseudo-Dionysius) and Martin Heidegger, Christos Yannaras argues that, on a certain reading, the Heideggerian analysis of European nihilism and its "death of God" actually shows this "internal crisis" of metaphysics to constitute a form of theological apophaticism. According to such a reading, a version of which returns in Jean-Luc Marion, the destruction of all metaphysical conceptions of God, or all "rational idols," reaches its culmination in Nietzsche and opens anew the possibility of thinking and expressing the inconceivable and ineffable transcendence of God as previously developed within theological traditions reaching back to Pseudo-Dionysius in the early sixth century.[2] The death of God, on this reading, would effect the disappearance of all those rational screens that block a true vision of the invisible, a true language of the ineffable, a true thought of the inconceivable.

Other early, primarily philosophical, studies of mysticism that are influenced significantly by Heideggerian perspectives include those by Reiner Schürmann and John D. Caputo, who will focus less on the foundational figure of Dionysius and more on later thinkers, such as Thomas Aquinas and Meister Eckhart, who nevertheless maintain a Dionysian lineage. In his *Meister Eckhart: Mystic and Philosopher* (French version, 1972; English version, 1978), Schürmann connects Heidegger's existen-

2. Originally written in Greek, Yannaras's book appeared in 1971, in a French translation by Jacques Touraille, as *De l'absence et de l'inconnaissance de Dieu d'après les écrits aréopagitiques et Martin Heidegger* (Paris: Éditions du Cerf, 1971).

tial understanding of *Gelassenheit*, or "releasement," to the practice of *gelâzenheit* in Meister Eckhart's mysticism. Similarly, in his attempts to relate Heideggerian philosophy and classic theological traditions, Caputo argues both that Heideggerian philosophy itself has a "mystical element" issuing from the influence of figures like Eckhart (in *The Mystical Element in Heidegger's Thought*, 1978) and that the *intellectus* central to the metaphysics of Aquinas himself proves in fact to be a religious and mystical form of thinking that would *not* fall under the Heideggerian critique of metaphysics (in *Heidegger and Aquinas*, 1982).[3]

In more recent, historically and psychoanalytically inclined approaches to the operations of negativity in mystical thought and spirituality, the influence of Heideggerian perspectives is mediated in crucial ways by Michel Foucault and Jacques Lacan. Here, the extraordinary work of Michel de Certeau stands out. Focusing on post-Reformation transformations in mystical spirituality (from Teresa of Avila through Johannes Scheffler), de Certeau's *Mystic Fable* (French, 1982; English, 1992)[4] argues, among other things, that the disintegration of the medieval world and the birth of modernity give rise to historically new forms of spirituality in which a deep obscurity or "absence" of God is experienced through mystical movements of mourning and desire. In other, related work, Foucault's analyses of the "death of man" have been interpreted as a contemporary form of "negative theology,"[5] and Lacan's psychoanalytic thought has been read in light of the Christian mystical traditions.[6]

3. Reiner Schürmann, *Meister Eckhart: Mystic and Philosopher* (Bloomington: Indiana University Press, 1978); John Caputo, *The Mystical Element in Heidegger's Thought* (Athens: Ohio University Press, 1978), and *Heidegger and Aquinas* (New York: Fordham University Press, 1982).

4. Michel de Certeau, *La Fable mystique, I: XVIe–XVIIe siècle* (Paris: Gallimard, 1982); *The Mystic Fable*, vol. 1: *The Sixteenth and Seventeenth Centuries*, trans. Michael B. Smith (Chicago: University of Chicago Press, 1992).

5. On Foucault and negative theology, see James Bernauer, "The Prisons of Man: An Introduction to Foucault's Negative Theology," *International Philosophical Quarterly*, vol. 27, no. 4 (December 1987): 365–80.

6. On the "apophatic" rhetoric of Lacan (and its relation to the "prophetic" rhetoric of Freud), see David Tracy's essay, "Mystics, Prophets, Rhetorics: Religion and Psychoanalysis," in Françoise Meltzer, ed., *The Trial(s) of Psychoanalysis* (Chicago: University of Chicago Press, 1988). Here I agree in particular with Tracy's assertion that a serious consideration of the apophatic carries one beyond the simple (or simplistic) alternative between "theism" and "atheism" (see esp. pp. 271–72). On Lacan and the questions of language and desire in theology, see Edith Wyschogrod, David Crownfield, and Carl A. Raschke, eds., *Lacan and Theological Discourse* (Albany: State University of New York, 1989).

The Heideggerian or post-Heideggerian slant of the contemporary interest in apophatic and mystical theology becomes nowhere more apparent than in the numerous attempts to relate such theology to Jacques Derrida and deconstruction. Among such attempts, two tendencies predominate. On the one hand, writers suggest that Derridean thought as such constitutes a form of negative theology.[7] Derrida himself was one of the first to raise this suggestion—in order immediately to deny or denegate it. Already in 1968, in his seminal essay "Différance," Derrida writes that "the detours, locutions, and syntax in which I will often have to take recourse will resemble those of negative theology, occasionally even to the point of being indistinguishable from negative theology. [. . .] And yet those aspects of *différance* which are thereby delineated are not theological, not even in the order of the most negative of negative theologies."[8] As I will argue below, it remains an open question—and especially for Derrida himself—whether this kind of denial of negative theology might not itself belong (without belonging) to negative theology.[9] In his superb recent study of Derrida, John Caputo has exploited precisely this openness of the question in order to argue not only that Derridean thought leaves open the possibility (or impossibility) of negative theology but also that it allows one to push the unsettling force of apophatic logic and language beyond strictly theological spheres—for example, into the ethical and political.[10] On the other hand, a writer such as

7. For example, in an article entitled "Open Secrets: Derrida and Negative Theology" (in Robert P. Scharlemann, ed., *Negation and Theology* [Charlottesville: University of Virginia Press, 1992]), David Klemm suggests that deconstruction would represent a theological "negative way" to which hermeneutics would correspond as a "positive way." Passing *between* this negative and positive way, the naming of God would constitute a language—much like Dionysius's third, mystical mode of theology—of "overturning": "'God' would name the explicit overturning at the limit of both the negative and the affirmative ways. [. . .] The unity of the two senses of 'God' would manifest the movement of thinking that aspires to God but ever fails to reach God" (p. 22).

8. Jacques Derrida, "Différance," in *Margins of Philosophy*, trans. Alan Bass (Chicago: University of Chicago Press, 1982), p. 6. "Différance" was first delivered as a talk on January 27, 1968, and was published both in *Bulletin de la société française*, vol. 62 (1968) and in *Théorie d'ensemble*, coll. Tel Quel (Paris: Editions du Seuil, 1968).

9. Thus, the straightforward manner in which someone like Brian Ingraffia accepts this assertion of disjunction between deconstruction and negative theology seems to me misguided. On this, see Ingraffia's treatment of Derrida in Brian Ingraffia, *Postmodern Theory and Biblical Theology* (Cambridge: Cambridge University Press, 1995).

10. John Caputo, *The Prayers and Tears of Jacques Derrida: Religion without Religion* (Bloomington: Indiana University Press, 1997). My own attempt to relate negative theology and negative anthropology would bear strong affinities with Caputo's very powerful and far-reaching approach to the apophatic.

the theorist and poet Kevin Hart suggests not simply that deconstruction could amount to, or leave open, a negative theology, but rather that the traditions of apophatic theology deriving from Pseudo-Dionysius themselves already operate "deconstructively."[11] In a rich and nuanced reading of apophaticism in both historical and contemporary terms, Hart argues that a "general" (as opposed to "restricted") economy of negative theology deconstructs the simple alternative in which negative theology would merely reverse affirmative theology and thus remain bound to its logic.[12] This reading of a double negativity in the Dionysian context offers a powerful corrective to the common misreading of negative theology according to a simple binary logic.

Now, in my own approach here to contemporary inquiry concerning classic theological forms of negative thought and language, I aim not so much to identify those forms with or within any specific contemporary figure such as Lacan, Foucault, or Derrida, but more to situate them with respect to the horizon shared by most all of the relevant contemporary theorists: the horizon of Heideggerian thought itself.[13]

Thus, the book takes its orientation from the most recent debate among post-Heideggerian philosophers and theologians concerning the relation between, on the one hand, metaphysics as Heidegger interprets it (namely, as "onto-theological") and, on the other hand, the traditions of apophatic and mystical theology reaching back, in the Christian traditions, to the early sixth-century writer Pseudo-Dionysius.

From the perspective I develop, the central question of that debate is fairly simple: do certain figures from the (largely medieval) traditions of apophatic and mystical theology stand in continuity or in disjunction with what Heidegger identifies as the onto-theological character of

11. See Kevin Hart, *The Trespass of the Sign* (Cambridge: Cambridge University Press, 1989).

12. Hart's distinction here goes back to Derrida's important essay on Bataille and Hegel, "From Restricted to General Economy: A Hegelianism without Reserve," in *Writing and Difference*, trans. Alan Bass (Chicago: University of Chicago Press, 1978). See esp. pp. 194–206 in Hart, *Trespass of the Sign*.

13. For another recent study that attempts to situate the medieval mystical traditions (specifically, Bonaventure, Eckhart, Tauler, and Ruusbroec) in relation to Heidegger, see Sonya Sikka, *Forms of Transcendence: Heidegger and Medieval Mystical Theology* (Albany: State University of New York Press, 1997).

Western thought? Or, more specifically, does the operation within apophatic and mystical theology of a "Good beyond Being" exceed or undo the primacy accorded in metaphysics to the role of "Being"?

The significance of this question, or what is at stake in any response to it, remains less clear. The book seeks, then, to elucidate what might be at issue in deciding on the continuity and/or discontinuity between the thought of "the Good" in apophatic and mystical theologies, on the one hand, and the thought of Being in onto-theology as defined by Heidegger, on the other.

Through such an elucidation, I show that the decision on whether or not apophatic or mystical theology eludes onto-theology concerns the possibility or impossibility of a thought and language of "pure gift," "absolute giving," or "unconditional givenness."[14] Such a giving or givenness might be understood in several senses. It might concern the kinds of giving that occur (or not) between human persons (an ethical giving); it might concern the kinds of giving that occur (or not) between a God and human being (a theological giving); or, finally, it might concern the sheer givenness of all phenomena—the world as such, without any specifiable "giver" (phenomenological givenness). While my analyses here concentrate on theological and phenomenological understandings of gift and giving, they also have important implications for ethical thought insofar as such a concentration leads me to the question of negative anthropology.

The two figures on whom I focus from the contemporary debate, Jacques Derrida and Jean-Luc Marion, agree that onto-theology fails to think "the gift," "giving," or "givenness" absolutely or unconditionally. They disagree, however, concerning the success of negative theology in thinking and expressing such a gift and, thus, in eluding the bounds of onto-theology. Marion asserts a clear break between onto-theology (a thought primarily of Being) and negative theology (a thought of the absolutely generous "Good beyond Being"), whereas Derrida suspects a deeper continuity between the Being of onto-theology and the "hyperessential" (ὑπερούσιος) God of negative theology.

In order to address this tension between the positions of Derrida and

14. The general question of "the gift" has been crucial especially to twentieth-century French thought, from Marcel Mauss's sociological analyses in *The Gift*, through George Bataille's writings on sacrifice and expenditure, to the analyses of exchange in Claude Lévi-Strauss's structural anthropology, and on into the work of contemporary philosophers such as Emmanuel Levinas, Jacques Derrida, and Jean-Luc Marion.

Marion, I seek to establish indispensable background to those positions within Heidegger's critique of onto-theology and within the Dionysian foundation of negative theology. The central issue from Dionysius here proves to be the generous, causal Good which, because beyond Being, would remain ineffable and inconceivable. The central issue in Heidegger's critique, I argue, is that of finitude. Thus, within the post-Heideggerian context, very traditional debates over the naming of God (either according to the primacy of Being or according to the primacy of Goodness, Charity, Love, etc.)[15] are brought to bear on modern and contemporary interpretations of subjectivity and its finitude. These contemporary considerations of negative theology, then, must be seen in light of the Heideggerian critique of metaphysics generally (philosophy from Plato through Nietzsche) and, more specifically and more importantly, of modern metaphysics (primarily, Descartes to Hegel) and its interpretation of Being in terms of subjectivity. The modern attempt to establish a thoroughly self-grounding subject—an attempt to establish the rational and ethical autonomy of the ego (e.g., in Descartes, Kant) and even, eventually, the absolute freedom of an absolute subject (Hegel)—is opposed by the Heideggerian insistence on the radical finitude of Being-in-the-world.

In light of this background, the book works to establish a remarkable analogy between, on the one hand, the manner in which the thought of *goodness* or gift from negative theology might resist onto-theology, especially in its modern form, and, on the other hand, the manner in which the Heideggerian conception of *finitude* resists such onto-

15. Within such traditional debates, the naming of God according to Being finds its primary biblical source in Exodus 3:14 (I AM) and its strongest traditional expression in Thomas Aquinas (*Summa Theologica*, I, q.13). The naming of God according to Love finds a primary biblical source in 1 John 4:8 (God is *agape*), and a foundational formulation in Pseudo-Dionysius. These two tendencies are expressed together in Bonaventure's *Itinerarium mentis in Deum* (in *Bonaventure*, trans. Ewert Cousins, New York: Paulist Press, 1978)—which, in christocentric terms, finally sides with Dionysius:

> By these cherubim we understand the two modes or stages of contemplating the invisible and eternal things of God: one is concerned with the essential attributes of God and the other with those proper to the persons. The first method fixes the gaze primarily and principally on Being itself, saying that God's primary name is *He who is*. The second method fixes the gaze on the Good itself, saying that this is God's primary name. [. . .] Therefore, Christ our teacher, wishing to raise to evangelical perfection the youth who had observed the Law, attributed to God principally and exclusively the name of goodness. For he says: *No one is good but God alone*. Damascene, therefore, following Moses, says that *He who is* is God's primary name; Dionysius, following Christ, says that the Good is God's primary name.

theological thinking. It is with a view toward defining and developing such an analogy that I seek to clarify and elaborate the significance of the contemporary debate. In moving toward that goal, I focus on 1) the role of finitude within Heidegger's critique of the metaphysical, and especially modern, conception of Being in terms of subjectivity; 2) the Dionysian interpretation of gift as causal Goodness, which constitutes an ineffable and inconceivable "Good beyond Being"; and finally, 3) the limits and possibilities for a contemporary reading of Dionysian conceptions of the Good carried out in light of a post-Heideggerian understanding of finitude—and vice versa.

Of course, these specialized theological and philosophical questions arise within a broader horizon of social, cultural, and intellectual developments. It is no mistake that the relation between negative theology and metaphysics becomes a pressing question primarily for those who find themselves at, or in the wake of, the "end" of metaphysics. Likewise, contemporary interest in the negative forms of thought and language that are found in traditional religious contexts must be seen, it seems to me, against the background of the complex "negative" phenomena (closely related to the "end" of metaphysics) such as secularization, nihilism, and the death of God.

Thus, in the first chapter, I situate the debate over negative theology and metaphysics with respect to these more general concerns and developments. I try to locate, in particular, the philosophical and theological underpinnings of the "death of God" in G. W. F. Hegel. Hegel here strikes me as decisive in at least two ways. First, he actually offers us the first thoroughly developed theological and philosophical expression of the "death of God,"[16] and, second, that "death of God" itself is intimately related to Hegel's status as the thinker who brings metaphysics to "completion." By locating the death of God in the figure who "completes" metaphysics, I am able to situate the contemporary discussion of apophatic theologies not only with respect to the general critique of meta-

---

16. The formulation of a "death of God" occurs prior to Hegel in the famous Lutheran hymn, "O Traurigkeit, O Herzeleid" (1641) by Johannes Rist: "O grosse Not, Gott selbst liegt tot. Am Kreuz ist er gestorben; hat dadurch das Himmelreich uns aus Lieb' erworben" (for references and discussion, see David Kolb, ed., *New Perspectives on Hegel's Philosophy of Religion* [Albany: State University of New York Press, 1992], pp. 57 and 97). Hegel, however, remains the first to develop this formulation in systematic theological and philosophical form—and it will be Hegel's death of God (or a very Hegelian reading of Nietzsche's) that grounds the work of the most powerful modern theologian of the death of God, Thomas J. J. Altizer.

physics, but also more specifically with respect to the death of God.[17] Thus, having established the centrality of the "death of God" in Hegel's philosophy, I turn to the question of finitude in Heidegger's engagement with Hegel.

In addressing that question, I attempt to explicate the basic elements in Heidegger's reading of Hegel according to which the Hegelian conception of subjectivity in terms of infinite Being (or of Being in terms of absolute subjectivity) would mark the fullest positive expression, or the "completion," of modern metaphysics as onto-theology. By developing an understanding of modern onto-theology as it appears in its culminating figure, Hegel, I seek insight into what might be at stake in resisting or surpassing it. Within his interpretation of Hegelian philosophy as onto-theology, Heidegger stresses that metaphysics, generally, and Hegel's embodiment of it, specifically, fail to articulate the finitude of existence in a sufficiently fundamental manner. To "overcome" metaphysics, then, one would need to articulate a finitude that metaphysics ignores.

With the goal of explaining the significance of such an ignorance, I examine Heidegger's analyses concerning the Hegelian conception of the temporal experience of consciousness (chap. 2) and a Heideggerian

---

17. At this level, the task would be to determine the relation between the "absence and unknowability" of God within the classic theological traditions and the "absence and unknowability" of God ensuing from the "death of God." Here one finds at least two differing theological positions. On the one hand, a figure like Marion (or Yannaras before him) will argue that the "death of God" amounts only to a destruction, within the history of philosophy, of concepts that were never anything other than "idols." On this reading, the death of "God" (an idol) leaves the true God untouched and frees thought to approach that God more truly. On the other hand, a figure like Thomas J. J. Altizer will insist that the "death of God" has a significance reaching beyond the limits of philosophy into the spheres of modern culture and society. For Altizer, one would need to distinguish between classic forms of divine unknowability and ineffability, on the one hand, and, on the other, the modern poverty—or even sheer absence—of discourse and thinking on God. "Obviously," Altizer writes, "there is an overwhelming and uncrossable distance between an unknowability which is a mark or sign of the transcendence of God and an unknowability which is simply and only unknowability" (*Total Presence* [New York: Seabury Press, 1980], p. 26). For Altizer, the contemporary ignorance of God must be distinguished fundamentally from the ignorance of God to which the traditions of mystical unknowing or *agnosia* aspire. "We can sense the truth of this judgment," Altizer suggests, "by noting the distinction between a negative attribute of God, or a negative naming of God, and the absence of all naming whatsoever" (*Total Presence*, p. 26).

critique of the philosophical language that would articulate the truth of such experience (chap. 3). Temporality and language, then, provide two key structuring categories for the overall argument: the Hegelian conception of time's sublation through the realization of absolute self-consciousness (addressed in chap. 2) will be answered (in chap. 4) by Heidegger's insistence on Dasein's radical finitude and the insurmountability of time; the Hegelian language that would fully name the absolute and so exorcise the ineffable (as discussed in chap. 3) will be contrasted (in chap. 5) by the Dionysian insistence on God's ineffability.

Now, in his critique of Hegel, Heidegger argues that the Hegelian interpretation of consciousness and language is based in a conception of time that annuls, by seeking to overcome, the true finitude of temporal existence. In conjunction with this insufficient conception of temporality, Heidegger notes, the Being of consciousness and its articulation in language prove in Hegel to be characterized essentially by their closed *circularity* (the insistence of which proves central to many of the most seminal twentieth-century readings of Hegelian philosophy—from Alexandre Kojève to Jacques Derrida).[18] For Hegel, the true Being of consciousness, that is, infinite Being, consists in the return of consciousness to itself in and through every "other" of consciousness. By finding itself in any otherness, or in its own self-difference, consciousness returns fully to itself as infinite self-consciousness. This circular return of thought to itself occurs in and through the spiritual, historical process that Hegel understands to constitute the temporal experience of consciousness. As Heidegger stresses, and as Hegel himself affirms, such a return finally annuls time, for time as such in the Hegelian framework consists in the existence of consciousness in a self-differentiated form, the persistence of an otherness or difference in which consciousness has not *yet* found itself.

This annulment of time through the experience of consciousness, I go on to argue, is reflected—or enacted—in the Hegelian conception of representation and language: the initial opacity to consciousness of

18. On Kojève's reading, see his *Introduction to the Reading of Hegel: Lectures on the Phenomenology of Spirit*, trans. James H. Nichols Jr. and ed. Allan Bloom (Ithaca, New York: Cornell University Press, 1969), and the major chapter left out from the English version of the book but published separately, "The Idea of Death in the Philosophy of Hegel," trans. Joseph J. Carpino, *Interpretation* 3 (1973): 114–56. On Derrida's reading, see esp. his *Glas*, trans. John P. Leavey Jr. and Richard Rand (Lincoln: University of Nebraska Press, 1986).

representational and linguistic forms must finally be elucidated by consciousness in such a way that consciousness finds its own rationality in and through that very opacity. Within this Hegelian perspective, the subject of experience, the subject of consciousness and language, proves to be a subject who, in its most essential Being, returns to itself in self-consciousness and thereby "annuls" time. Heidegger will resist this closed, self-referential circularity of Being operative in Hegelian consciousness and language with his own articulation of finitude. A more fundamental finitude, Heidegger insists, resists or undoes the circular return of the conscious, speaking subject to itself.

By elaborating these key issues from Heidegger's encounter with Hegel, the book establishes indispensable groundwork for an attempt to address contemporary debate concerning the "gift," since, for Derrida most notably, the closed figure of the circle (especially as in the circular Being of Hegelian consciousness and language) returns over and again to establish an "economy" that would transform giving (which, if absolute, would remain "without return") into exchange—into an economic give-and-take that would threaten to annul the gift as gift. In this way, circularity would pose the most serious threat to any thought or language of absolute giving.

From the perspective developed here, Hegel would have conceived such circularity most rigorously (in the infinite Being of the subject), and Heidegger would have defined its onto-theological character (indicated especially in the misunderstanding of fundamental finitude). Thus, I suggest, one might seek to resist or surpass onto-theological thinking via either 1) a thought of radical finitude, which would remain irreducible to the circularity of infinite self-consciousness (Heidegger), or 2) some thought of gift or giving that would, similarly, remain irreducible to the circular economy of Being, language, and consciousness (Derrida, Marion). Just as Heidegger sets radical finitude in opposition to the circular Being of language and consciousness (as seen in Hegel), so Derrida (or Marion) posits an antagonism between the unconditional gift and the circular economy.

The question here becomes the following: if a Heideggerian or post-Heideggerian thought of finitude resists the essentially circular or economic character of metaphysics' consummate thinking (Hegel), what might be the relation of such finitude to an unconditional gift or giving that would likewise resist economic thought and language? It is through this specific question that I approach the contemporary debate over the relation between the thought and language of Goodness in Dionysian theology and the thought and language of Being within the metaphysics whose essential circularity Heidegger defines.

Before entering into my own analysis of the thought and language of giving in Dionysian theology (chap. 5), I seek in chapter 4 to explicate the foundations for Heidegger's articulation of finite existence. While in his works dedicated to Hegel, Heidegger understands finitude primarily in terms of "ontological difference," I suggest that such an understanding of finitude, which informs Heidegger's ongoing engagement with Hegel (from the 1930s through at least 1968), must be seen also in relation to the earlier analysis of Dasein's finitude as set forth in *Being and Time* (1927). Within Heidegger's analysis of existence, or Dasein, as "Being-in-the-world," I stress the essentially ecstatic and potential character of that being's temporal structure: in its defining ex-istence, Dasein always "stands" (*sistit*) "out" (*ex-*) beyond itself in the projection of its possibility. By addressing this ec-static, potential character of Dasein's existence, I seek, more specifically, to explicate the decisive role played by "Being-toward-death" (*Sein zum Tode*) within the structure and movement of Dasein's possibility. For Heidegger, death represents Dasein's "ownmost possibility," but as such it gives Dasein "nothing to be 'actualized,' nothing which Dasein, as actual, could itself *be*" (SZ 307; H 262). In this sense, death constitutes the possibility of an absolute impossibility, a possibility that can never pass into actuality for the being whose possibility it nevertheless is.[19] Thrown into an existence that it cannot itself ground, Dasein finds itself fundamentally oriented toward a possibility (death) that it cannot realize. My explication of the paradoxical logic of this "possibility of impossibility" sets the ground for the analogy I establish between Dasein's Being-toward-death in Heideggerian thought and the created soul's naming of the unnameable in a Dionysian framework.

As in Heidegger, where the being of Dasein is articulated ecstatically between a past that it cannot ground and a future that it cannot realize, so in Dionysius, I argue, the being of the soul is essentially ecstatic.

19. In stressing this aspect of Heidegger's thought, I should call to mind also the famous remark of Wittgenstein: "Death is not an event in life: we do not live to experience death. If we take eternity to mean not infinite temporal duration but timelessness, then eternal life belongs to those who live in the present. Our life has no end in just the way in which our visual field has no limits" (*Tractatus Logico-Philosophicus*, trans. D. F. Pears and B. F. McGuinness [London: Routledge and Kegan Paul, 1961], 6.4311). For Heidegger too, death is not "an event in life"; however, as we will see, Dasein cannot simply live "in the present," for its very Being is articulated in and through the *three* equiprimordial ecstases of temporality.

Called into being from nothing or nonexistence by a God who, as cause (αἰτία), remains irreducibly transcendent, the soul exists ecstatically between that nonbeing from which it is called and that cause for whom it endlessly yearns. Thus, having drawn out the structure and significance of finite "Being-toward-death" in Heidegger, I go on in chapter 5 to examine the paradoxical logic according to which Dionysian theology names and thinks this God who remains by definition ineffable and inconceivable.

Dionysius develops this paradoxical logic within the complex interplay of affirmative thought and language (kataphatic theology) and negative thought and language, which take two forms: apophatic and mystical theology (the mystical being a redoubling of the apophatic). These fully interdependent modes of theology articulate the relation of the created soul to its God, and within that relation, the soul would tend, through a movement of double negation, to transcend itself and its world toward God. That is, by negating affirmative statements and thoughts about God, which are based analogically on a knowledge of created beings, and by negating in turn the security of its own negations, the soul ecstatically transcends all beings. This ecstatic function of negation answers to the radical self-giving of a God who remains both "all in all" (as creative cause) and finally "nothing in anything" (as *transcendent* cause). The doubly negative thought and language of Dionysius, we will see, answer to the radical donation of a God who, as self-giving cause of all beings, transcends all beings caused, a God *beyond* being who, as cause of all things, "is" no thing among things. While Heidegger understands the ecstatic structure of finite existence in terms of its "Being-toward" a death that cannot be realized or made manifest, Dionysius understands the ecstatic movement of the created soul in terms of its movement toward a God who cannot be known or named—a God who is, strictly speaking, no-thing and thus "without truth" (as MT 1048A indicates: οὔτε ἀλήθεια ἐστιν). In the penultimate and concluding chapters, I draw out the analogy between such a nullity of death and such a nullity of God—in their irreducibility to the truth of presence.

In my use of analogy here, I stress that the analogy is one of relation, not attribution: the relation of Dasein to its impossible death in Heidegger is likened to the relation of the created soul to its unnameable God in Dionysius. Like Caputo's earlier use of analogy in a similar context, where he compares the relation between human thought and Being in Heidegger to the relation between the soul and God in Eckhart, the analogy I develop "suggests a similarity of structures, not of content. It is not *what* is related but the *how* which is comparable."[20] My own use of analogy does differ from Caputo's, however, in one important respect: while Caputo will clearly indicate that "*what* is related in each case is quite different" (i.e., Being is not "really" God, or vice versa), I find myself prohibited, by the very terms of the analogy, not only from identifying those terms *but also* from distinguishing them—for the terms themselves cannot be given determinate, identifiable content; indeed, lacking the determinacy or identity of any "what," the terms indicate that which would remain, in and of itself, unknown and unknowable. The similarity of relation can be established, on my view, precisely because the final term in each relation can be neither identified with nor distinguished from the final term in the other. Thus, through the analogy I attempt to establish, I do not intend to imply that the Dionysian God is equivalent to Heideggerian death (or vice versa). Nor, however, can I wholly separate that God from that death—and for the same reasons that prohibit an identification: in both cases the term "in itself" remains, strictly speaking, indeterminate, and thus beyond the consciousness and language in which either an identification or distinction might ever be made. It is in this sense that an "indiscretion" grounds the (groundless) analogy, and it is on the basis of such indiscretion that the analogy itself proves to be an "apophatic analogy": that is, an unsettled and unsettling analogy between two figures of the unknowable and ineffable. In the conclusion I signal some important ways in which such an apophatic analogy might allow for contemporary philosophical understandings of death and traditional mystical understandings of God to illuminate one another—and I suggest, further, how the unsettling force of such analogy might eventually be used to extend the aporetic logic of apophaticism beyond the theological and thanatological spheres.

Toward that end, in chapter 6, I assess the contemporary discussion concerning the relation between the Being of onto-theology and the "Good beyond Being" from Dionysian theology. Within that discussion, I focus on the confrontation between Derrida and Marion, who represent the strongest competing positions. To begin, I explicate Marion's theological reading of the gift in Dionysius and of givenness in phenomenology, and I suggest that a certain ambiguity persists in Marion between the theological and the phenomenological thought of uncondi-

20. Caputo, *The Mystical Element in Heidegger's Thought*, p. 144.

tional givenness. To elucidate and exploit that ambiguity, I take up Derrida's challenges both to Marion's reading of Dionysius and to any thought of the unconditional gift. On the basis of my engagement with these two thinkers, I am able to argue that Marion's phenomenological thought of givenness—because of the indeterminacy such a thought itself demands—might better answer Derrida's concerns about Marion's theological position (insofar as that position might involve a determination that would threaten a thought of the unconditional). A twofold ambiguity remains in Marion, however, to the degree that his theology already wants to proceed phenomenologically, and insofar as his phenomenology seems still indebted to a thought of givenness that is itself given first only in the theology. Exploiting rather than resolving this ambiguity, I argue that the radical indeterminacy of givenness implies a thought of finitude according to which one might sustain an indecision or undecidability, indeed, an indiscretion, between the theological and the thanatological—an indiscretion that could illuminate and enrich our approach to both. In cultivating such an indiscretion, one would remain faithful, I believe, to the rigors of radical "unknowing." A contemporary retrieval or rereading of classic theologies of inconceivable, ineffable goodness, therefore, benefits by taking into account these post-Heideggerian understandings of finitude—and vice versa.

Thus, in my concluding chapter, I situate the naming of the unnameable Good in negative theology with respect to these contemporary understandings of gift and finitude, which, we will have seen, are figured largely in terms of "the impossible": like the death in which Dasein cannot be self-present, so an absolute gift would mark a point where the subject of consciousness and language cannot return to itself. While both "death" and "gift" thus remain irreducible to the experience of a self-present subject of consciousness and language, they nevertheless remain intimately bound to such experience—because, precisely, they open the space for it. The death that marks the absolute impossibility of my existence at the same time opens or gives the very possibility of that existence; the absolute giving that would mark "the impossible" for a subject of experience remains at the same time that around which all possible experience turns.

In this sense, then, for those who take seriously the Heideggerian critique of metaphysical and especially modern conceptions of subjectivity, the question of finitude becomes crucial and leads necessarily to the question of what or who comes *after* the subject as it has been conceived within metaphysics and its modern consummation.[21] Among post-Heideggerians, the response to this question is formulated almost invariably in terms of what *precedes* and thus "undoes" the subject in its modern, self-grounding form. In other words, the response is formulated in terms of what belongs inextricably to the constitution of the finite, speaking "I" but remains radically prior and finally irreducible to the conscious, intentional thought and language of the autonomous (or absolute) subject. In the contemporary understandings that I address, "gift" or "givenness" provides one of the primary terms according to which such responses are made, and that "gift," itself understood according to "the impossible," always stands in indiscrete proximity to death. Following the critique of the modern subject, therefore, these contemporary understandings allow for a creative rereading of negative theology that will tie its thought of the ineffable Good to a thought of death and of all that death gives.

In order to read classic apophatic theologies, generally, and Dionysian theology, specifically, in light of the Heideggerian critique of the modern subject, one might fruitfully develop my proposed analogy between the logic of negative theology's "naming of the unnameable" (a logic dependent on the thought of God's self-donation) and the structure of the finite being whose death signals "the possibility of impossibility." If the thought of finitude and death is integral to the Heideggerian critique of metaphysics and its culmination in the Being of the modern (Hegelian) subject, then so too—as far as the proposed analogy proves effective—might the thought of donation that determines negative theology's logic and language provide a similar path for reconceiving the human subject *after* the Being of the modern subject and, correlatively, after the death of the metaphysical God. After the death of God and the destruction of the subject who consumes that God, the thought of gift and finitude allows those who are theologically committed to reassess very traditional thinking about God, and it allows those who remain uncommitted theologically to approach in contemporary terms the possible significance of naming God.

This conclusion, I think, proves significant both for the contempo-

---

21. The question "Who comes after the subject?" serves as the title for an illuminating collection of essays treating the interpretation of subjectivity among contemporary French (and primarily post-Heideggerian) writers: Cadava, Connor, and Nancy, *Who Comes after the Subject?* (New York: Routledge, 1991).

rary philosophy of religion and for historical studies in the traditions of mysticism—and for the interplay between these two spheres. In particular, the proximity within contemporary philosophy between a language of absolute gift and a language of death would call for further historical investigation concerning approaches to "death" within those theologies where the absolute self-donation of an ineffable, inconceivable God goes together with the "death" or dissolution of the thinking and speaking subject of experience. In other words, moving indiscretely along the borders of the theological and the philosophical, between the historical and the contemporary, a thinking that would approach negative theology in all of its paradox would need also to articulate the negative anthropology such paradox might imply—and vice versa. By exploiting points of indiscretion between negative theology and negative anthropology, between the historical and the contemporary, we might open new fields of discussion—bringing together, on the one hand, traditionalists who may have thought they had nothing to learn from postmodern negativities and, on the other, postmoderns who may have decided too quickly that they were at an end with the naming of God.

ONE

The Deaths of God in Hegel:
Overcoming Finitude and
Religious Representation

*W*hile many would first hear (or not hear) the proclamation of God's death in the cry of Nietzsche's madman (1882) or in Zarathustra's gospel parody (1885),[1] a conceptually developed "death of God" appears already as a central element in the thought of G. W. F. Hegel (1770–1831), who traces the philosophical significance of the death of God to its theological—that is, its christological and trinitarian—ground.[2] The "death of God," then, emerging from the religious sphere itself, comes to its first full, philosophical expression in the thinker who, as we will see with Heidegger, brings metaphysics, or onto-theology, to its highest positive completion. The completion of metaphysics and the death of God thus go hand in hand—and, as I will show in the present chapter, that death of God implies an attempt to overcome both the finitude of death and its correlative: the representational form of thought and language that defines religion. Because the present work as a whole is concerned to articulate the significance of finitude and religious language following the end of metaphysics and its death of God, the work must begin with Hegel.

Two Meanings and Two Developments

Like everything in Hegel, his thought on the "death of God" is complex, for it carries at least two interrelated meanings. On the one hand, God

1. See the famous § 125 (as well as § 108) in Friedrich Nietzsche, *The Gay Science* (1882), and the whole of *Thus Spoke Zarathustra* (completed 1885).

2. The significance of this theological ground of the death of God in Hegel has been recognized and developed by contemporary religious thinkers of varied orientation. See, e.g., Eberhard Jüngel, whose helpful overview of the "death of God" in Hegel's texts stresses its specifically theological origins, in *God as the Mystery of the World*, trans. Darrell L. Guder (Grand Rapids, Michigan: William B. Eerdmans Publishing Company, 1983), p. 63 ff.; and Thomas J. J. Altizer, all of whose work, from *The Gospel of Christian Atheism* (Philadelphia: Westminster Press, 1966) through *The Genesis of God* (Louisville: Westminster/John Knox Press, 1993) relies on a deeply Hegelian approach to the death of God. Likewise the philosophical study of Hegel has long recognized the death of God as central—from Jean Wahl's *Le Malheur de la conscience dans la philosophie de Hegel* (Paris: Les Editions Rieder, 1929) through Roger Garaudy's *Dieu est mort: Etude sur Hegel* (Paris: Presses Universitaires de France, 1962) to Delan S. Anderson's recent *Hegel's Speculative Good Friday: The Death of God in Philosophical Perspective* (Atlanta: Scholars Press, 1996).

is called "dead" insofar as God can seem or remain thoroughly remote
and thus unknowable; on this view, the enlightenment rationality that
reaches a high point in Kant and the pietistic feeling so influential in a
Jacobi or Schleiermacher would equally condemn God to the lifelessness
that ensues from the abstraction of the unknowable, from a lack of
determinate content, for "the Enlightenment of the understanding and
Pietism volatilize all content" (LPR 487; 5:267–68). On the other hand,
Hegel opposes this unknowable and thus lifeless God in terms of a second "death of God." On this second understanding, God empties or negates precisely his own abstraction or emptiness, moving out of his remoteness and unknowability in order thus actually and concretely to live.
For Hegel, these two meanings of the death of God must be interpreted
in light of one another.

In terms of the first meaning, but already opening into the second,
Hegel offers his earliest formulation of the "death of God" in his important early work on the philosophy of subjectivity in Kant, Jacobi, and
Fichte, *Faith and Knowledge* (1802): "But the pure concept or infinity as
the abyss of nothingness in which all being is engulfed, must signify the
infinite grief [of the finite] purely as a moment of the supreme Idea, and
no more than a moment. Formerly, the infinite grief only existed historically in the formative process of culture. It existed as the feeling
that 'God himself is dead,' upon which the religion of more recent
times rests."[3] Here the first sense of the death of God, according to
which God remains an unknowable abyss separate from the finite subject, already signals the second, according to which that separation and
unknowability constitute only a moment within the idea of a God who
"dies"—that is, departs from the abyss of his separation—so as to make
himself manifest and known—as ultimately identical—to the finite
subject.

This second sense is developed more fully in the *Phenomenology of
Spirit* (1807) and perhaps most fully in the Berlin *Lectures on the Philosophy
of Religion* (1821, 1824, 1827, 1831), where in both cases the "*abstraction
of the divine Being*" is put aside through the kenotic death of that Being.[4]
Here God dies in the sense that his abstraction and unknowability are
negated and thus overcome. Such a death proves absolutely necessary

3. *Faith and Knowledge*, trans. Walter Cerf and H. S. Harris (Albany: State University of New York, 1977), p. 190.
4. See esp. PhG 471, 476; 416, 419, and LPR 464–68; 5:245–50.

to the divine life and, indeed, it always falls within the greater force of that life.

The first death of God (abstract unknowability), then, relates to the second (kenotic self-giving or manifestation) as a moment within it. In his overview of the "death of God" within Hegel's texts, Eberhard Jüngel nicely summarizes this relation:

> By designating the feeling that "God himself is dead" as a moment of the supreme Idea, talk about the death of God gains a twofold meaning. First of all, in talk about the death of God, the situation of absolutized finitude expresses itself, which corresponds to abstract infinitude as empty negativity. Once that feeling is grasped as a moment of the supreme Idea, then the death of God is understood as an event of the *self-negation* of God, who does not desire to be "in and for himself" and does not desire to forsake the world in its finitude.[5]

As clearly explicated here by Jüngel, the two senses of the death of God go together inextricably, for the second operates only as a negation and surpassing of the first, while the first assumes its actual meaning only by passing into the second.

This death of God, which conveys two essentially interrelated senses, involves from the perspective of my concerns two key developments. On the one hand, the phrase "God is dead" indicates that any separation or remoteness of the absolute with regard to human consciousness in this world, any otherness or unknowability of the absolute, is thoroughly erased or overcome. God dies in his abstract transcendence and unmoving eternity so as to become temporally immanent and thus concretely known to this world and its history. On the other hand, correlatively, through the realized presence of the absolute in this world and its history, the finitude of humanity itself will prove untrue or inessential, a transitory moment that is sublated or raised up within the realized infinitude of the absolute. Annulling human finitude in this way, the death of God in Hegel ultimately effects the death of death itself, a *mors mortis* according to which God dies so that death as such might be overcome.[6]

---

5. Jüngel, *God as the Mystery of the World*, p. 74.

6. Within his discussion of the theological ground of the Hegelian death of God, Jüngel stresses the specifically Lutheran character of the terminology surrounding the "death of death": "In using the term 'death of death' Hegel enters directly into the theological terminology of Luther. We find the expression 'death of death' (*mors mortis*)

For Hegel, this death of death would mark the central teaching of Christianity, and by extension its logic proves foundational to Hegelian philosophy as a whole.

The death of God, then, occurs through the radical *kenosis* of the absolute, the self-giving of the absolute into its own most extreme otherness, into finitude and death. In and through that self-giving, divine nature and human nature finally achieve substantial unity within the realized knowing of absolute subjectivity. Within the circle or circuit that is absolute subjectivity, consciousness actualizes itself as spirit—as that which knows and maintains itself in all otherness and so returns to itself in the infinite freedom of absolute self-consciousness. Insofar as absolute subjectivity passes beyond all unknowable otherness, God dies (in his abstract unknowabilty) and the finitude of humanity (as the correlate of the abstract, unknowable God) is overcome.

Death of God and the Annulment of Finitude

Now, within this Hegelian framework, such a death of God and annulment of finitude represent specifically Christian achievements, which means that they conclude and complete both the specific history of religions and the broader history of spirit as such, for religion is the penultimate stage within the overall unfolding of spirit (and, accordingly, the science of religion is the final science within philosophy) (LPR 113; 3:265). In and through that history, spirit progressively and teleologically externalizes or concretizes itself; it comes to know itself fully and actually as absolute subjectivity by returning to itself from and through its self-externalization: "[T]he series of forms that we have passed through [within the philosophy of religion] is a succession of stages that follow upon one another; but these forms are encompassed within the infinite, absolute form, in absolute subjectivity, and only the spirit so defined as absolute subjectivity *is* spirit" (LPR 410; 5:193). Spirit is realized as absolute subjectivity first and only in the religion where God or the absolute is known explicitly as spirit—that is, in Christianity. While all previous religions would know God implicitly as spirit, only Christianity knows God as spirit fully and explicitly. Thus, marking the teleological consum-

---

a number of times in Luther, and its essence is also found in a genuine Luther hymn [*Evangelisches Kirchengesangbuch*, no. 76, verse 4: 'The Scriptures have proclaimed how one death devoured another; death has been scorned. Hallelujah.']" (*God as the Mystery of the World*, p. 93).

mation of religious history itself, the "revealed" or "consummate" religion alone finally teaches human beings *what* God *is:* the concept that reveals itself explicitly as spirit.

Within this view according to which Christianity alone knows God fully as spirit, spirit itself is defined as the (essentially trinitarian) movement of self-manifestation through self-division or self-othering. "For Spirit," writes Hegel in the *Phenomenology of Spirit*, "is the knowledge of oneself in the externalization of oneself; the being that is the movement of retaining its self-identity in its otherness" (PhG 459; 405). "Spirit is essence," Hegel writes in the *Lectures on the Philosophy of Religion*, "but only insofar as it has returned to itself from out of itself, only insofar as it is that actual being which returns and is at home with itself, that being which posits itself from itself as at home with itself. This positing produces the distinctive determinations of its activity, and those distinctive determinations are the forms through which spirit has to move" (LPR 410; 5:194). Spirit's movement of self-externalization and self-return is essential to revelation or manifestation as such—both the manifestation of the infinite to the finite and the manifestation of the infinite, through the finite, to itself. For Hegel this movement of manifestation achieves its fullness only in Christianity, which means that Christianity alone reveals the very essence or nature of revelation, makes manifest the movement of manifestation itself. In short, Christianity illuminates the very nature of spirit to spirit.

Thus, spirit appears in Christianity as "a self-manifesting, a being for spirit" (LPR 90; 3:74), as "the activity of *self*-manifesting" (LPR 102; 3:85), a self-determining, self-objectifying and self-finitizing movement through which spirit essentially negates itself and returns to itself through that negation. Only in such return is spirit spirit, for "It *is* spirit only by virtue of the fact that it is for itself as the negation of all finite forms, as this absolute ideality" (LPR 109; 3:91). In its self-manifestation, spirit is for an other, and as such a being-for-other, spirit necessarily enters into its own determination, limitation, and finitude. At the same time, spirit by its very definition endures that limitation, it overcomes or sublates that finitude and returns to itself through it. Indeed, spirit realizes itself only to the extent that it posits and maintains itself in its own self-difference.

An essentially circular or circuitous process, spirit's movement of self-realization through self-difference is traced through the historical and conceptual unfolding of consciousness generally (as in the PhG) and of religious consciousness specifically (as in the LPR), and it reaches its

fullness in Christianity alone (the ultimate stage of religious consciousness and the penultimate stage of consciousness as a whole). Through
that circular process, consciousness will return fully to itself in being
elevated to the self-consciousness of absolute, infinite subjectivity:

> The last stage, however, is that this concept, this subjectivity for
> which spirit is, is not to remain something external to spirit, but
> rather is itself to be absolute and infinite subjectivity, infinite form.
> The infinite form is the circuit of this determining process; the con-
> cept is spirit only because it has achieved determinacy through this
> circuit, has moved through it. This is how it first becomes concrete.
> This means on the one hand a stripping away of the mode of fini-
> tude, and on the other hand a self-diremption and a return to self
> from diremption; only so is it posited as spirit. [. . .] It is spirit only
> as that which dirempts itself and returns into itself again—i.e., only
> after traversing this circuit. What we have traversed in our treat-
> ment is the becoming, the bringing forth of spirit by itself, and only
> as such, or as eternally bringing itself forth, is it spirit. This course
> is, therefore, the grasping or comprehension of spirit. It is the con-
> cept that determines itself, and takes these determinations back into
> itself, as the concept; in this way the concept is infinite subjectivity.
> What results is the concept that posits itself, and has itself as its
> content. This then is the absolute idea. The idea is unity of concept
> and reality; it is concept *and* objectivity. Truth consists in objectivity
> being adequate to the concept; but what is adequate to the concept
> is only the concept itself insofar as it has itself as its counterpart or
> object. The content as idea is truth. (LPR 411; 5:194–95)

As this movement of self-diremption and maintenance of self in diremption or, better, return to self through diremption, as this movement
of spirit which, significantly, Hegel will equate with love in the religious
sphere, God himself is "the concept." The logic of that concept, the logic
of God and thus a theo-logic, governs all of Hegelian thought—and it
is conceived first in Christianity because in Christianity first God reveals
himself explicitly as spirit to spirit:

> [The concept] is immediately this universal that determines and par-
> ticularizes itself—it is this activity of dividing, of particularizing and
> determining itself, of positing a finitude, negating this its own fini-
> tude and being identical with itself through the negation of this fi-

nitude. This is the concept as such, the concept of God, the absolute concept; this is just what God is. (LPR 184–85; 3:325)

Within the historical and conceptual unfolding of religion, according to Hegel, only Christianity teaches fully *what* God *is*, and the being so known is the concept itself—the self-conceiving concept. Hegel determines God fundamentally according to being and the conceptual knowledge, or self-knowledge, of that being.

Conceptual Knowledge and the Trinity: The Determination of God

It is precisely in terms of such (self-) knowing that Hegel will interpret the central Christian doctrine of the Trinity. According to Hegel the self-dividing and self-reconciling movement of the concept that exists as spirit is represented religiously in the triune God revealed through the Christ:

> The reconciliation in Christ, in which one believes, makes no sense if God is not known as the triune God, [if it is not recognized] that God *is*, but also is as the other, as self-distinguishing, so that this other is God himself, having implicitly the divine nature in it, and that the sublation of this difference, this otherness, and the return of love, are the Spirit. (LPR 469; 5:251)[7]

These moments within the triune God, moments "which establish that humanity has become conscious of the eternal history, the eternal movement which God himself is" (LPR 469; 5:251), represent religiously the

7. Of the many parallels to this trinitarian and christological conception of spirit, see especially LPR 392; 5:178; LPR 412–13; 5:196; LPR 417–18; 5:201; LPR 426–27; 5:209–10. Within the essentially threefold movement of the divine, which Hegel interprets according to the trinitarian God revealed through the Christ, one can also discern a deeply Neoplatonic (especially Proclean) tendency. Consider, e.g., these passages from Hegel and Proclus: "[The universal] is also not an inert, abstract universal, however, but rather the absolute womb or the infinite fountainhead out of which everything emerges, into which everything returns, and in which it is eternally maintained" (LPR 122; 3:272); "every effect remains in its cause, proceeds from it, and reverts upon it" (*Elements of Theology*, proposition 35). Among others, Gadamer has noted the Neoplatonic aspects of Hegel's thought, following Feuerbach, who labeled Hegel "the German Proclus." See Hans-Georg Gadamer, *Hegel's Dialectic*, trans. P. Christopher Smith (New Haven, Connecticut: Yale University Press, 1976), pp. 21, 32–33, and § 29 of Feuerbach's *Principles of the Philosophy of the Future*, trans. Manfred H. Vogel (Indianapolis: Hackett Publishing Company, 1986).

logical moments of the concept as such, the concept with which God is equated.[8]

Within this comprehension of God as and through the concept, Hegel rejects the prohibitions or restrictions of his day, operative in otherwise competing tendencies of both the Enlightenment and Pietism, and discernible in such figures as Kant and Jacobi, against any determinate knowledge of God's *nature*, any knowledge of what God is *in himself.* This rejection grows out of Hegel's conviction that religious faith and practice remain forms of thought, and indeed forms of knowing, that, being such, must have determinate content. For Hegel, it is precisely *thought* that distinguishes humans from animals, and religion is a specifically human exercise. If religion does indeed concern feeling, that feeling is a *thinking* feeling and thus distinct from the unreflective feeling of the animal: "Religion has its seat and soil in the activity of thinking. The heart and feeling that directly sense the truth of religion are not the heart and feeling of an animal but of a thinking human being; they are a thinking heart and a thinking feeling, and whatever [measure] of religion is in this heart and feeling is a thought of this heart and feeling" (LPR 399; 5:184). Were religion limited to purely subjective feeling or opinion, it would lose any justifiable content and thus any objective truth, for "the purely subjective standpoint recognizes no content and hence no truth" (LPR 487; 5:267–68). Religion for Hegel consists not simply or primarily in the *relation* of a finite subject to God, as it is variously interpreted in Kant, Jacobi, or Schleiermacher, but in *knowledge*—and indeed absolute knowledge—of God. That knowledge can actually be knowledge only through its concrete, determinate content.

If the religious is limited to the subjective, as Hegel believes it is in such figures, then the center of religion, God, loses all content, becoming either the indeterminate correlate of feeling, or else a guiding idea that cannot actually be known. Such a limitation, for Hegel, results in an empty, abstract God, on the one side, and an unfulfilled, divided subject, on the other. But for Hegel, religion concerns, precisely, a determinate knowledge whose content is the absolute itself. Having defined religion as an objective *knowing*, and not simply as a subjective relating, Hegel insists that the object of religion, God, is indeed known determinately,

---

8. For the logical exposition of the dialectic of the concept, see G. W. F. Hegel, *Science of Logic,* trans. W. H. Johnston and L. G. Struthers (London: George Allen and Unwin, 1966), 2:234–57.

concretely. Christianity achieves and completes such concrete knowledge by revealing its very nature and ground in spirit.

Now, when God is known, and known as spirit, God is known as the movement of self-positing in determinate, finite form, and the return to self through the negation or sublation of such finitude. Only within such a process does God cease to remain abstractly "beyond" human consciousness, its world and its history. Thus, it is precisely through the process in which God "dies," through the movement in which God sacrifices his abstract otherness, that God becomes fully known or comprehended—and known or comprehended as the very ground and nature of all knowledge. The annulment of finitude that occurs through the movement of spirit will go hand in hand with an exorcism of the unknowable or incomprehensible.

With regard to the contemporary debate over apophatic and mystical theologies, such an annulment and exorcism mark a primary significance of the Hegelian death of God: the "mystery" of Christianity is, for Hegel, not a "secret"; it is not unknowable or incomprehensible. Rather, the truth expressed by Christianity—that is, speculative knowledge of God as the absolute—appears to be unknowable or incomprehensible only to the limited gaze of sensible cognition or understanding: "The nature of God is not a secret in the ordinary sense, least of all in the Christian religion. In it God has made known what he is; there he is manifest. But he is a secret or mystery for external sense perception and representation, for the sensible mode of consideration and likewise for the understanding" (LPR 422; 5:205).[9] The reason that God might appear incomprehensible or unknowable within the revealed religion has to do not with the content of that religion, which for Hegel proves absolutely knowable, but with the form of religion as such: "One of the circumstances contributing to the assertion that the divine idea is inconceivable is the fact that, in religion, the content of the idea appears in forms accessible to sense experience or understanding, because religion is the truth for everyone" (LPR 425; 5:208–9). One can see here that the reduction or exorcism of the mystery, according to which Christian revelation implies the full knowledge of God, will occur in conjunction with an overcoming or dissolution of the representational form—an overcoming, that is, of that form's limitation or finitude. Before turning

9. On Hegel's view of the mystery, see esp. LPR 422–25; 5:205–9; LPR 130; 3:278–79; LPR 193; 3:333; and PhG 437; 386.

to the significance of Hegel's movement beyond representation, however, I need to address first the knowledge conveyed *within* the representational form—the divine idea of Christianity, which in Hegel exorcises
the unknowable through the death of God and the annulment of human
finitude.[10] The logic according to which representation is overcome in
fact governs, already *within* the sphere of representation, the central
Hegelian interpretation of the Christ.

The Determination of God in the Christ

Because God is known fully only in the revealed or manifest religion, the
"death of God" necessary to such knowledge will constitute a distinctively Christian achievement. In this sense, then, the "death of God"
must be interpreted, precisely, in terms of the Christ's incarnation, death,
and resurrection.[11]

10. Though I focus here on specifically theological and philosophical meanings of
the "death of God," the issues at stake would relate significantly to the diverse social and
cultural developments associated with the process of "secularization." When consciousness reaches that point where it encounters nothing that in principle remains irreducibly
opaque to it, when philosophy or science has exorcised the world of anything insurmountably secret or incomprehensible, the social and cultural processes of "secularization" necessarily enter into play. On this, Weber's "disenchantment" of the world
remains a fundamental starting point: "The increasing intellectualization and rational-
ization do *not*, therefore, indicate an increased and general knowledge of the conditions
under which one lives. It means something else, namely, the knowledge or belief that if
one wished one *could* learn it at any time. Hence it means that principally there are no
mysterious incalculable forces that come into play, but rather, that one can master all
things by calculation. This means that the world is disenchanted" (Max Weber, "Science
as a Vocation," in H. H. Gerth and C. Wright Mills, eds., *From Max Weber: Essays in
Sociology* [New York, Oxford University Press, 1946], p. 139).
11. Among those to stress the christological origin and meaning of the "death of
God" in Hegel are, of course, Thomas J. J. Altizer, whose entire thinking might be seen
as a radical Hegelian understanding of the incarnation, but also figures who remain
critical of the "death of God theology." Among the latter would be Eberhard Jüngel,
according to whom "the systematic *connection* of the christological source of the idea of
the death of God with the epistemological-metaphysical problematic of modern atheism
could be Hegel's most significant achievement for theology" (*God as the Mystery of the
World*, p. 97), and Hans Küng, according to whom "we might even say that Hegel sees
theology itself as defined in terms of Christology, as christomorphic theology." For
Küng, in the Hegelian interpretation of the death of God, "for the first time there is
posed with radical clarity the basic problem which has always constituted the one specifically theological aspect of the disputed sphere of classical Christology [. . .]: in the
event that God were to empty himself in such a way into this immanent reality, into

The incarnate Christ in Hegel presents in religious, representational form the content of philosophical, conceptual truth. In Christ, the reconciliation of finite and infinite spirit appears religiously as the reconciliation of human and divine nature: "the substantiality of the unity of divine and human nature comes to consciousness for humanity in such a way that a human being appears to consciousness as God, and God appears to it as a human being" (LPR 454; 5:236).

The two key movements or moments of the Hegelian death of God here appear in their religious center. On the one hand, through incarnation, the abstraction of the divine Being, the separation or remoteness of the absolute from the actuality of this world, has been put aside, negated, or overcome; God, the absolute, takes on human actuality even in its finitude and death. On the other hand, through the death and resurrection of the Christ, the limitation or deficiency of human being, its finitude or negativity, is itself negated and raised to identity with the infinitude of the absolute.

These two movements first become present and available to human consciousness in the form of a sensibly existing individual who is both human being and God. Only through such an existing individual is the divine idea of reconciliation made available to the *experience* of consciousness, and experience alone first accords truth its certainty:

> In other words, this content—the unity of divine and human nature—achieves certainty, obtaining the form of immediate sensible intuition and external existence for human kind, so that it appears as something that has been seen in the world, something that has been experienced. It is essential to this form of nonspeculative consciousness that it must be *before* us; it must essentially be *before* me— it must become a certainty for humanity. (LPR 455; 5:237–38)

For Hegel, the Christian consciousness constitutes the highest form and last moment of the nonspeculative, re-presentational consciousness that characterizes religion in general, the consciousness that sets *before* itself the truth of consciousness itself. Through this final moment of religious

---

history, into humanity, in the event that we can in fact talk of an incarnation of God and of a death and resurrection of God—how must this God himself be understood? What, on these presuppositions, do suffering and death mean for God . . . ?" (*The Incarnation of God: An Introduction to Hegel's Theological Thought as Prolegomena to a Future Christology*, trans. J. R. Stephenson [New York: Crossroad, 1987], pp. 162, 169).

consciousness, all humanity gains access to the content of a conceptual truth whose most adequate expression would occur only in the form of speculative philosophy. The passage from representational conscious- ness to conceptual reason, a movement from a limited, finite conscious- ness to unlimited, infinite self-consciousness, will involve overcoming the finitude, limitation, or one-sidedness of the representational form.

The conceptual logic of that movement, however, is already pre- sented *within* the sphere of representation itself, in the figure of the Christ, since the finite, sensible existence of that individual, through which alone the divine puts aside its abstraction and so realizes itself concretely, must at the same time be overcome or sublated if humanity is to be reconciled with the divine and if the divine is itself to prove absolute. In the sensible existence of Christ, the divine empties itself of its abstract universality to realize itself as a concrete individual, present to humanity. At the same time, the finitude of humanity itself will be raised thereby to the infinitude of the divine—but only insofar as the sensible Christ is ultimately overcome.

In putting aside its abstraction, in exiting from its abstract universal- ity and eternity, the divine Being enters into the concrete particularity of temporal, finite human being. But the extreme and confirmation of such finite being, indeed, its defining limit, will be found nowhere else than in death: "It is the lot of human finitude to die. Death is the most complete proof of humanity, of absolute finitude; and indeed Christ has died the aggravated death of the evildoer [. . .]. In him, humanity was carried to its furthest point" (LPR 465; 5:246). By taking on humanity to the defining extreme of death, God has most radically emptied himself and, in this specific sense, has died. The death of the finite being of Christ, therefore, will signify not only the death of an existing individual, but first the death of God himself in God's having become such an indi- vidual. That is, through the death of the existing individual, Christ, God passes into the extreme of temporal finitude, which implies the death of the abstract universality and eternity of the absolute Being.

Thus, as Hegel makes clear both in the *Lectures on the Philosophy of Religion* and already in the *Phenomenology of Spirit*, the death of the partic- ular individual, Christ (or the Mediator), who is the representation or "picture thought" of the idea of reconciliation, involves "at the same time the death of the *abstraction of the divine Being* which is not posited as Self. That death is the painful feeling of the Unhappy Consciousness that *God Himself is dead*" (PhG 476; 419). Here in Hegel's words one might hear Nietzsche himself: "*God has died, God is dead*—this is the most frightful of all thoughts, that everything eternal and true *is not*, that negation itself is found in God. The deepest anguish, the feeling of complete irretrievability, the annulling of everything that is elevated, are bound up with this thought" (LPR 465; 5:246). Through the incarnation and death of Christ, God has achieved the most thorough negation or reversal of his abstract Being. In that incarnation, whose confirmation death is, the elevated has been brought low, the universal has become particular, the eternal has entered time.

According to the dialectical movement of reason, however, the universal and the particular, the eternal and the temporal, the infinite and the finite, cannot remain antithetical. Such unresolved antitheses, indeed, stand at the center of Hegel's critique of the subjective philosophy of reflection (see, e.g., LPR 96–97; 1:80). According to the dialectical necessity of reason, these opposites essentially imply and depend on one another, for "we call something 'necessary' when, if one [element] exists, the other is thereby posited" (LPR 154; 3:301). Thus, in a third movement of double negation, opposites pass beyond mere antithesis to prove substantially identical. Religiously, this third movement is represented by the resurrection of Christ and the subsequent community of spirit.

The resurrection, on this view, presents in representational form the dialectical movement of double negation. In taking on finitude even unto death, the absolute has negated itself, emptied itself, become other to itself. That otherness or negation, however, must itself be negated if the absolute is to realize and maintain itself in and through that otherness or self-difference. The other-being of the absolute, the negation of the absolute, must itself be a moment within the absolute. Otherwise, the absolute would remain limited by and thus relative to that which remains other than itself, but in such a case, the absolute would simply no longer be absolute. Thus, God maintains himself in and through the negation signaled by Christ's death—which for this reason is already resurrection: "The [absolute essence] has thereby come to be its own Self in its sensuous presence; the immediate existence of actuality has ceased to be something alien and external for the absolute essence, since that existence is superseded, is universal. This death is, therefore, its resurrection as Spirit" (PhG 471; 415).

God, the absolute, endures, passes through, and thus elevates the very finitude or negation of which death is the extreme, and in this sense death itself is negated: "God [. . .] maintains himself in this process [of death], and the latter is only the death of death. God rises again to life, and thus things are reversed" (LPR 465; 5:246). The reversal of God's

death through the resurrection and glorification of Christ constitutes the
very death of death and, as such, gives the fullest significance of the
"death of God" in Hegel. If death belongs to human finitude, the reconciliation of God and humanity essentially annuls that finitude through
the reversal of death within the resurrection to life.[12]

This annulment of finitude marks the conclusion of that history in
which, through the self-explication or unfolding of the divine, the human realizes its own identity with the divine. That divine self-
explication, the reconciling history of spirit or the spiritual history of
reconciliation, follows the triune, rational movement of spirit from the
abstract, universal idea immediately in itself (representationally, God the
Father), through the determination of that idea in the otherness of finite,
sensible particularity (Christ the Son, incarnate), through the negation
and sublation of the sensible and finite within the now fully realized universality of the self-conscious idea (the final realization of spirit).[13]

The twofold movement of death—from the divine into the human
and from the human up to the divine—structures the entire movement
of that history:

> This history is the explication of the divine nature itself. If in the
> first sphere we grasped God in pure thought, then in this second
> sphere we start from the immediacy appropriate to intuition and
> sensible representation. The process is now such that immediate
> singularity is sublated: just as in the first sphere the seclusion of God
> came to an end, and his original immediacy as abstract universality,
> according to which he is the essence of essences, has been sublated,
> so here the abstraction of humanity, the immediacy of subsisting

12. The fundamental significance of resurrection here renders Hegel's conception
of death very different, I think, from that of Heidegger, for whom Dasein lives toward
death but does not survive it. In light of this contrast, my reading of the Hegelian conception of death would be at odds with the classic reading of Kojève, for whom "the
Spirit that Hegel has in view is essentially finite or mortal. It is in introducing the idea
of death [into the Christian Spirit] that one transforms theology into anthropology. And
it is in taking this idea literally, that is, in suppressing the notions of survival and of
resurrection, that one ends up at the true, or Hegelian, anthropology" (Kojève, *Introduction à la lecture de Hegel* [Paris: Gallimard, 1947], p. 573 [my translation]). Despite the
real power and productivity of Kojève's anthropological reading, it seems to me to go
too far by denying the deep consistency of Hegel's thought with a Christian conception
of resurrection.

13. The triune logic of specifically Christian consciousness structures also the
broader philosophy of religion (Concept, Determination, Consummation), or even of
systematic philosophy as a whole (Logic, Nature, Spirit).

singularity, is sublated, and this is brought about by death. But the death of Christ is the death of this death itself, the negation of negation. (LPR 466; 5:247)[14]

The death of Christ, as the death of death or the negation of negation, spells the very end—that is, both the goal and the overcoming—of finitude. The finite appears finally as untrue, inessential; through its necessary negation it is elevated to the infinite and thereby to its truth. The death of God in Christ, then, ultimately signifies the death of a humanity that is only finite, the elevation of that humanity to identity with God, who himself takes up and internalizes the external and the negative (LPR 468; 5:250).

The "death of God" in its two aspects, the entrance of God into finitude and the movement of humanity to infinitude, constitutes a fundamental structuring principle for that entire history in which human consciousness becomes conscious of its own nature as and through spirit:

> The truth to which humans have attained by means of this history, what they have become conscious of in this entire history, is the following: that the idea of God has certainty for them, that humanity has attained the certainty of unity with God, that the human is the immediately present God. Indeed, within this history as spirit comprehends it, there is the very presentation of the process of what humanity is, what spirit is—implicitly both God and dead. (LPR 468; 5:250)

Humanity is itself "both God and dead" only insofar as God himself dies. God dies by taking on the human, and in that death, which confirms God's humanity, the human is made identical with God.[15] At the same

14. This same twofold movement of death—the negation of divine abstraction through incarnation and the negation of incarnate particularity—appears clearly also in the *Phenomenology*'s interpretation of absolute religion. See PhG 476; 419.

15. Figures such as Karl Barth, of course, will stress the degree to which Hegel fails to maintain the *distinction* of divine nature and human nature. As Barth will indicate, "the identification of God with the dialectical method, even if it did not signify that he was identified with man's act of life, implies a scarcely acceptable limitation, even abolition of God's sovereignty [. . .]. This God, the God of Hegel is at least his own prisoner. Comprehending all things, he finally and at the highest level comprehends himself too, and by virtue of the fact that he does this in the consciousness of man, everything God is and does will be and is understood from the point of view of man, as God's own necessity" (*Protestant Thought: From Rousseau to Ritschl* [Salem, New Hampshire: Ayer Company, 1987], p. 304). Following Barth, Jüngel will note that "Hegel's God needs man, who thereby becomes divine himself. It may be that the God who is in the process

time, the death of that God-made-human is itself reversed or undone and thus marks the negation of the human, the overcoming or sublation of the finitude that characterizes the human. In this sense, in the Christ, humanity is not only God but also, thereby, dead.

The Meaning and Content of Death: The Idea of Love

Within this perspective, I should stress, death does not indicate a simple negative limit or deficiency. Death here is not empty. Rather, through the work of double negation, death is given positive content or meaning, the positive content or meaning of the idea.

The imperative that death receive such content or meaning, that its negativity not be sheer negativity and nothing more, constitutes a central line of thought running through Hegel's philosophy. In the *Lectures on the Philosophy of Religion*, the positive determination of death, its fulfillment as meaningful, clearly issues within a specific conception of Christianity's truth. In the *Phenomenology*, death is, more broadly, a driving force essential to the meaning of history as such.

In the *Phenomenology*, one can see the significance of Hegel's attempt to fill death with meaning when, for example, he will critique the form of death operative within the "Absolute Freedom and Terror": "the sole work and deed of freedom is *death*, a death too which has no inner significance or filling, for what is negated is the empty point of the absolutely free self. It is thus the coldest and meanest of all deaths, with no more significance than cutting off a head of cabbage or swallowing a mouthful of water" (PhG 360; 320). The empty, sheerly negative form of death operative in the Terror marks a moment that for Hegel *must* be surpassed within the movement toward a fulfilled negation, toward a meaningful death—which is achieved in Christianity and its history. That history will take up and surpass all empty or incomplete forms of negation such as those apparent in the absolute freedom of the Terror, which is a freedom whose "negation is the death that is without meaning, the sheer terror of the negative that contains nothing positive, nothing

---

of coming to himself uses man [. . .]. It may be that man uses God while en route to the depths of the spirit, so that . . . he elevates himself to his true height [. . .]. It is irrelevant whether man is the being who uses God or God is the being who uses man—the latter is the more likely one—, the concrete distinction between God and man is jeopardized in either case" (*God as the Mystery of the World*, p. 95).

that fills it with a content" (PhG 362; 322). For Hegel, the death that is filled with a content, the death that contains the positive, is, precisely, the death of God, which effects the death of death.

I should stress, furthermore, that Hegel expresses this positivity of death philosophically as *idea* but religiously as *love*. Hegel's ultimate conception of death as positively meaningful goes hand in hand with a very specific conception of love: in terms of the unity or identity of opposites. Within this conception, it is out of love and through love that God has taken the finitude of humanity upon himself "in order to put it to death by his death":

> As the monstrous unification of these absolute extremes, this shameful death is at the same time infinite love. It is out of infinite love that God has made himself identical with what is alien to him in order to put it to death. This is the meaning of the death of Christ. It means that Christ has borne the sins of the world and has reconciled God [with the world (2 Cor. 5:18–19)]. (LPR 466; 5:247)

The reconciliation of God with the world through the death that is endured out of love constitutes the religious expression of the speculative idea that infinite spirit and finite spirit are identical.

Within that reconciliation, the infinite does indeed enter into finitude, but it is finally the finite that will be raised to the infinite. That is, the finite finds its essential truth only in the infinite and thus constitutes a fleeting, inessential moment. This is precisely the truth of the idea that Hegel discerns within the Christian story: "finitude is reduced to an inessential status, and is known as inessential. For in the idea, the otherness of the Son is a transitory, disappearing moment, not a true, essentially enduring, absolute moment" (LPR 474; 5:255).

The interpretation within which this annulment of finitude occurs, within which death is given a positive, infinite content, conceives love as that through which consciousness returns to itself, finds and realizes itself in its other. While love, according to Hegel, consists in a movement toward the other, that movement is not one of self-loss or insatiable yearning but rather one of self-realization and self-satisfaction:[16]

---

16. In this respect, we might say that Hegel comes closer to the satiety of Origen than to the *epektasis* of Gregory of Nyssa. On these figures and issues, see my discussion of Dionysius in chap. 5.

> For love is a distinguishing of two, who nevertheless are absolutely
> not distinguished for each other. The consciousness or feeling of
> the identity of the two—to be outside of myself and in the other—
> this is love. I have my self-consciousness not in myself but in the
> other. I am satisfied and have peace with myself only in this other—
> and I *am* only because I have peace with myself; if I did not have it,
> then I would be a contradiction that falls to pieces. (LPR 418; 5:201;
> see also LPR 428; 5:211)

Departing from or ignoring those traditions wherein love might signal
divine incomprehensibility and the utter loss of self (traditions to which
my central argument will return), Hegel takes love to express, precisely,
the full comprehensibility of the divine (equated with the concept) and
the discovery of self, the recovery of self, the satisfaction of self therein.

Now, both this conception of love as return to self in the other and
the correlative conception of death as filled with content or meaning
issue within the Hegelian conception of religion in terms of knowledge.
As I showed above, religion for Hegel is primarily a form of thought and
knowing. Two results of that primacy can be seen here in the interpretation of death and of love: death will be filled with meaning, and love will
mean self-recovery and self-satisfaction. In order to situate these results
with respect to Hegel's conception of religion, one needs to understand
the relation of religion to philosophical thinking, for the movement of
thought according to which death has positive meaning and content, the
movement according to which finitude is raised to the essential truth of
infinitude, is recapitulated within the relation between, on the one hand,
religious thought as such, where the sublation of finitude comes to light
representationally in terms of love, and, on the other hand, speculative
philosophy, where alone the sublation of finitude achieves the fully adequate form of the rational idea.

Vorstellung and *Begriff*:
The Passage from Religion to Philosophy

In religion, which according to Hegel offers the primary means of access
for human beings to God or the absolute, the absolute is not fully conceived (*begriffen*) but is rather only represented (*vorgestellt*): "For human
beings, God *is* primarily in the form of representation (*in der Form der
Vorstellung*). [Representation is] a consciousness of something that one
has before oneself (*vor sich*) as something objective" (LPR 144; 3:291–

92). In the form of representation, God stands before consciousness and thus seems separate from and opposed, or objective, to consciousness. This objective status wherein God stands over against consciousness is necessary but also provisional.

On the one hand, the objective character of representation is necessary insofar as it gives determinate, objective content to an otherwise indeterminate, purely subjective feeling of certitude or faith: "The form of feeling is the subjective aspect, the certainty of God. The form of representation concerns the objective aspect, the content of that certainty" (LPR 144; 3:291). Through representation, which introduces to consciousness the otherness or difference of the objective, subjective religious feeling and its immediate certitude are given an identifiable, determinate shape, an objective sense or meaning that is not limited to the purely subjective sphere. Such objective content remains indispensable to the concrete realization of subjective feeling and, correlatively, to the justification of religious truth, since "feeling is still nothing justificatory, for everything possible is capable of being in feeling" (LPR 151; 3:198). Only determinate content can provide the ground for legitimating an otherwise arbitrary feeling, and it is representation that contains the objective, or that "constitutes the contents or determinacy of feeling" (LPR 151; 3:198). Representation thus gives to religious feeling the content and determinacy that are necessary for the justification of religious cognition as true and, thus, for the true realization of religious subjectivity. Only according to such determinate content can an otherwise arbitrary feeling be justified in its necessity.

On the other hand, however, such objective content cannot remain insurmountably opposed to consciousness, as if it were wholly separate from or independent of consciousness, for were the objective aspect to remain opposed to consciousness in that way, it would mark a limit to the realization of subjectivity in its freedom—an obstacle, therefore, to the realization of the absolute itself. If religious consciousness remains divided from or opposed to its object, such a division marks an inward split that resists the completion of absolute self-consciousness. Consciousness must rediscover itself fully as self-consciousness in order that spirit be realized in and as absolute subjectivity.

The representational *form*, then, insofar as it involves this objective aspect, this seeming independence and separation vis-à-vis consciousness, has *not yet* been comprehended fully as the activity of consciousness itself, and thus as an embodied form of self-consciousness. Religion here relates to philosophy according to an identity of content and a difference

of form. Religious consciousness represents to itself or sets before itself
the conceptual truth that only philosophy actually conceives in wholly
rational form. In religion, the *form* of representation "is not yet Spirit's
self-consciousness that has advanced to its Concept *qua* Concept: the
mediation is still incomplete. [. . .] The *content* is the true content, but all
its moments, when placed in the medium of representation (*Vorstellens*),
have the character of being uncomprehended (*den Charakter, nicht begriffen zu sein*)" (PhG 463; 408). Thus, in passing through the analysis of
religion, the task of philosophy will be to clarify that true, conceptual
content by removing or overcoming the inadequacy of the religious, representational form.

The central question here concerns the precise status of religion
vis-à-vis philosophy. While some commentators would hold that the
philosophical expression of the conceptual truth first revealed in religion
finally eliminates the need for, or even possibility of, that religion,[17] others would insist that philosophy does not cease to depend on religion, or
even that philosophy in its Hegelian form is itself thoroughly religious.[18]

17. Forms of this position, of course, arise in both the Feuerbachian and Marxist
critiques of Hegel and are developed in later Hegelian commentators such as Kojève
and Hyppolite. Within scholarship on Hegel's philosophy of religion, the contention
that Hegelian philosophy leads necessarily to the surpassing of religion is articulated
with some force by Walter Jaeschke, for whom the speculative understanding of religion
"can, to be sure, only legitimate religion on condition of its being sublated into thought.
And this, finally, is the very step that conjures up the end of religion" (in David Kolb,
ed., *New Perspectives on Hegel's Philosophy of Religion* [Albany: State University of New
York Press], p. 16).

18. The hermeneutic view that religion and philosophy remain in a relation of
mutual dependence is perhaps best articulated by Paul Ricoeur in his article, "The Status of *Vorstellung* in Hegel's Philosophy of Religion": "For my part, I tend to interpret
absolute thought less as a final stage than as the process thanks to which all shapes and
all stages remain thoughtful. Absolute knowledge, consequently, is the thoughtfulness
of picture-thinking. [. . .] As a result, we have the possibility of reinterpreting the hermeneutics of religious thinking as an endless process thanks to which representative and
speculative thought keep generating one another" (in Leroy S. Rouner, ed., *Meaning,
Truth, and God* [South Bend, Indiana: University of Notre Dame Press, 1982], p. 86).
Among those who insist on the religious character of Hegelian philosophy itself, see
Quentin Lauer, *Essays in Hegelian Dialectic* (New York: Fordham University Press, 1977),
and *Hegel's Concept of God* (Albany: State University of New York Press, 1982); Emil
Fackenheim, *The Religious Dimension in Hegel's Thought* (Chicago: University of Chicago
Press, 1967); and the masterful new study by Cyril O'Regan, *The Heterodox Hegel* (Albany: State University of New York Press, 1994). For a helpful assessment of current
debate on the status of determinate religion in Hegel, see Louis Dupré, "Transitions
and Tensions in Hegel's Treatment of Determinate Religion," in Kolb, ed., *New Perspectives on Hegel's Philosophy of Religion*.

The fundamental issue of the question is not simply "philosophy" or "religion" but the relation of the conceptual to the representational, and for Hegel the representational form of thinking does prove clearly inferior to the conceptual—in which alone the representational finds its actual truth. The representational consciousness, on Hegel's view, remains burdened with finitude and so has not achieved absolute self-consciousness; the conceptual, by contrast, marks the realization of absolute self-consciousness and thus the overcoming of the finite forms of representation.

Because religion first introduces to human consciousness the true content that philosophy alone will articulate conceptually, philosophy depends on religion but must at the same time overcome it, for "the content of religion proclaims earlier in time than does Science, what Spirit is, but only Science is its true knowledge of itself" (PhG 488; 430). The science of religion, then, on which philosophy depends even as it passes beyond the religious form, constitutes the final science within philosophical science (LPR 113; 3:265). At the same time, religion depends on and therefore remains *in need of* philosophy for the adequate articulation of its own truth, the spiritual content that it represents to itself but cannot conceive.

In the movement from representation to conception, according to which thought passes beyond the representational form of religion, the work of philosophy appears similar to the *aphairetic* operation of the theological traditions going back to Pseudo-Dionysius; as distinct from those traditions, however, the "removal" of the image or representation in Hegel serves and *ends in* the concept, rather than also removing and passing beyond the concept itself (I will return to this in Dionysius):

> Philosophy does nothing but transform our representation into concepts. The content always remains the same. [. . .] The difficult thing is to separate out [*zu trennen*] from a content what pertains only to representation [*Vorstellung*]. The reproach made to philosophy is that it pares away [*abstreicht*] what belongs to representation [*Vorstellung*] and that the content is then also taken away with it. This transformation is therefore held to be a destruction [*Zerstörung*]. (LPR 145; 3:292)

On Hegel's view (as distinct from that of the apophatic and aphairetic traditions), the removal of the representation serves to clarify and attain the concept, not to pass beyond it. Within this perspective, resistance to the removal of representational forms mistakes the determinate, finite shapes of religious consciousness for the essential truth-content that they present. Only by removing and transcending the former, Hegel insists, can philosophy fully clarify and conceive the latter. But precisely *what* in the religious form of representation remains inadequate with regard to the articulation of conceptual truth? In order to approach this question, I should explicate briefly the nature and function of representation as Hegel interprets them.

Like the great traditions of "spiritual exegesis" reaching back to Origen, and also like the modern counterparts of those traditions, the schools of critique and analysis following Marx and Freud, Hegel's philosophical interpretation of religious consciousness depends on the fundamental distinction between manifest and latent content, form and substance, letter and spirit. The 'letter' of religious representation, its shapes or forms, can be divided into two main types: religious representation can consist either in the "sensible forms or configurations" of "images" (LPR 145; 3:293) or in "nonsensible configurations" where the "spiritual content" is represented "in its simple mode—an action, activity or relationship in its simple form" (LPR 148; 3:295). The images or figures used in the first form of representation (e.g., symbols, allegories, metaphors, analogies, similes) involve the explicit consciousness "that we have before us something twofold, first the immediate and then what is meant by it, its inner meaning. The latter is to be distinguished from the former, which is the external aspect" (LPR 145–46; 3:293). The philosophical paring away of the representational or figurative form will seek to eliminate the external so as to reveal the internal, to overcome the immediate through the mediated concept, to pass beyond an incomplete meaning so as to attain the fullness of what is meant. The inward content that is meant and mediated by any external image or figure is for Hegel, precisely, the spiritual.

What holds here for representational shapes like images or figures holds likewise for all representational movement, that is, all narrative— which includes both the evidently mythical and the historical itself, which, as distinct from the mythical, might not at first appear manifestly figurative. As essentially governed, or indeed constituted, by spirit, the historical proves to be not only a literal or external narration of events, but also, more fundamentally, a spiritual and inward comprehension of their rational unfolding. This twofold aspect of history reaches its consummation in the religious figure that centers all of Christian consciousness: "The story of Jesus is something twofold, a divine history. Not only [is there] this outward history, which should only be taken as the ordinary story of a human being, but also it has the divine as its content: a divine happening, a divine deed, an absolutely divine action. This absolute divine action is the inward, the genuine, the substantial dimension, and this is just what is the object of reason" (LPR 147; 3:294). Both with the shapes of images or figures and with the movement of mythical or historical narrative, religion presents 'externally'—that is, according to the limits of space and time—a truth whose inward substance philosophy alone will articulate adequately—that is, in a manner whereby thought passes through those limits so as to find itself.

Thus, religious consciousness at one and the same time presents absolute truth to itself representationally and *conceals* that truth from itself through its failure to see the representational form as its own activity:

> For ordinary consciousness [. . .] religion exists essentially in these modes, as a content that primarily presents itself in sensible form, as a series of actions and sensible determinations that follow one another in time and then occur side by side in space. The content is empirical, concrete, manifold, its combination residing partly in spatial contiguity and partly in temporal succession. But at the same time this content has an inner aspect—there is spirit within it that acts upon spirit. To the spirit that is in the content the subjective spirit bears witness—initially through a dim recognition lacking the development for consciousness of this spirit that is in the content. (LPR 148; 3:295)

On this view, the spiritual truth given in religion is both present to and *not yet* fully realized by consciousness (hence, as I will show in the next chapter, an essential tie between religion and time). Within religion, spirit has not yet fully recognized itself; the spiritual content set forth in and by religious consciousness still seems, due to the form of that consciousness, to stand objectively independent of it. Even at the highest level of religious consciousness (that of the revealed or absolute religion), "Spirit has indeed attained its true shape, yet the shape itself and the representation (*die Gestalt selbst und die Vorstellung*) are still the unvanquished aspect from which Spirit must pass over into the Concept (*die unüberwundne Seite, von der er in den Begriff übergehen muß*), in order wholly to resolve therein the form of objectivity, in the Concept which equally embraces within itself its own appearance" (PhG 416; 368). The "unvanquished" objectivity of representation, the aspect that thought must overcome and pass beyond, constitutes the most significant character of such representation in relation to philosophy.

The second form of representation, that of "nonsensible configurations," presents the same inadequacies seen in sensible shapes and movements, but it does so in a less evident manner, for here the clear difficulties involved in sensible externality, the limits of space and time, and so
on, are no longer operative. Instead, at this level, the spiritual itself still
seems to remain external and objective to consciousness. Thus, "God"
himself, though not limited by external sensibility in space and time,
nevertheless remains a representation, and thus subject to the limitations
of the representational form: "God himself is this [sort of] representation. God, after all, is the universal that is determined in manifold ways.
In the form of representation, however, God is in this simple manner in
which we have God on the one side and the world on the other" (LPR
149; 3:295–96). When represented thus, God and his relation to the
world still seem external and contingent. Consciousness does not yet
realize the necessary coimplication of these two related terms.[19]

The conceptual thought that distinguishes itself from, and thus passes beyond, representational consciousness does so precisely in that it
overcomes the particular determinacy, the isolation and apparent contingency that characterize the content within representational form. Only
thus does it raise the content of that form to universality: "As we last said
above, representing holds all sensible and spiritual content in the mode
in which it is taken as isolated in its determinacy. [. . .] But the general
form of thought is *universality*" (LPR 152; 3:299). The universality of
thought, through which the contingency of the particular will be overcome, implies, first, "reflection," and then "concept" (LPR 152; 3:299)—
that is, it requires a passage beyond the seeming immediacy of the represented form and realization of the thoroughly mediated character of its
content.

To comprehend the content of religious consciousness, then, philos-

19. Likewise, the determinations made of this separated God within himself ("God
is all-wise, wholly good, righteous," etc., LPR 149; 3:297) seem themselves to remain
external to or independent of one another. This results precisely from the representational form in which God's determinations are approached, for "to the extent that [the
determinations of God] are not yet analyzed internally and their distinctions are not
posited in the way in which they relate to one another, they belong to [the realm of]
representation" (LPR 149; 3:296). The contingency apparent in the representational
form—where the determinations of God are not yet grasped in their essential interrelation—will be "stripped away," Hegel insists, "only in the form of the concept" (LPR
150; 3:297), and the concept is fully articulated only at the level of thought that removes
or rises above the form of representation.

ophy must remove or overcome the inadequacy of its representational form so as to transform a (limited) mode of consciousness into its truth as (infinite) self-consciousness. Such a transformation can be effected only by passing beyond the objectivity, externality, and sensibility inherent to the religious form of representation.

Now, as I have suggested, the logic underlying this passing-over or passing-beyond, this *Übergehen*, operates already *within* the representational sphere that presents the history of that central religious figure, the Christ or Mediator. Within the representational telling of that figure's story, the truth of the figure is achieved or comprehended only insofar as his sensible, external, objective existence has been negated and overcome. While God has become a particular *this*, while "the moment of the *Dieses* has been placed at the very center of theology," it is at the same time necessary, precisely here, "that the supreme being, after having presented itself as *Dieses*, suppress this *Dieses*."[20]

Within the representational sphere itself, in other words, a truly universal, spiritual consciousness begins only with the *death* of the sensibly existing Christ, for it is at the boundary of death that a distinction can and must be made between an irreligious, merely historical consciousness—according to which the Christ is "a human being in accord with his external circumstances" (LPR 458; 5:239)—and an actually religious consciousness—which consists in "the perspective that occurs in the Spirit or with the Spirit" (LPR 458; 5:239). Only through the removal of the immediately given, sensuous Christ does consciousness attain wholly to this second perspective, the truly religious perspective. Indeed, "It is this second view that leads us for the first time into the religious sphere as such" (LPR 464; 5:245), and it is "precisely in [Christ's] death that the transition to the religious sphere occurs" (LPR 464; 5:245).

Thus, death and its temporality are here put into the service of spirit and its truth. Only the *dead* Christ, the sensible, existent individual who *has been*, opens the way for a fully spiritual consciousness of the reconciliation effected in and through the Christ:

> This individual man, then, which absolute Being [*das absolute Wesen*] has revealed itself to be, accomplishes in himself as an individual the movement of sensuous Being [*des sinnlichen Seins*]. He is the *immediately* present God; consequently, his *"being"* passes over into *"having*

20. Jean Wahl, *Le Malheur de la conscience dans la philosophie de Hegel*, pp. 112, 113.

been" [*dadurch geht sein Sein in Gewesensein über*]. Consciousness, for
which God is thus sensuously present, ceases to see and hear Him;
it *has* seen and heard Him; and it is because it only *has* seen and
heard Him that it first becomes itself spiritual consciousness. Or, in
other words, just as formerly He rose up for consciousness as a *sensuous existence*, now He has arisen *in the Spirit*. (PhG 462; 407–8)

The death of Christ, then, operates within Hegel's conception of
truly essential time as the time of the "having-been"—the time which is
fully recollected and thus comprehended in and through the spiritual
movement of consciousness. This conception of time (to whose analysis
I turn in the next chapter) determines already Hegel's approach to representation and thus language (whose significance I then unfold in chap.
3). Within this conception, the figure of Christ can be seen to constitute,
in fact, the figure of figures as such—the figure of the singular *this* which
is necessarily annulled in and through the Hegelian movements of time
and language toward the universal. Within the story of the particular
Christ himself there unfolds the logical movement essential to all representation—namely, the movement of "passing-over," the movement of
overcoming the external, the objective, the particular, and the sensuous
in order to raise it to or reconcile it with the internal, the subjective, the
universal, and the spiritual: "For a consciousness that sensuously sees
and hears Him is itself a merely immediate consciousness which has not
overcome the disparity of objectivity, has not taken it back into pure
thought: it knows this objective individual, but not itself, as Spirit" (PhG
462; 408). The movement from the objective externality and individuality of the immediately present God to the inward comprehension of that
God in terms of spirit's absolute subjectivity is a movement from an incomplete to a complete self-consciousness. As long as God stands objectively before consciousness, as God necessarily does even in the highest
form of religion, consciousness has not achieved the fullness of self-
consciousness. The otherness inherent to the representational form
marks a remaining division within consciousness, a division of consciousness from itself.

Religion, then, is *not yet* the fullest expression of a truth that it nevertheless *already*—and first—presents. The temporal dynamic of this
"already . . . not yet" in Hegel characterizes, beyond the specifically religious sphere, the experience of consciousness as such. I have attempted
here to situate the significance of that dynamic in relation to the Hegelian death of God and the correlative annulment of finitude and over-

coming of representation. In order to begin interpreting these in their onto-theological character, I turn now to Heidegger's engagement with Hegel, an engagement where the central issue will be that of finitude, and the central field for engagement that of the temporal experience of consciousness.

TWO

The Temporal Experience of
Consciousness: Hegel's Difference
of Consciousness and Heidegger's
Ontological Difference

*I*f the Hegelian "death of God" marks a historical-conceptual development wherein the knowledge of absolute reconciliation annuls or sublates finitude, thereby effecting the "death of death" itself, then one must relate that development to the temporal experience of consciousness in and through which it would occur—for it is only in and through the trial of temporality that finitude is actually assumed in such a way as to be overcome. By approaching in light of Heidegger's reading of Hegel the relation in Hegel between temporal experience and the overcoming of finitude, I aim to illuminate the sense in which that relation is determined by the onto-theological character of the thinking that Hegel brings to completion.

According to Heidegger, Hegel's interpretation of Being in terms of absolute subjectivity completes the characteristically modern approach to Western philosophy's guiding concern to understand "beings as beings," a concern reaching back to Aristotle's investigation of ὄν ᾗ ὄν.[1] From within that guiding concern, on Heidegger's view, philosophy has presupposed but failed to articulate sufficiently the difference between the ontological question of Being (*das Sein*) and the ontic question of being or beings (*das Seiende*).[2] This confusion or ambiguity between the ontic and the ontological is operative already in Aristotle's formulation of first philosophy, where the participial τὸ ὄν, which indicates a being, or something that is, is taken also as the starting point for an investigation of being *as such*—in its *Being*.

---

1. Aristotle treats the question of "being as being" notably in books 4 and 6 of his *Metaphysics* (1003a21–1005a18; 1025b3–1026a32), where one sees already the distinction being made between *a* being or a part of being, on the one hand, and being as such, on the other: "There is a science which investigates being as being and the attributes which belong to this in virtue of its own nature. Now this is not the same as any of the so-called special sciences; for none of these others deals generally with being as being" (1003a21–25). The question of being as being, furthermore, will be tied essentially to the question of first principles or causes: "Now since we are seeking the first principles and the highest causes, clearly there must be some thing to which these belong in virtue of its own nature. [. . .] Therefore it is of being as being that we must also grasp the first causes" (1003a26–31).

2. Throughout the book, the capitalized "Being" will indicate the substantive use of the infinitival form (*das Sein*) in its distinction from the participial "being" (*das Seiende*), which will appear in the lower case.

On Heidegger's view, philosophy has failed to articulate the Being of beings and the implied difference of the two because it has failed to clarify the "as" according to which beings are *as* beings—in their Being. Leaving the "as" in obscurity, philosophy perpetuates the confusion or nondifferentiation of beings and Being. In the case of Hegel, this insufficient interpretation of the "as" would occur within his fundamental conception of subjectivity and representation: beings will appear *as* beings in Hegel only on the basis of the subjectivity that represents them and, finally, rediscovers itself in and through that representation.

Now, how does this conception of Being/beings in terms of subjectivity relate to the question of onto-theology? According to Heidegger, the confusion of beings and Being, the insufficient conception of the "as" according to which beings are *as* beings, in their Being, betrays philosophy's failure to articulate what he names the "ontological difference" between beings and Being. This failure to articulate the ontological difference will constitute the very ground on which onto-theology operates. Thus, I will seek here, broadly, to investigate the significance of the ontological difference in light of onto-theology's failure to think it; but, more specifically, I will trace that difference and that failure within Hegel's philosophical conception of subjectivity. In order to do this, I need to develop the question of ontological difference in relation to the Hegelian conception of temporal consciousness and experience, for it is on the basis of that conception that subjectivity in Hegel is constructed.

Within that construction of subjectivity, I will show, Hegel conceives the ontic and the ontological in terms of a difference—between "natural consciousness" and "real knowledge"—that the temporal experience of consciousness finally resolves and thus overcomes. But by interpreting the difference of the ontic and the ontological, which Heidegger takes to remain irreducible, in terms of a difference whose movement achieves resolution, Hegel misses the irreducible finitude which ontological difference would imply. The failure to clarify the ontological difference goes hand in hand, then, with a failure to articulate finitude in a sufficiently radical manner, and Hegel's failure to interpret finitude in a radical manner here plays itself out within his conception of Being according to the absolute subjectivity that, as fundamentally circular, "annuls" time. In these terms, then, I can relate the annulment of finitude that I traced in the Hegelian death of God to onto-theology's characteristic insufficiency regarding the thought of ontological difference and the interpretation of time.

Hegel and the Heideggerian Definition of Metaphysics as Onto-theology

From Heidegger's perspective, Hegel represents the modern completion (*Vollendung*) of traditional approaches to the guiding question of philosophy and thus marks the highest positive expression of what Heidegger terms the "onto-theological constitution" of metaphysics.[3] Because I am concerned to develop the Heideggerian (and post-Heideggerian) thought of finitude in relation to onto-theology, I should briefly lay out here the terms that define onto-theology in Hegel.

While receiving numerous formulations over the course of Heidegger's career, the definition of onto-theology remains, with differing emphases, relatively stable in its basic elements. As the term itself indicates, onto-theology concerns the interplay of ontological or ontic thought concerning Being and beings (τὸ εἶναι, τὸ ὄν; *das Sein, das Seiende*), theological thought concerning God and the divine (ὁ θεός, τὸ θεῖον), and the reasoning or discourse (ὁ λόγος) that sustains such thought.

The unclarified difference or ambiguity between beings and Being, which for Heidegger runs throughout metaphysical thinking, is borne in particular by that thinking's discourse on the divine. Onto-theology articulates its God as a being who, because supreme, accounts for all beings and thus also Being as such. In the modernity that culminates in Hegel, it will be the absolute subject that functions as the supreme being on the basis of whom the Being of beings is conceived. The interplay within onto-theology of Being and beings, the divine, and subjectivity appears in several key texts from Heidegger's engagement with Hegel.

In "Hegel's Concept of Experience" (1942–43), Heidegger offers a definition of onto-theology that stems back to Aristotle and stresses the ambiguity involved in the identification of a supreme, divine being (τὸ θεῖον) with Being itself.[4] Ontology, which would constitute the science

3. For nearly forty years, Hegel's philosophy and its onto-theological character remained a persistent concern for Heidegger—from *Hegels Phänomenologie des Geistes* (a lecture course given in the winter of 1930–31), through *Hegels Begriff der Erfahrung* (from a seminar devoted to Hegel's *Phenomenology of Spirit* and Aristotle's *Metaphysics*, books 4 and 9, given in 1942–43), to "Die Onto-theologische Verfassung der Metaphysik" (based on a seminar concerning Hegel's *Science of Logic*, winter 1956–57). In 1958, Heidegger published "Hegel und die Griechen," and in 1968 he dedicated the summer seminar at Le Thor to Hegel's *Differenzschrift*. These, along with § 82 of *Being and Time*, constitute Heidegger's main writings on Hegel.

4. For an objection to the application of the onto-theological framework to Aristotle, see Pierre Aubenque's "La Question de l'onto-théologie chez Aristote et Hegel,"

of Being itself, proves to be equally theology, the science of a particular being:

> The Science Aristotle has described—the science that observes beings as beings—he calls First Philosophy. But first philosophy does not only contemplate beings in their beingness [*Seiendheit*]; it also contemplates that being which corresponds to beingness in all purity: the supreme being [*das höchste Seiende*]. This being, τὸ θεῖον, the divine, is also with a curious ambiguity called "Being" [*Sein*]. First philosophy *qua* ontology, is also the theology of what truly is. It should more accurately be called theology. The science of beings as such is in itself onto-theological. (HCE 135; 179)

Insofar as it accounts for Being in terms of what most *is*—that is, the highest being, τὸ θεῖον—ontology is also inextricably theology or theiology, and thus the ontic science of a being. Within such a framework, the conception of the divine betrays a confusion between the ontic and the ontological, an unstable differentiation between a (highest) being and Being as such. The thinking that understands Being in terms of a supreme being leaves unclarified the nevertheless implied difference of beings and Being.[5]

From Heidegger's perspective, this intimate tie between the logic of the divine and the logic of beings in their Being will dominate philosophical thought from Aristotle, who "already brought philosophy in the genuine sense in very close connection with θεολογικὴ ἐπιστήμη, without being able to explain by a direct interpretation what the relationship is between the question concerning ὃ ᾗ ὄν and the question of θεῖον" (HPS 98; 141–42), through Hegel, who himself will state that "philosophy, too, has no other object than God—and thus is essentially rational theology—and service to God in its continual service to the truth" (Hegel, quoted in HPS 98; 141). The connection that is established but not explicated in Aristotle becomes Hegel's explicit achievement: the conception of Being in terms of a science that is at once philosophical and theological, a science of the absolute. For Hegel, that science is a science of spirit, whose conceptual unfolding will determine Being in terms of absolute subjectivity.

---

in *La Question de Dieu selon Aristote et Hegel* (Paris: Presses Universitaires de France, 1991), p.281 ff.

5. For a similar definition, according to the manner in which Being and λόγος are determined by a supreme being or absolute god, see HPS 98; 141–42.

As throughout onto-theology, the absolute in that science, subjectivity, will bear the unclarified ambiguity between beings and their Being. Absolute subjectivity remains a being whose manner of Being determines all beings, but the science of that absolute subjectivity will leave unclarified, precisely, this implied difference between the ontic and the ontological. In order to understand this onto-theological character of Hegelian subjectivity, one needs to consider Heidegger's interpretation of "ground."

In his classic essay "The Onto-theological Constitution of Metaphysics" (1956–57), Heidegger articulates the unclarified difference between beings and their Being in terms of "ground." Because the supreme being in metaphysics is understood as first cause, and vice versa, the metaphysical conception of ground will involve the ambiguity seen to characterize that supreme being. Heidegger argues that such an ambiguity involves a twofold notion of ground that becomes definitive for the onto-theological constitution of metaphysics.

According to that twofold notion, Being is understood to ground all beings in their Being while at the same time the highest being, understood as cause, accounts for beings as a whole—and thus also Being:

> Because Being appears as ground, beings are what is grounded; the highest being, however, is what accounts in the sense of giving the first cause. When metaphysics thinks of beings with respect to the ground that is common to all beings as such, then it is logic as onto-logic. When metaphysics thinks beings as such as a whole, that is, with respect to the highest being which accounts for everything, then it is logic as theo-logic. (ID 70–71; 63)

The onto-theological constitution of metaphysics is thus defined by the ambiguity of the ontic and the ontological within the central function of ground. That function is divided between, on the one hand, the grounding of all beings in the Being common to them and, on the other hand, the causation of all beings by another, supreme, being. The ambiguity of being/Being is thus borne by the God who, as supreme being, is taken as cause and thereby accounts for all beings as such—in their Being. Now, how does this conception of ground relate to Hegel?

In modernity, generally, and in Hegel, more precisely, the conception of ground will shift from the transcendent causality of the *causa sui* to the immanent ground of absolute subjectivity. That shift occurs in and through the characteristically modern development of a rationally autonomous subject, the subject whose freedom Hegel will seek to render absolute. In modernity, in other words, the thought of the absolute becomes "ego-logical."

This understanding of ground in terms of the ego-logical proves decisive for the interpretation of Hegel's modernity as the completion of onto-theology. For Heidegger, it is precisely Hegel's *Phenomenology of Spirit* that, by establishing the subjective standpoint of the absolute, attempts to realize and justify the fully modern approach to the question of Being. In doing so, Heidegger argues, the *Phenomenology* becomes the juncture at which "the decisive approaches and lines of inquiry into the problem of Being (*Seinsproblem*) in Western philosophy are gradually gathered into one":

> The inquiry into the ὄν was onto-logical ever since its beginning with the ancients, but at the same time it was already with Plato and Aristotle onto-theo-logical [. . .]. Since Descartes the line of inquiry becomes above all ego-logical, whereby the ego is not only crucial for the logos but is also co-determinant for the concept of θεός as it was prepared anew in Christian theology. The question of Being [*Seinsfrage*] as a whole is onto-theo-ego-logical. It is important in this regard that the term "logical" is repeated everywhere. The apt expression of these relations in their original formation and their concise justification lies in the fact that for Hegel the absolute (i.e., the true being, the truth) is *spirit*. Spirit is knowledge, λόγος; spirit is I, ego; spirit is God, θεός; and spirit is actuality, beings purely and simply, the ὄν. (HPS 126; 183)

On Heidegger's reading, Hegel brings onto-theology to expression and completion as a characteristically modern ego-logy wherein the guiding question of philosophy—the question of beings as beings, the question of the reality or truth of beings—is answered in terms of the logic of spirit, which comprehends the knowing I, or subjectivity, and the absolute, or God, in their essential identity—which above we saw achieved through the "death of God." Insofar as it determines beings *as* beings, this identity of subjectivity and the absolute in Hegel will be determinative for the Being of beings as such. Because, or to the extent that, the Being of beings is conceived by Hegel in terms of absolute subjectivity, Being as such goes unthought in its *irreducible* difference from beings; in this measure, Hegel's philosophy of spirit will prove onto-theological.

How, precisely and concretely, does this failure to think the ontological difference occur in Hegel? The ambiguity between a thought of beings and a thought of Being assumes form in what Hegel names "the difference of consciousness (*Unterschied des Bewußtseins*)" (PhG 490; 431): the gap that, by distinguishing the various shapes of consciousness within spirit's unfolding, engenders the tension or dynamism of that unfolding. The difference of consciousness spurs and sustains the fundamental movement, within spirit's unfolding, from "natural consciousness," which simply encounters beings in their (seeming) immediacy or givenness, to "real knowledge," which conceives the wholly mediated ground of beings (and therefore their Being) in and through absolute subjectivity. If Hegel distinguishes, at least implicitly, between the ontic and the ontological, he does so in terms of this "difference of consciousness," the difference between natural consciousness and real knowledge—and to the extent that Hegelian dialectic *resolves* the difference of consciousness, it has not interpreted the ontological difference radically. The significance of this appears especially within the Hegelian conception of temporality, where, unlike the ontological difference in Heidegger, which remains irreducible, the difference of consciousness is ultimately resolved. Only on the basis of that resolution will Hegel be able to interpret time and the finitude implied by time in such a way that the self-conceiving concept achieves an infinitude that would "annul" time. How precisely is that annulment realized?

Time and the "Difference of Consciousness"

In bringing onto-theology to culmination as ego-logy, Hegel conceives Being in terms of absolute subjectivity, and according to that conception he will establish infinite Being as the essence of time. This determination of time has an important result: to the extent that the infinite Being of absolute subjectivity comes to full conception, time as such is annulled. From this perspective, the modern consummation of onto-theology as egology would "annul" time.

This annulment of time within the thought of absolute subjectivity marks precisely the point at which Hegel cannot account for a radical finitude or difference. Indeed, the thinking that would annul time must be a thinking that conceives finitude in such a way as to negate it, establishing thereby its identity with the infinite. The point at which Hegel overcomes or sublates finitude by conceiving infinite Being as the essence of time marks the point at which he differs most fundamentally from Heidegger, for whom time, as radically finite, is the essence of Being.

Now, in the *Phenomenology of Spirit*, where the standpoint of absolute subjectivity is to be established, Hegel interprets time as the "existence of the concept," the *Dasein* of the *Begriff*. To say here that the concept *exists* is to indicate that thought stands outside of itself, appears to itself in determinate, objective shapes or forms. In and through such appearance, in and through the historical development of its interrelated, determinate thought-forms, consciousness unfolds progressively toward self-consciousness and its rational comprehension. This unfolding is driven by the negativity of consciousness, or consciousness's self-difference, in and through which the forms of consciousness move from lesser to greater adequacy, from lesser to greater self-comprehension. The consummation of this movement will consist in the absolute self-consciousness of the concept, or the idea.

The movement of consciousness toward the ideal self-consciousness of the concept constitutes the fundamental movement of spirit in its history. Spirit is historical precisely insofar as it falls "into" time, insofar as the conceptual shapes of consciousness exist and so develop toward their own self-comprehension. For Hegel, that history or conceptual development is governed by the immanent, rational teleology of the absolute. The telos of spirit's history is the rational self-certainty of the self-conscious subject, or absolute knowing.

In reading this history, one must stress the fact that consciousness *becomes* "certain that it is all of reality" precisely because it is *not* immediately so. The significance of time lies precisely in the movement of that becoming and in the negativity out of which it issues. In and through time comprehended historically, consciousness proceeds from its most empty, abstract, immediate forms (beginning with sense-certainty) to its fullest, most concretely mediated forms (culminating in the conceptual realization of spirit's absolute self-knowledge).

One can say, then, that time in Hegel constitutes the dynamic tension of the absolute that is "already" but also "not yet." Because the unfolding of consciousness is governed by the rational teleology of spirit, thought is in some sense always already the absolute. At the same time, because consciousness exists temporally, because it actually, explicitly develops or becomes, it is also *not yet* what it essentially, implicitly is (the *realized* absolute).

The existence and unfolding of consciousness, which are engendered and sustained by the negativity of consciousness's self-difference, are thus characterized by the lag between the consciousness and the *self*-consciousness of absolute spirit. That lag persists to the extent that consciousness remains opaque to itself, or has not yet recognized itself in its own shapes or forms of embodiment. Within its existence and temporal movement, then, consciousness remains unaware of the self-activity that is its actual ground and truth. Time moves, time is at issue, only insofar as consciousness and self-consciousness are implicitly identical (in substance) but explicitly non-identical (in form).

This formal gap between the consciousness and self-consciousness of spirit drives spirit's temporal development toward the realization of its full self-consciousness. The substantial identity of consciousness and self-consciousness can be actualized, then, only through a form of thinking, realized in and through historical time, that surmounts the formal lack or insufficiency of consciousness vis-à-vis self-consciousness. In this way, through the dynamism of temporal consciousness, which is driven by the difference of consciousness, thought passes from sense-certainty through the moments of perception and understanding into the fullness of self-conscious spirit and reason.

As I showed in chapter 1, in the penultimate moment of the unfolding of consciousness—that is, in the transition from religion to philosophy, thought passes, by way of its temporal existence, beyond the abstract or one-sided principles governing its representational form (*die Vorstellung*) to the fully rational form of the concept (*der Begriff*). In and through this transition, the consciousness in which self still remains concealed from itself is clarified or enlightened in such a way that consciousness becomes fully self-conscious—for it finally conceives itself in and through all those representational forms where it appears to itself.

The Annulment of Time as a Resolution of Difference

In Hegel's concluding statements on time in the *Phenomenology*, time appears as the existence of the concept that does *not yet* grasp itself in and as self-consciousness. Progress toward self-consciousness, therefore, which resolves the difference of consciousness, moves toward the fulfillment and overcoming of time itself. How? The movement of time marks the existence of the concept as merely presented or represented to consciousness; conceptual comprehension of that representation will resolve the self-difference of consciousness that spurs the very movement of time. Time's circle thus annuls time.

The philosophical explication of the concept's existence, then, concerns the temporal-historical realm of appearance, the realm where the objects of consciousness are outwardly manifest, where conceptual thought takes on external shape in order eventually to be comprehended.

Fully to grasp or comprehend inwardly the outward, objective shape of the concept will be to "annul time": "Time is the Concept itself that is there (*der da ist*) and which presents itself (*sich . . . vorstellt*) as empty intuition; for this reason Spirit necessarily appears in Time and it appears in Time just so long as it has not *grasped* its pure Concept (*seinen reinen Begriff*), i.e. has not annulled (*tilgt*) Time" (PhG 487; 429).

As the existence or there-being of the concept, time is the spiritual movement whereby consciousness stands outside of itself, over against itself—in the deficiency or negativity of its self-difference. The concept stands out, exists, shows itself in actual, determinate shapes only as this movement of time, which in a sense is a fallen movement, a movement driven by lack. To exist temporally is to struggle toward an as yet lacking comprehension of the concept, and to grasp the concept is finally to have fulfilled and thus annulled time—to have paid its price in full, like a debt, or to have wiped it away, like sin.

As the realm of the concept's appearance, existence, and movement, time depends intimately on the representational forms of thought that are time's very embodiment and punctuation (and for this reason, as I indicated above, religion and time would be intimately bound). The movement of consciousness, which becomes incarnate and determinate through time, issues from the negativity of the difference in which such forms stand with respect to a fully and purely conceptual self-consciousness. In other words, time marks "the difference of consciousness" (PhG 490; 431) that has not yet been resolved. The negativity of time proves essential to the realization of consciousness, and, at the same time, it finally resolves itself in and through that realization.

While the lag between the mere consciousness and the rational self-consciousness of spirit marks a lack or deficiency, a poverty or negativity of consciousness, such a negativity is also the very basis for consciousness's self-realization. The negativity of consciousness, its finitude and self-difference, is essential to its dynamism. Neither contingent nor accidental, that negativity or finitude of consciousness vis-à-vis self-consciousness constitutes a "destiny" and a "necessity":

> Time, therefore, appears as the destiny [*Schicksal*] and necessity [*Notwendigkeit*] of Spirit that is not yet complete [*vollendet*] within itself, the necessity to enrich the share which self-consciousness has in consciousness, to set in motion the immediacy of the in itself, which is the form in which substance is present in consciousness; or conversely, to realize and reveal [*realisieren, offenbaren*] what is at first

only inward (the in-itself being taken as what is inward), i.e. to vindi-
cate it for Spirit's certainty of itself. (PhG 487; 429)

The self-certainty of Spirit, which constitutes the truth and end of time,
is realized for Hegel in the full conversion of consciousness into self-
consciousness. In the end, no finitude or negativity can persist that
would limit the self-certainty of spirit's rational self-consciousness. The
overcoming of all such limitation is equivalent with the disclosure or
revelation of spirit to itself.

Thus, while time, like representation, is essential to the existence,
unfolding, and realization of the concept, the persistence of time indicates a remaining deficiency of the concept's form, an outstanding divide
or distance between consciousness and its own objective shapes, on the
one hand, and, on the other hand, the conceptual self-consciousness that
is to discover itself in those shapes. Time marks the persistence of a
thinking that is not yet purely conceptual, a still divided thinking that
remains burdened with the opacity of its own other-being. While the
concept does and must appear in time in order to realize itself, the persistence of time indicates the incompletion of that realization.[6]

The fullness of spirit's appearance in time, the complete realization
of the concept's existence as time, will "annul" time by overcoming the
representational thought that constitutes time's body. Such annulment
and overcoming, which stand at the heart of the Hegelian death of God,
occur to the precise extent that self grasps itself in the movement of the
Aufhebung:

> [Time] is the outer, intuited pure Self which is not grasped by the
> Self [*das äussere angeschaute vom Selbst nicht erfaßte reine Selbst*], the
> merely intuited Concept [*der nur angeschaute Begriff*]; when this lat-
> ter grasps itself it sublates [*hebt . . . auf*] its Time-form, comprehends
> this intuiting [*begreift das Anschauen*], and is a comprehended and
> comprehending intuiting [*begriffnes und begreifendes Anschauen*].
> (PhG 487; 429)

The persistence of the uncomprehended self in face of the comprehending (*begreifendes*), the opacity of what is merely represented (*vorgestellt*),
seen, or intuited, but not (yet) thoroughly conceived, the incompletion
or deficiency of the self's consciousness of itself—these characterize the

---

6. In light of this conception of time, the tie would be inextricable between time
and religion, for time implies the representational form of thinking that characterizes
religion.

time-form (*Zeit-form*) whose essential dynamic issues in and as the "not yet" of absolute spirit.

As implied by the notion that the time-form might be sublated or annulled, the "not" in this "not yet" is not radical, for the difference it signals is not insurmountable. Indeed, if the persistence of time marks the "not yet" of the self's self-comprehension, or the negativity of self-difference, then the annulment of time or the sublation of its form through self-comprehension will mark the negation of that "not yet," the resolution of that difference.

The temporal negativity or difference of the "not yet" is provisional insofar as it is the "not," precisely, *of* the absolute. As Heidegger stresses, consciousness in Hegel is not-yet-absolute only insofar as it is *already* absolute. The negativity of the not belongs to the absolute essentially:

> The not-absolute *is* not yet absolute. But this "not-yet" is the not-yet *of the absolute*. In other words, the not-absolute is absolute, not in spite of, but precisely because of its being *not*-absolute. The "not" on the basis of which the absolute can be relative pertains to the absolute itself. It is not *different* from the absolute. It is not finished and lying dead *next to* the absolute. The "not" in "not-absolute" does not express something which exists in itself and lies *next to* the absolute, but expresses a mode of the absolute. (HPS 33; 47–48)

This "not," then, indicates a negativity that is not simply opposed to the absolute, standing opposite the absolute as if external to it or independent of it; rather, the negativity indicated is integral to the being of the absolute as such. In my first chapter, this essential role of negativity *within* the life of the absolute appeared in the "death of God" according to which, in order to be known to and thus realized by human consciousness, the absolute had to pass through the most extreme negation of itself; only the God who endures the negation of other-being is actually and truly the absolute. Here, that "not" or negativity comes to light within the dynamic of time, whose annulment would relate fundamentally to the annulment of finitude effected in and through the death of God. Indeed, the annulment of finitude through the death of God and the annulment of time through the realization of self-consciousness would constitute two expressions of an identical conceptual development.

According to the logic of that development, the negativity of the "not" marks the lag between the consciousness and self-consciousness of spirit, the persistence of an opaque in-itself that stands (only apparently) over against the self of consciousness. So understood, this lag marks the self's ignorance of its own representational activity. Insofar as consciousness has its true ground and end in self-consciousness, such a lag and its representational form remain—like the negativity they signal—only provisional. The overcoming of the "not-yet" will occur in and through the self's insight into its own representational activity, and through that insight, representation is abandoned for conceptual thought.

Thus, time in Hegel is the concept that exists but has not yet been comprehended by and as the self-consciousness of spirit. The embodied, temporal forms of the concept, which appear to consciousness in the objective form of representation, must be comprehended in their truth, which is self-consciousness. Spirit achieves absolute self-certainty to the degree that consciousness becomes self-conscious and the representational form is overcome. This overcoming of the representational form marks an overcoming of finitude, and the fulfillment of time's circle constitutes an annulment of time.

Infinity and Egology in Heidegger's Engagement with Hegel

This annulment of time and overcoming of finitude point toward the central issue in Heidegger's engagement with Hegel. "In our obligation to the first and last inherent necessities of philosophy," Heidegger writes, "we shall try to *encounter* Hegel on the *problematic of finitude*" (HPS 38; 55). Within that encounter, Heidegger will argue that the finitude Hegel overcomes or sublates cannot be—for that very reason—a fundamental finitude:

> Was it not Hegel, in fact, who ousted finitude from philosophy in the sense that he *sublated* [*aufhob*] it by *putting it in its proper place?* Certainly. But the question is whether the finitude that was determinant in philosophy before Hegel was the *original and effective finitude installed* in philosophy, or whether it was only an incidental [*beiläufige*] finitude that philosophy was constrained to take up and transmit. The question must be asked whether *Hegel's conception of infinitude* did not arise from that *incidental* finitude, in order to reach back and absorb it. (HPS 38; 55)

In elaborating this question, Heidegger will claim that a finitude that can be sublated or overcome, a finitude that one can reach back to grasp and exhaust, can finally be only an incidental (*beiläufige*) finitude, not a radical one. What Heidegger himself means by a nonincidental finitude becomes clear when one relates the Hegelian conception of infinitude to Heidegger's interpretation of "idealism" and its egological ground.

Explicating Hegel's approach to self-consciousness as the "Truth of Self-Certainty," Heidegger argues that the movement in Hegel from consciousness to self-consciousness, which constitutes the return of Being to itself in and through the thought that thinks itself, is possible only when Being is conceived as infinite or absolute: "It is only from out of this genuine [i.e., absolute] Being that self-Being (*Selbstsein*) in its various stages unfolds to its own truth, to *Spirit*, which is the absolute, so much so that Spirit is Concept" (HPS 141; 203). The conception of Being as absolute, as that which essentially returns to itself in self-thinking thought, is grounded, precisely, in the thinking "I."

Thus, the Hegelian conception of Being, according to Heidegger, brings together the ancient determination of Being according to "εἶδος" or "idea," and therefore according to "seeing, knowing, and λόγος," with the modern, Cartesian ego—the "I" on whose basis being is assured: "Therefore, philosophizing as inquiry into the Being of beings is *idealism*, a title which should not be taken as the label for an epistemological orientation and viewpoint, but as a designation for the basic approach to the problem of Being" (HPS 141–42; 204). For Heidegger, the "idealistic" form of thinking concerns not simply a determination of grounds or conditions for knowing, but rather, in light of that determination, a decision concerning the meaning of Being. On this broad understanding, "idealism" determines Being according to εἶδος—that which appears to the seeing/thinking "I."

As a basic approach to the problem of Being, this idealism for Heidegger involves the logical determination of Being that in Hegel will be equally theo-logical (as throughout metaphysics) and ego-logical (as especially in modern thought). The egological development of traditionally ontological and theological thought, a development that begins for Heidegger with Descartes and comes to Hegel via Kant and Fichte, "receives its comprehensive and explicitly absolvent foundation (*Begründung*) in Hegel's *Phenomenology*" (HPS 126; 182–83). Within Hegel's idealism, the relation of the I to the not-I "shows nothing other than—to use an expression of Husserl's—the 'egological' foundation for the fact that and the manner in which consciousness of the thing, thinghood, and objectivity is possible only as self-consciousness" (HPS 125; 181).

This egological foundation of the relation between consciousness and self-consciousness comes to light in Hegel's analysis of understanding, and it is precisely there that the infinitude of the "I" or self emerges. While understanding as such remains unaware of this egological foundation, the speculative reason that knows absolutely discerns in self-consciousness the true ground and end of understanding:

> The *interior of things* into which understanding penetrates is the interior of the genuine interior, the *interiority of the self.* Only because the interior of things is basically the same as the interior of the self, is understanding constantly satisfied with its explanation. In the belief that it is doing something else in its explanation, understanding "in deed" hovers around only with itself and enjoys itself. (HPS 125; 182)

To ignore the equivalence between the interior of things and the interior of the self, to ignore the fact that "as I, the I posits what has the character of the not-I (*Nicht-Ichkeit*)" (HPS 125; 181), is to ignore the true nature of infinity, for "by itself understanding is incapable of grasping infinity as such. Understanding happens upon infinity and comes against it, but it does not discover infinity as such" (HPS 124; 180). While finding satisfaction in its explanations of reality, the understanding implicitly enjoys its own truth (i.e., self-identity in otherness, the identity, finally, of the finite and the infinite), but in taking the reality it explains as independent of itself, understanding does not yet realize that truth—which occurs only when "consciousness becomes aware of the I which differentiates itself from itself and thus knows that it is not differentiated from itself" (HPS 124; 181). At the level of understanding, consciousness does not recognize that with which it struggles: the infinite identity of its self. That infinite identity is realized only in the form of self-consciousness, the consciousness in which the thinking I becomes its own object and sees in every object itself. When consciousness finds itself in its object, it overcomes the relativity of that object and thus also of its own knowing; in this way knowing becomes ab-solute, untied from anything other than itself that would hinder its infinitely free return to itself: "The illusion of the relative is dissolved in the truth of the first simple absolute, in the truth of the *infinite*" (HPS 126; 182).

Now, the path to this egological realization of the infinite is indeed a path—it is a becoming that passes necessarily through the temporal-historical experience of consciousness, which is driven by the negativity of the difference of consciousness. Within the comprehended time of experience, consciousness is driven by its own self-difference to realize its truth as self-consciousness, the infinite truth of the self that grounds all consciousness. The lag between consciousness and self-consciousness constitutes the very existence and movement of time, and the experience of consciousness both embodies or enacts that lag and realizes its final overcoming. It is experience that resolves or negates the difference or negativity that spurs its movement in such a way as to achieve the infinite truth of the self. To understand more closely the manner in which Hegel's conception of time in terms of the infinite Being of the I proves ontotheological, one must turn to Heidegger's analysis of Hegel's concept of experience. The key to that analysis resides in Heidegger's attempt to trace the natural consciousness and real knowledge of Hegelian dialectic to the ontological difference between beings and Being, and the center of that attempt is the question of representation and Hegelian subjectivity.

Heidegger on the Temporality of Consciousness in Hegel: Representation and Subjectivity

In "Hegel's Concept of Experience" (1942–43), Heidegger explicates three statements, presented by Hegel in the introduction to the *Phenomenology of Spirit*, that concern the basic structure and activity of consciousness.[7] All three of those statements are determined according to the dynamic of temporality to which I have pointed—that is, according to the lag between the consciousness and self-consciousness of spirit—and all three thus share an ambiguity that marks "the fundamental character of [consciousness's] essence: already to be something that, at the same time, it is not yet" (HCE 116; 167). This ambiguity between "being" and "not being" is embodied temporally in the tension between the "already" and the "not yet" of the absolute. Hegel articulates that tension epistemologically in terms of the difference and dynamic between "natural consciousness" and "real knowledge," while Heidegger will trace the Hegelian framework to the more fundamental difference between ontic and ontological consciousness.

The dynamic of both being and not being, of being "already" but "not yet," signals the essential negativity that drives the being of consciousness: "Consciousness in the sense of 'being conscious' means that this 'being' resides in the 'not yet' of the 'already,' such that the 'already' *is* present in the 'not yet.' To be, be present, is in itself a self-direction

---

7. "Consciousness is its own concept, and at the same time it is not"; "consciousness provides itself with its own standard, and at the same time it does not"; "consciousness examines itself, and yet again it does not" (HCE 115; 167).

toward the 'already'" (HCE 116; 167). As indicated above, the "not" involved here is the "not" *of* the absolute; it is always already taken up by the absolute—and in that sense already overcome. The realization of consciousness as absolute involves the overcoming or negation of its own "not yet" and, correlatively, the comprehension of its "already." To realize itself as absolute, consciousness must reach back and grasp the sense in which it is "already" absolute, and it does so precisely through a negation of the sense in which it is "not yet" absolute. The overcoming of the "not yet" here depends on the essentially past-oriented movement whereby consciousness realizes, through recollection, that which in essence it always already has been.

This self-direction toward the "already" would go hand in hand with Hegel's orientation toward the past as the essential dimension of time—as the dimension where Being returns to itself in the thought that thinks itself: "For Hegel, the former time, *the past*, constitutes the essence of time. This corresponds to the fundamental view of Being (*Sein*) according to which what is a genuine *being* (*eigentlich seiend ist*) is what has *returned to itself*" (HPS 146; 211). On this reading, the essence of time, essential time, is that through which being returns to itself in what genuinely is. The ground of that return is the infinite self or I, the I that is absolute. The return of being to itself in and through the self is always already dictated by the absoluteness of the self. The temporal movement of consciousness, then, would be the movement wherein consciousness realizes that return by comprehending itself recollectively as self-consciousness.

In other words, Hegel conceives essential time as the time wherein being returns to itself in and through the resolution of the difference of consciousness. Insofar as essential time resolves the difference of consciousness through the circular return of consciousness to itself, it annuls the very ground of time's movement. But how is the difference of consciousness resolved, and what exactly is onto-theological about that resolution?

The key to understanding the resolution of difference and annulment of time as onto-theological will lie in Heidegger's understanding of Hegelian "natural consciousness" and "real knowledge" as "ontic" and "ontological," respectively, but the key to understanding the relation between natural consciousness and real knowledge must be located first within the problematic of "representation."

The dialectical movement of the experience of consciousness in Hegel—driven by the negativity according to which consciousness is

"already" but also "not yet" absolute—moves between "natural consciousness," which takes beings in their immediacy, and "real" or "absolute" knowledge, which conceives them on the basis of absolute subjectivity. In and through this movement, consciousness comes progressively
to recognize explicitly that which for the most part remains implicit
within its own activity: the function of representation.

On Heidegger's reading, the representational activity of consciousness in Hegel will determine its ontological significance, for beings in
Hegel will be significant *as* beings only insofar as they are grounded in
the consciousness of the representing subject. To argue that consciousness always already represents its objects to itself, or that it is the "I" in
consciousness that always posits the "not-I," is to argue that, at bottom,
self always represents itself to itself in the objects of consciousness. From
Heidegger's perspective, to argue in this way is to have decided on the
Being of any possible being in terms of consciousness and its representational activity. The absolute "already" of consciousness in Hegel indicates the representing *self* that is essentially present in all consciousness.
Thus, what Heidegger will seek to interpret within the horizon of Being
in its difference from beings, Hegel interprets within the egological horizon of the representing subject.

Initially, of course, consciousness does not explicitly know or comprehend its own representational function. "Natural consciousness" represents to itself each of its objects in the mode of a present being, but it
remains ignorant to its own role in bringing that being to presence.
Hegel seeks, therefore, to lead natural consciousness to the real knowledge of its self-activity. While for Heidegger the presence of beings will
indicate the Being within whose light alone beings can appear "*as*" beings, for Hegel that "*as*" indicates the representational activity of consciousness itself, and thus the infinite *self*-consciousness that is consciousness's truth.

The egological character of the modern philosophy that Hegel
would complete is here specified in terms of representation; such a philosophy finds its terra firma in the "self-certainty of mental representation (*Selbstgewissheit des Vorstellens*) in respect of itself and of what it represents" (HCE 33; 121). In the representational consciousness that
characterizes such philosophy, the self-certain subject finally takes all beings as objects that it represents to itself. Here where the Being of beings
is conceived in terms of representation, and thus subjectivity, the relation
of subject to object is finally self-relation: "The subject has its being in
the representing relation to the object; but by virtue of being this relation

it also relates to itself in the mode of representation" (HCE 34; 121). Knowledge is conceived here in terms of the self-relation of a representing subject, and the Being of beings will achieve its meaning or significance only as a function of that knowledge: "Being (τὸ ὄv) *qua* being (ἡ ὄv) exists insofar as it is the mode of the unconditional self-knowledge of knowledge" (HCE 34; 122).

Now, this conception of being in terms of knowledge, and vice versa, is achieved in Hegel when the relation of subject to object becomes thoroughly reflexive; the representing/knowing subject thinks its object as itself and itself as its object. Within the subject-object relation, subjectivity at bottom represents itself to itself and comes to comprehend that representation as such—namely, as self. Representation constitutes the self-relation of the thinking subject, and the certitude of truth itself is conceived on that basis: "But, being certainty, truth now is intellectual representation itself (*das Vorstellen selbst*), insofar as the intellect represents itself, and assures itself of itself as representation (*als die Repräsentation versichert*)" (HCE 38; 124).

Within this framework, the task of philosophical science will be to present and explicate representation as such, for representation constitutes the self-relation of the subject in terms of which truth itself is defined in its certitude. That truth, however, must come to conceive representation—for the movement of representation is initially veiled to the consciousness whose activity it already is. Here again, consciousness is both already and not yet absolute—and this marks the peculiar difficulty Hegel confronts with regard to the starting point of his science: "We, within and therefore from within the *parousia* [i.e., the appearance of the Absolute, which consists in the unconditional self-certainty of the knowing subject], must bring forth our relation to the *parousia*, and bring it before the *parousia*" (HCE 44; 126–27).

Already within the light of the absolute (which consciousness implicitly is), science—which seeks explicit absolute knowing—appears by virtue of that light: "To appear by virtue of that radiance means: presence in the full brilliance of self-presenting representation (*Repräsentation*). The appearance is authentic presence itself: the *parousia* of the Absolute" (HCE 48; 130). In order for science to be realized as science, representation must undergo the scrutiny or the *skepsis* that will lead consciousness to the absolute knowing *in which it already is* implicitly. The path of such skepsis passes for Hegel, precisely, between natural consciousness and real knowledge.

The centrality of representation within the movement from natural

consciousness to real or absolute knowledge can be related back to the
tie that Heidegger discerns throughout Western thought between knowing (as representing) and seeing: within "idealism" (ἰδέα, form or look;
ἰδεῖν, to see), the perfect "I have seen" (οἶδα, *vidi*) grounds the present
"I know." Within this optic, the seeing/knowing of a present object in its
presence depends on the function of representation: "Representation
(*das Vor-stellen*) gathers from the start into an 'I have seen' (*co-agitat*). In
this gathering, what has been seen comes to presence (*In der Ver-
sammlung west das Gesichtete an*). *Conscientia* is the gathering into presence
of the kind in which that is present which is represented" (HCE 56; 133).
Consciousness (*Bewußtsein*) is the Being that represents and achieves
self-certainty in that representation. To represent here means to render
present, to gather the represented being or beings into the presence of
consciousness. On this view, beings are present only as represented,
which means that they appear only on the basis of the conscious subject,
the Being that represents.

Now, when consciousness is understood fundamentally in terms of
a re-presentational subjectivity, the manner in which beings might appear at all *as* beings has been predetermined according to that subjectivity. For Heidegger, this means that the very Being of beings as Hegel
conceives it becomes a function of the subject:

> The other term [i.e., in addition to consciousness] for this being that
> is in the mode of knowing is "subject"—that which underlies and
> hence precedes everything else, is always already present, and thus
> accompanies all consciousness: "subject" is that itself which, in its
> representing, puts things before us, that which refers to itself what
> it has put before us and so puts it aside. To put before us is to present
> in the mode of representation [*Das Vor-stellen präsentiert in der Weise
> der Repräsentation*]. (HCE 57; 134)

In every act of consciousness, as an act of representation, the subject's
knowing refers as much to the subject's representational function as to
the "object" that is represented and thus known by the subject. More
precisely, the ob-ject constitutes an expression of the subject defined as
re-presentational; the object refers the subject back to itself because the
subject alone has set the object before itself.

This primacy of the subject's representational function, this self-
referential presence of the subject that is always already present in any
object, defines the meaning of the "subjectness" that determines the Being of beings in the mode of present presence. To be, for an object, is to

be present and to be present to a subject: "The Being of the subject which precedes everything that is represented, insofar as it reflects the subject-object relation within itself, is called subjectness (*Subjektität*). Subjectness *is* presence in the mode of representation (*Repräsentation*)" (HCE 57; 134). In Hegel, subjectness and representation go together essentially. The presence of beings is founded in the representation that constitutes the fundamental mode of subjectness. Subjectness thus grounds the possibility of the appearance of all known objects, or beings, and Being itself is interpreted within the horizon of that subjectness.

To present "phenomenal knowledge" therefore means "to represent (*vorstellen*) knowledge which itself is nothing other than that which appears, in its appearance" (HCE 58; 134). In other words, not simply knowledge (a conscious knowing or representing of some known), but the consciousness of knowledge (the self-conscious presentation of representational knowledge as such) constitutes the primary concern of the *Phenomenology*. On this view, philosophy constitutes a presentation or explication of representation itself. That representation is the very being of consciousness that goes unclarified within the activity of natural consciousness. The passage to real knowledge, therefore, will be achieved only to the degree that representation as such is brought to light.

The being of consciousness, which will constitute the reality of the real, or determine beings as such, cannot merely fix itself immediately on beings that are represented, as occurs in natural consciousness. Rather, in its movement toward real knowledge, consciousness must represent beings *as* beings—which means *as* they are represented, or according to that *as*. Real knowledge will bring beings to appearance according to the very conditions of their appearance; it will represent the movement of representation itself:

> Real knowledge is that knowledge which always and everywhere represents beings in their beingness (reality), and represents phenomena in their appearance. This is why knowledge of the reality of the real is called real knowledge. If natural knowledge proves to be unreal knowledge, it means that it turns out to be that knowledge which everywhere represents not beings *qua* beings, but in its representing merely adheres to whatever is. (HCE 60; 136)

In failing to comprehend its own subjectivity, according to whose representational activity beings are taken *as* beings, natural consciousness simply "accepts" or "adheres to" present beings but does not explain their presence, does not bring the ground of their appearance to light.

However, even in remaining fixed on the present presence of its object, natural consciousness has *already* implicitly oriented itself with respect to the beingness of beings. "But even [natural knowledge] can
become absorbed in beings, and can regard everything everywhere as
beings, only if, unbeknownst to itself, it already has a general representation of the beingness of beings. Natural representation of beings necessarily implies this general representation of the beingness of beings without, however, any specific knowledge of the beingness of beings or the
reality of the real" (HCE 60–61; 136).

Natural consciousness's immediate acceptance of beings as present
or as given constitutes the characteristic stance of opinion, or δόξα. To
move beyond opinion (δόξα) to true thinking (νοεῖν)—to "that perception which specifically perceives what is present in its presence, and approaches it with that presence in mind" (HCE 106; 162)—thought must
pass through the σκέψις that Heidegger interprets, according to its
"original" meaning, as "seeing, watching, scrutinizing, to see what and
how beings are as beings. Skepsis in this sense pursues the Being of beings with its gaze" (HCE 65; 139–40). This skeptical gaze looks beyond
beings as merely present or given in order to investigate the manner in
which they have been given in presence.

The thinking that seeks to conceive presence or appearance as such,
and not simply that which is present or apparent, is the thinking wherein
"consciousness informs itself of its own nature, which is that it is science
in the sense of absolute knowledge" (HCE 77; 145). Informing itself of
its own nature, consciousness moves beyond its natural, one-sided mode,
where it remains captive of the apparent independence of the objects
that appear to it—but this does not mean that consciousness simply or
straightaway enters the mode of real knowledge. *No longer* simply natural
or immediate, *not yet* fully real or mediated, consciousness proves to be
this very tension of being "no longer" natural and "not yet" real (another
way of expressing the "already" but "not yet" absolute): "Consciousness
itself is neither merely natural consciousness nor merely real consciousness. Nor is it the mere coupling of the two. Rather, consciousness is the
original oneness of the two. Consciousness is in itself this tension of mutual distinction between natural and real knowledge" (HCE 77; 145).

This tension of the natural and the real, the difference of consciousness, defines the structure and drives the movement of consciousness as
such. Through that temporal-historical movement, consciousness progressively transcends itself so as to become fully self-conscious rationality. While Hegel interprets that movement in terms of the dynamic

between the natural and the real, Heidegger insists that it can be understood fundamentally only in terms of the difference of the ontic and the
ontological. How so?

Difference of Consciousness and Ontological Difference

Heidegger identifies the Hegelian natural consciousness, the consciousness that "goes straight to its object as a particular being, and in the same
way goes straight to its knowledge of it as a being," as "ontic consciousness" (HCE 105; 161), and for Heidegger that ontic consciousness is
specific to modern philosophy, where the ontic determination of being
as object is based on the ontological status assigned to the conscious subject. Such ontic determination thus relates fundamentally to the egological aspect of Hegel's onto-theology:

> When beings appear as the object, because beingness has come to
> light as objectivity, when Being is consequently regarded as non-
> objective, we are already basing ourselves on that ontology by which
> the ὄν has been determined as the ὑποκείμενον, the latter as the
> *subjectum*, and the Being of the *subjectum* in terms of the subjectness
> of consciousness. (HCE 105–6; 161)

According to the ambiguity already in the Greek, "τὸ ὄν," or "being,"
serves to indicate both particular beings *and* the beingness of those beings. The question of Being, then, is posed only in terms of beings. This
ambiguity, therefore, leaves Being as such unthought or unquestioned.
Heidegger frames the difference that grounds this ambiguity in terms of
the tension between δόξα and νοεῖν, between the thinking that merely
receives and accepts present beings immediately as objects of consciousness and the thinking that investigates the presence of such present beings, illuminating the way in which they come to presence.

Metaphysics for Heidegger is that thinking which has not clarified
but nevertheless depends on the difference between presence and what
is present: "In its ambiguity, ὄν designates both what is present and the
presence (*das Anwesende als auch das Anwesen*). It designates both at once,
and neither as such" (HCE 107; 162). The consciousness that takes beings immediately as present, that is, ontic consciousness, already implies
a consciousness of the presence of what is present—an ontological consciousness. For natural or ontic consciousness, which represents beings
(as beings) immediately, representation itself is not presented. But the
"as" that makes representation possible and characterizes its function

implies that beings have already been "gathered" within some pre-understanding of Being: "the representation of the object represents the object as object, although this fact is not grasped in thought. The representation has already gathered the object into its objectivity, and thus is ontological consciousness" (HCE 108; 163).

While ontic consciousness is *already* ontological, it is at the same time *not yet* ontological insofar as it has not examined the nature and possibility of its own representational activity, the subjective activity according to which alone the Being of beings has been brought to light. In other words, natural consciousness has already and at the same time not yet thought ontological difference:

> [B]ecause it does not think of objectivity as such, even though it already represents it, natural consciousness is ontological, and still is not yet ontological. We say that ontic consciousness is pre-ontological. Being such, natural ontic pre-ontological consciousness *is* in latent form the differentiation between the ontically true and ontological truth. Since consciousness, or *being* conscious, means *being* this differentiation, consciousness is by its nature the comparison of what is ontically with what is ontologically represented. (HCE 108; 163)

Heidegger's terminology here stresses the latent or implicit aspect of consciousness that, at one and the same time, is essential to its nature and impedes its attaining insight into that nature. "Always under way" and yet "constantly turning back," consciousness "does never attain what goes on constantly behind its back" (HCE 109; 163).

It is precisely the skeptical gaze that attempts to see "behind the back" of the natural, ontic, consciousness, behind the back of that consciousness which simply accepts present beings as given without inquiring into the manner whereby their presence has become possible. A true skepsis with regard to beings opens insight into the Being of beings. Looking into the background against which all beings are presented, it seeks the ontological truth of things that are ontically true.

This background, this ontological truth which gives all beings (and thus the possibility of the ontically true), is in some way closer to consciousness than are the beings that natural consciousness simply accepts in the immediate present. The attention of skepsis

> tries to see in truth what it is that, as truth, is behind the things that are true. Someday, the skepsis might even come to see that that

which for philosophical opinion remains "behind" is in truth "before." The truth of natural consciousness—which this consciousness can never find out because *it is its own background*—is itself, that is, in truth, the *foreground* of the light which *from the first* surrounds every mode of knowledge and consciousness, as a "having seen." (HCE 109; 163)

The "having seen" of idealistic consciousness, which grounds the present knowledge of any ontically true "I know" (οἶδα, *vidi*), occurs in Hegel against the ontological background of subjectivity and its representational function. To the extent that this background/foreground itself comes to light, natural consciousness and the opinion based on it lose their immediately compelling truth. Skeptical consciousness will thus take as its object not simply the object, but objectivity itself: "Now objectivity is the object; and what is now called object can no longer be determined on the basis of previous opinion concerning objects" (HCE 111; 165).

When objectivity becomes the issue, then so too does the subjectivity in terms of which objectivity is defined. The examination of objectivity that arises in the dialectical movement of consciousness will trace objectivity to its subjective ground, and thus it names what Hegel understands by "experience."

Ontological Difference, the Difference of Consciousness, and Dialectic

Heidegger identifies Hegelian "experience" as a name for the "as" that underlies all consciousness in its representational character. Because the "as" marks a condition of possibility for any access to beings as such, it finally names the Being of beings insofar as Hegel conceives it—that is, in terms of the subject's subjectness. Heidegger here takes the question of experience in Hegel to be primarily ontological, not epistemological:

> The term "experience" in Hegel names that which appears, insofar as it appears, the ὄν ἧ ὄν. The ἧ is implied in thought in the word "experience." In virtue of the ἧ (*qua*, as), beings are thought of in their beingness. Experience is now no longer the term for a kind of knowledge. Experience now is the word of Being, since Being is apprehended by way of beings *qua* beings. Experience designates the subject's subjectness. (HCE 113; 166)

Being is apprehended in the function of the "as" according to which beings appear *as* such. Implicit in that "as" lies the distinction between ontic and ontological consciousness, and for Heidegger the "as" functions only on the basis of that distinction. Functioning on that unclarified basis, the "as" presupposes some ontological comprehension of Being, but the ontological is not thought as such insofar as the consciousness based on the "as" remains preoccupied immediately with beings. The tension of this distinction is maintained in and by the differentiated unity of consciousness, whose very movement is grounded in the distinction.

It is precisely in this sense that Heidegger interprets the dialectical character of Hegelian consciousness: "Consciousness is *qua* consciousness its own movement, for it is the comparison between ontic-pre-ontological knowledge and ontological knowledge. The first lays claim to the second. The second lays claim to the first. Between (διά) the one and the other, there is the uttering of these claims (*Ansprüche*), a λέγειν" (HCE 118; 169). Hegelian consciousness thinks and speaks (λέγειν) between (διά) the ontic and the ontological, which circle one around the other, each calling for the other.[8] Consciousness gathers the two and holds them together in their difference—in order finally to sublate that difference. For Hegel, the dialectic between natural consciousness and real knowledge culminates in their reconciliation; the real will grow out of the natural, which itself is thus raised to its truth. That truth grows

8. As I will show in the next chapter, the circling of the ontic and the ontological, their gathering in the difference that joins them—in short, the dialectical character of consciousness—relates consciousness essentially to its form of articulation, its utterance or statement. Such statement is grounded, for Hegel, in the primacy of the I, itself taken as infinite, and it brings to light, for Heidegger, the essential thrust of λόγος in metaphysics: "For Hegel, as the completion of Western metaphysics, the entire dimension of the problem of Being is oriented toward the λόγος. [. . .] The truth of what is spoken ultimately lies in the I, the subject, or spirit" (HPS 65–66; 93). The I-orientation of the spoken and the thought—the λόγος in dialectic—characterizes the Absolute Idea, wherein the I thinks itself absolutely. The exposition of this self-referential λόγος within itself marks the achievement of the *Science of Logic*, which "represents the self-movement of the Absolute Idea only as original *word* [. . .]. The self-determination therefore in which alone the Idea is, is to hear itself speak: it is in pure thought, where the distinction is not yet any otherness, but is and remains completely transparent to itself" (G. W. F. Hegel, *Science of Logic*, trans. W. H. Johnston and L. G. Struthers [New York: Humanities Press, 1966], 2:467). In the *Phenomenology*, the self-referential character of thought and expression operates not at the level of pure thought, but at the level of experience; only through the labor of experience is that self-referential character of thought and language achieved explicitly.

essentially out of the Hegelian conception of subjectivity. Subjectivity is the name for that which reconciles or resolves the difference out of which the experience of consciousness moves; it names the presence that would endure and overcome that difference.

According to its dialectical character, experience is always already ahead of itself, and in this sense it is not within itself, not present to itself—but at the same time, it has always already arrived, has always been present to itself in subjectivity: "Experience is the process of reaching forth, reaching, arriving (*Das Erfahren ist das auslangend-erlangende Gelangen*). Experience is a mode of being present (*eine Weise des Anwesens*), that is, of Being" (HCE 120; 170). As a mode of *Anwesen*, experience is that in terms of which Hegel conceives Being in its truth. As the manner in which beings become present, as the presence or presencing of being, experience indicates the "truth of what is true," the appearing of what appears. The presentation of this truth or appearing is nothing other than the presentation and comprehension of the subject that represents: "Experience is the presentation of the absolute subject that has its being in the representation, and so absolves itself. Experience is the subjectness of the absolute subject. Experience, the presentation of the absolute representation (*die Präsentation der absoluten Repräsentation*) is the *parousia* of the Absolute" (HCE 120; 171).

This *parousia* of the absolute, wherein absolute representation is itself presented or brought to light, effects the overturning or inversion, the destruction or the very "death" of natural consciousness. The uprooting effected by *skepsis*, through whose insight "natural is carried off into real knowledge," is "the death of natural consciousness" (HCE 80; 147), but, at the same time, "[i]n this constant dying consciousness sacrifices itself, so that it may by the sacrifice gain its resurrection into its own nature" (HCE 80; 147). The death of natural consciousness, then, is conceived only already within the horizon of resurrection; it *belongs to* the absolute subjectivity of which it is only a passing moment, the absolute subjectivity within which difference is a path to reconciliation or resolution.

The dialectic between natural consciousness and real knowledge operates according to the same logic governing the death of God, and thus it means finally the sacrifice and elevation of the finite to the infinite: "The course of the dialogue [i.e., the dialogue—which experience is—between natural consciousness and absolute knowledge], reaching and arriving, is the way of despair, the way by which consciousness at each moment loses what in it is not yet true and sacrifices it to the real appearance of the truth" (HCE 146; 186). This way of despair is the path along which natural consciousness gains insight into its foundation in the subject that always represents itself to itself; through such insight, natural consciousness "dies" only to be resurrected in the reality or truth of the absolute.

The death of natural consciousness, then, occurs within "the theology of the Absolute, in respect of the Absolute's *parousia* in the dialectical-speculative crucifixion. This is where the absolute meets death. God is dead. And this means everything except 'there is no God'" (HCE 146–47; 186). God dies precisely insofar as representational consciousness is finally conceived and thus overcome. Through that overcoming, natural consciousness is sacrificed to the truth of real knowledge. The difference of consciousness is thus resolved and so proves not to be a radical or irreducible difference.

Such an overcoming and resolution, however, would prove problematic to the degree that the difference of consciousness indicates but does not clarify a more fundamental difference, itself irreducible. This difficulty brings me to a conclusion concerning the Heidegger-Hegel engagement.

Explicating the original title of the *Phenomenology*—"Science of the Experience of Consciousness"—Heidegger insists on the irreducibly twofold meaning of the genitives. While natural consciousness takes the genitives objectively, as indicating that experience is the object of science and that consciousness is the object of experience, the science that is itself named effects the inversion of precisely such consciousness. For this reason, the genitives must be read not only as *genitivus objectivus* but also as *genitivus subjectivus* such that "strictly understood, neither takes precedence over the other. Both designate the subject-object relation of the absolute subject, in its subjectness" (HCE 140; 182).

Here Heidegger signals the manner in which Hegel's thought implies but does not or cannot clarify the difference starting from which the inversion of consciousness itself becomes possible:

> In either reading, the genitives indicate that relation of which the inversion makes use *without ever giving thought to it* specifically: the relation of Being to particular beings as the relation of particular beings to Being. The dialectical movement establishes itself in that domain which has been opened up by the inversion, but which is also concealed by it precisely *qua* openness of that relation. (HCE 140; 182)

This passage sums up the central point on which Heidegger differs from Hegel. The dialectic of absolute knowing, driven by the negation of the negation, which overcomes the difference of consciousness and operates within a conception of Being as infinite subjectivity, implies a difference that would prove more fundamental than the Hegelian difference of consciousness and its negativity.

Just as that difference is implied by the Hegelian conception of temporal experience, even as that conception would ignore or annul it, so too would the Hegelian conception of language turn on the unthought difference and so bear the characteristic ambiguity of onto-theology. To that conception of language I now turn.

THREE

The Naming of God in Hegel's
Speculative Proposition:
The Circle of Language and
Annulment of the Singular

*A*s the immeasurably influential commentaries of Alexandre Kojève and Jean Hyppolite[1] made remarkably clear, and as subsequent scholarship has not ceased to emphasize, language is essential to the very life or movement of Hegelian thought—the two are realized only in and through one another. Language for Hegel is the embodiment of thought, and thought is necessarily linguistic. Thus, the present chapter turns from the temporal experience of consciousness and its circular annulment of time and finitude to the language whose circularity would articulate or embody the truth of such experience. Just as absolute subjectivity in Hegel would annul time and finitude so as to give even death a fullness of meaning, so the philosophical language that articulates or embodies such subjectivity will name or express the absolute in a fullness that annuls all singularity. By thus relating Hegel's language of the absolute, which constitutes his naming of God, to his annulment of finitude, or his "death of death," I can go on then (in chaps. 4 and 5) to consider, by contrast, the possible relation between a thought of irreducible finitude (in Heidegger) and a language of the unnameable (in the Dionysian framework). Just as I will argue that the "death of death" in Hegel is tied essentially to the fullness or completion of his naming of God, so I will argue that the insurmountability of death in a Heideggerian perspective might be tied to a naming of God that remains empty or impossible.

The Speculative Proposition and the Theology of the Absolute

The form of language to embody the essentially circular movement of Hegel's thinking is the speculative proposition (*der spekulative Satz*). Hegel's development of that proposition proves at once egological and theological, which means that the articulation of the absolute through the speculative proposition will concern not only the interpretation of human subjectivity but also the fundamental manner in which Hegel

---

1. From Jean Hyppolite, see not only his commentary *The Genesis and Structure of Hegel's Phenomenology of Spirit*, trans. S. Cherniak and J. Heckman (Evanston, Illinois: Northwestern University Press, 1974) but esp. *Logique et existence* (Paris: Presses Universitaires de France, 1953).

names God. Hegel's naming of God in terms of absolute subjectivity, or, conversely, his conception of absolute subjectivity in theological terms, goes hand in hand with his conception of language in terms of the "absolvence" effected by the speculative proposition. Not only does the absolvence of human language render it appropriate to the naming of God, but such absolvence actually gives to language a "divine" character.

Of course, the conception of God in terms of the absolute and the conception of the absolute according to the infinite Being of subjectivity are not self-evident, but rather constitute characteristically Hegelian achievements. Stressing the link between the absolute and the speculative proposition in Hegel, Jean Beaufret indicates that to name God the absolute is, indeed, "to Hegelianize":[2]

> Like method for Descartes, the speculative proposition is only one side of [Hegel's] metaphysics. The other side, like Descartes' non-deceiving God, is the connection of the speculative proposition itself with what Hegel names the *absolute*. Such is, according to him, the most proper name of God, who has changed his name so many times since, as Heidegger says, he "entered into philosophy." (HLP 122–23)

The parallel drawn here between, on the one hand, the relation of God and method in Descartes and, on the other hand, the relation of the absolute and the speculative proposition in Hegel stems from Hegel's inheritance of the Cartesian definition of truth in terms of certitude. In seeking to establish the certitude of truth for the thinking I, Hegel renders the predicative form of language speculative, as Beaufret notes: "For spirit as reason is the 'certitude . . . of being all reality' as well as all 'presence,' but inasmuch as 'raised to the level of truth,' that is, to the level of the 'dialectical movement of the proposition'" (HLP 121). "Against Descartes," but nevertheless as a Cartesian seeking truth as egological certitude, "Hegel honors, higher than mathematics, the λόγος as proposition, in his speculative interpretation of the proposition" (HLP 122).

On Beaufret's reading, which I will follow here, the certitude of truth issuing in the dialectical movement of the proposition relates essentially both to Hegel's egology and to his theology. The "theology of the absolute" would be for Hegel "the indispensable reverse of that of which the

<hr/>

2. See Jean Beaufret, "Hegel et la proposition spéculative," in *Dialogue avec Heidegger: Philosophie moderne* (Paris: Editions de Minuit, 1973); hereafter cited parenthetically as HLP. Translations are mine.

speculative proposition is the obverse" (HLP 123). The theology of the absolute and the egology of the speculative proposition must therefore be thought together.

The speculative proposition and its egology prove Cartesian in the sense that, within that proposition, the Being of the "I" is conceived on the basis of consciousness and knowledge. As I noted in the previous chapter, Heidegger insists that this egological conception modifies but at the same time grows out of antiquity's ontology: "To put it in historical terms, the new orientation toward consciousness in modern philosophy since Descartes is not a radically new beginning over against antiquity, but only its extension and transference to the subject. [. . .] The egological orientation of the ontological still remains bound to the tradition in the form of the I as 'ego cogito,' 'I think,' 'I know, 'I state'" (HPS 136; 196). In the modernity that issues from Descartes, the ancient interpretation of Being in terms of λόγος occurs as an interpretation of Being based on the ego's logic. Being thus becomes that which is known and stated by the I—namely, the "I think" itself. "I think," or "I know," is essentially tied to the "I state."[3] In Hegel, the fullest form of such statement will consist in the speculative proposition, which articulates egologically the absolute conception of the absolute. Thus, the "I state" of Hegel's egology remains inseparable from his theology of the absolute.

Defined as a being-delivered, or absolved, from any relation in which it would constitute only one side relative to another, the absolute in Hegel is conceived as the infinite—the specifically "good" infinite. As absolute, or truly infinite, God is delivered from the one-sidedness or relativity that would set the infinite apart from the finite. The speculative proposition, correspondingly, will aim to free the language or expression of the absolute from the one-sidedness of simple predicative statement, where subject and predicates are taken as independent of one another.

Now, while the speculative proposition (insofar as it will concern the Being of what is) and the absolute (insofar as it will concern the Being of the highest being) mark two sides of an indivisible unity, that unity also involves an unclarified difference. Having noted that the theology of the absolute in Hegel is indispensable to the speculative proposition,

---

3. Indeed, Descartes makes this connection in his Second Meditation: "finally it is necessary to conclude, and to hold as constant, that this proposition, 'I am, I exist,' is necessarily true *every time that I pronounce it*, or that I conceive it in my mind" (Second Meditation, in *Oeuvres de Descartes*, ed. Charles Adam and Paul Tannery [Paris: Vrin-C.N.R.S., 1964–76], 9:25; my translation and my emphasis). The performative character of the *ego cogito* has not escaped commentary.

Beaufret goes on to mark out the ambiguity that we saw to structure onto-theology for Heidegger: the ambiguity between the Being of beings, on the one hand, and the highest being among beings, on the other: "Metaphysics is thus a dissymmetrical connection between a mode of the Being of being that is *generically* its radiant summit, and the essence of being that determines it *communally*, but according to a radically *transgeneric* community, such that the two determinations are equally fundamental" (HLP 123–24).

The interconnection of these two different but equally fundamental determinations can be formulated also in terms of the classic problem concerning "the one and the many." To make such a formulation, Beaufret refers here to Heraclitus, in whose fragment "it is not in a symmetrical manner that, το ἐκ πάντων ἕν, Heraclitus adds: καί ἐξ ἑνὸς πάντα" (HLP 123, n. 52). Here, the ambiguity of the ontological and the ontic within the ground of metaphysics comes to light in the ambiguity of the one and the many, the unique and the universal. The one can be understood as the gathering of all into a universality *and* as the unique from which all comes. This ambiguity, according to Heidegger, characterizes the very λόγος of metaphysics:

> Being becomes present as λόγος in the sense of ground, of allowing to let lie before us. The same λόγος, as the gathering of what unifies, is the ἕν. This ἕν, however, is twofold. For one thing, it is the unifying One in the sense of what is everywhere primal and thus most universal; and at the same time it is the unifying One in the sense of the All-Highest (Zeus). The λόγος grounds and gathers everything into the universal, and accounts for and gathers everything in terms of the unique. (ID 69; 61)

The highest being, the one source of all beings, is (as cause) essentially related to, but distinct from, the one, universal Being shared by all beings. In this manner, the λόγος of metaphysics both joins and separates the theological and the ontological.

As onto-theology, metaphysics displays the "dissymmetrical connection" between the highest being understood as first cause of beings as a whole, on the one hand, and the Being of such beings, understood as ground of all beings (including the highest), on the other. Metaphysics is thus characterized by the unclarified difference according to which this dissymmetry is structured. The expression of the absolute within the speculative proposition will bear this ambiguity and depend on that unclarified difference insofar as the absolute can be thought both as a term within the proposition (God, a being, is . . .), *and,* at the same time, as the entirety of what the proposition aims to express (the Being of beings is the absolute).

The manner in which Hegel's theology of the absolute relates to the dialectical movement of the speculative proposition here calls for explication. The absolute is, as such, ab-solved, removed, or untied from any relation in which it would constitute only one side of, and thus a relative term within, that relation. In a sense, the absolute would constitute the very "relating" of any relation, never a term within such relation. To this removal or ab-solvence of the absolute from any relativity must correspond the speculative recasting of the standard propositional form of language. How so?

Within standard propositional language, going back to Aristotle, subject and predicates seem to persist independently of one another and would be related externally as separate terms; predicates are understood to inhere in the subject much like accidents are understood to inhere in a substance that remains itself without those accidents. The relation of subject and predicate here remains, precisely, accidental or contingent. In other words, the difference of the predicates from the subject to which they seem to be related externally has not yet been conceived as the very *self*-difference of the subject; the predicates have not been seen in their essential, necessary relation to the subject.

In the speculative proposition, by contrast, the subject is related essentially to its predicates in the sense that they mark the very embodiment or self-realization of the subject itself. The subject passes over into, or even "loses" itself, in its predicates only in order to return to itself and find itself in them. The predicates of the subject here mark an otherness or difference that proves essential to the subject itself; they mark, precisely, the otherness in and through which alone the subject finds and realizes itself. Choosing the "example" of God, the logic of whose absoluteness would in fact govern *all* speculative language, Beaufret nicely explicates this Hegelian movement beyond the standard propositional form of language:

> When I say, for example, *God is Being*, or just as well, *God is dead*, I am not attaching to a fixed subject, namely God, the predicates of Being or non-Being [. . .]. Rather, in the subject's journey to the predicate, which is not simply a logical addition for the subject, but much rather an antagonistic pole, the subject loses its substantial base and enters so to speak into "the night of disappearance." How-

ever, the midnight of that night is, in the predicate, the counterblow
[*Gegenstoss*] that sends the proposition back from the predicate to
the subject, but in such a way that the subject to which it returns,
leaving off from the predicate, is no longer that from which it had
left in order to go to that predicate. In other words, the third concept (God), although homonymous with the first (God), is no longer
the latter, even if it seems to be so still. (HLP 116)

On this interpretation, the proposition does not constitute an empty tautology of abstract identity, but rather articulates the concrete, dialectical
movement of the spiritual "is." That concrete movement constitutes the
self-realization of the absolute in and through its own self-othering; the
speculative proposition alone would offer that self-realization its adequate expression because it alone articulates the mutual, essential implication of the subject and its predicates.

The speculative proposition thus seeks to express the truly restless,
absolvent character of what otherwise might appear as a static, abstract,
or empty "is." The restlessness brought to expression by the speculative
proposition, a restlessness opposed to the spiritless, abstract thinking
that would view subject and predicate as simply different rather than essentially different (that is, identical in their mutual implication), issues
in the fundamental negative movement of the *Aufhebung*, which raises
the difference of terms to a unity that at once preserves and resolves
the difference:

> the subject *is* the predicate, the word *is* no longer being the *geistloses
> Ist*, the simple copula of the judgment, but, as the between of the
> subject and the predicate, the properly "spiritual" *is* of a movement
> whose most proper name is: *the dialectical movement of the proposition*.
> Such a movement is at first only *transition* [*Übergang*]. But it is above
> all *Aufhebung*. (HLP 116–17)

As the actual embodiment of the *Aufhebung* and its negativity, the speculative proposition realizes the fundamental Hegelian movement of self-
realization through self-difference—the movement, that is, of spirit. To
set the abstract or spiritless "is" into motion, to engender the truly concrete, restless, and absolvent character of the spiritual "is," would constitute, from the Heideggerian perspective, the "whole task" of Hegel's
philosophy. The question of the speculative language form, then, is not
"simply" a question of language, but of Hegelian thought as such and of
its central movement (the double negativity of the *Aufhebung*):

[I]n speculative "philosophical" propositions, the simple difference between subject and predicate is not abolished through identity, but rather is sublated. This is the absolvent proposition. In the proposition "is" is stated. Hegel brings the absolute restlessness of absolvence into the quiet "is" of the general proposition. The *whole work of his philosophy is devoted solely to making this restlessness real.* (HPS 66; 93)

Now, insofar as the whole of Hegel's philosophy seeks to make real the restlessness of absolvence, the whole of that philosophy can be read as a treatise on the naming of God in and through the speculative proposition. The dialectical movement of the speculative proposition, the movement of the spiritual "is," is embodied in that very history where God or the absolute enters into self-difference (creation, history) so as to achieve self-realization. To that historical unfolding would correspond the unfolding of a philosophical language that progressively realizes the conceptual content or meaning of what otherwise would remain the empty name of God.

Hegel's dialectical development of the proposition, then, seeks to pass beyond what in less adequate thought and language forms (e.g., especially, the form and logic of the judgment) would appear as a mere, empty name awaiting the addition of predicates. The actualization of the name of the absolute depends on the dialectical movement of the *is*, which occurs in and as the history of spirit. For Hegel, that entire history embodies the conceptual realization and fulfillment of the (at first "mere") name of God. Thus, the speculative proposition, which passes beyond the mere name by realizing it substantially, functions in essential conjunction with the Hegelian theology of history.

Without this dialectical interpretation of the *is*, and without the speculative proposition that would articulate Hegel's ontology and theology of history, the name of God would remain empty and meaningless: "Whoever has not entered into the dialectical secret even of the divine essence can well form sentences about God such as *God is the Eternal* or *God is love.* But posed in this way immediately as subject, God is only a sound deprived of meaning, a simple denomination" (HLP 125). To this simple denomination Hegel will oppose precisely the language of the dialectical movement that drives the very history of spirit. That history wherein the name of God is filled conceptually is a history in which the language of God, theology, is related essentially to the language of Being as such, ontology, "for this theology is such, in its turn, only in its con-

trasted unity with an ontology whose fundamental trait is, in the proposition, the dialectical interpretation of what Kant named the 'particle of
relation' (*Verhältniswörtchen*) *is*" (HLP 126).

The dialectical interpretation of the copula, the particle of relation,
or the "is," unfolds on the basis of a history that proves fundamentally
theological. The dialectical unfolding of the "is," then, proves identical
with the unfolding of what God himself is. Religiously, that history is
understood starting from creation—that is, starting from the self-
negation, even unto death, of the absolute: "God is God only through
the movement of descending dialectically below himself, not only in order to vanish utterly in Being (*s'anéantir jusqu'à l'être*), as the *Logic* lays
out, but as far as to assume, as Malebranche said, 'the base and, so to
speak, humiliating condition of the Creator'" (HLP 125). The speculative proposition in and through which Hegel develops his dialectical interpretation of the copula thus corresponds to the movement of the creator into creation—the movement of God into that history where God
is fully realized in and through his death. Only through the movement
of God into creation and history, only through God's passage into the
negativity of other-being, only through the death that achieves meaning
through its own ultimate negation—only thus will the empty name of
God be realized and fulfilled. This tension between the mere name of
God and its conceptual fulfillment, a tension essential to the speculative
proposition that constitutes the essential language of Hegel's thought as
a whole, is first set out in the opening pages of the *Phenomenology of Spirit*.

A Grammar of Consciousness: The Name and the Concept

In his Preface to the *Phenomenology*, Hegel establishes several key principles for the role that language will play in his subsequent thinking. His
statements on language in the preface explicitly raise the question that
concerns me here—that regarding the relation between the naming of
the absolute, on the one hand, and conceptual thought, on the other.
Within his remarks on this relation, Hegel introduces the fundamental
distinction between the predicative form of discourse (the discourse of
everyday opinion as well as most philosophy) and the speculative form
of his own philosophical discourse.

Hegel's interpretation of language, generally, and his naming of God
as absolute, specifically, must be viewed in conjunction with the fundamental insight of the *Phenomenology* that "everything turns on grasping
and expressing the True, not only as *Substance*, but equally as *Subject*"

(PhG 10; 18). Substance can be grasped and expressed as Subject only to the extent that one comprehends the role that negativity plays in the movement of consciousness. For Hegel, thought always moves, by way of double negation, 1) beyond the empty simplicity of abstract immediacy, 2) through the determination of other-being (which is at bottom *self-othering*), 3) to recollection in a realized self-identity, which constitutes a mediated immediacy, a concrete, inwardly differentiated unity.

This fundamental movement of consciousness would correspond to the movement of language wherein 1) an initially empty grammatical subject, a mere name, is 2) "lost" in or passes over into its predicate, and 3) returns eventually from the predicate into itself as a self that now is concretely realized, filled with determinate content. As J. P. Surber suggests in his article "Hegel's Speculative Sentence,"[4] this parallel between the grammatical subject and the subject of consciousness is not coincidental. In reading Hegel, one must take seriously the fact that "the grammatical subject can reflect what is otherwise also understood by 'subject': consciousness as a process of self-articulation and development" (SUR 215).

This tie between the grammatical subject and the subject of consciousness indicates the essential role of language in rational self-consciousness: both at the level of language and at the level of thought, the subject (grammatical or conscious) realizes itself in and through its own self-othering. Within such a perspective, "the crucial point is that any adequate account of the basic form of language must reflect the, for Hegel, essentially *active* and *self-developing* nature of consciousness" (SUR 216). Like the movement between the grammatical subject and predicate within the propositional structure, a movement wherein the subject develops out of an initial simplicity or emptiness, the movement of consciousness is a movement between the loss and retrieval of self, between departure from the immediate simplicity of self, on the one hand, and return to the mediated unity of self, on the other.

At the level both of language and of consciousness, such movement depends on the negativity that defines the truth of the Hegelian subject:

> This Substance is, as Subject, pure *simple negativity*, and is for this very reason the bifurcation of the simple; it is the doubling which sets up opposition, and then again the negation of this indifferent

---

4. Jere Paul Surber, "Hegel's Speculative Sentence," *Hegel-Studien* 10 (1975); hereafter cited parenthetically as SUR.

diversity and of its antithesis [the immediate simplicity]. Only this self-*restoring* sameness, or this reflection in otherness within itself—not an *original* or *immediate* unity as such—is the True. (PhG 10; 18)

The movement of the Hegelian subject is a movement of self-positing or self-othering, a negative thetic activity in which the subject at one and the same time becomes other than itself, remains identical with itself in its otherness, and returns to—or fully becomes—itself in its concretely actualized self-identity.[5] Within this movement, truth consists in the mediated unity of self-identical subjectivity.

Such subjectivity, I have noted, is at the same time conceived theologically, for Hegel understands the subjective movement of self-positing and self-restoration in terms of the "life of God and divine cognition," the movement of God through creation and history. In other words, the negative movement in which substance becomes subject, a movement where self proves identical with itself in and through all otherness, is the historical movement of divine spirit. In a much quoted passage, and according to the logic I have been highlighting, Hegel insists on this inclusion of the negative within any true conception of the divine life; that inclusion of the negative, I showed above, is precisely what is at stake in the Hegelian "death of God," which, along with the correlative conception of love, is essential to the concretion and fulfillment of what otherwise would remain an abstract and empty understanding of the divine: "Thus the life of God and divine cognition may well be spoken of as a play of Love with itself (*ein Spielen der Liebe mit sich selbst*); but this idea sinks into mere edification, and even insipidity, if it lacks the seriousness, the suffering, the patience and the labor of the negative" (PhG 10; 18). For Hegel, the life of God must from the start be understood within the conception of substance as subject. The negativity that is essential to subjective consciousness thus governs Hegel's dialectical reinterpretation of language in general and of the naming of God in particular.

Within the becoming-subject of substance, which constitutes a movement from abstract or simple universality, through determinate self-negation or self-othering, to concrete self-identity, the absolute comes to be seen according to the aspect in which it is *result*. In the

5. Again, one might discern in Hegel's substantial subject a resonance or echo of the Proclean triad of μονή, πρόοδος, and ἐπιστροφή as expressed in the famous Proposition 35 of Proclus's *Elements of Theology*.

Phenomenology, the implicit self-identity of the absolute is explicitly developed and fully realized only over the course of the temporal-historical experience of consciousness that I explicated in chapter 2.

Such a conceptual movement grounds an initial statement on language: "The beginning, the principle, or the Absolute, as at first immediately enunciated, is only the universal. Just as when I say '*all* animals,' this expression cannot pass for a zoology, so it is equally plain that the words, 'the Divine,' 'the Absolute,' 'the Eternal,' etc., do not express what is contained in them" (PhG 11; 19). The immediate universal is the simple that has not yet been developed; it has not yet passed through its own self-positing or self-othering, has not mediated itself in and through its own otherness. At the same time, however, it already contains such mediation implicitly. Only on the basis of this *already* can Hegel maintain that the words Divine, Absolute, Eternal, and so on, do not yet express what in fact is already contained in them. This "not yet" characterizing the articulation of the absolute belongs, precisely, to that which is destined to be expressed, for it is the "not yet" *of* the absolute.

For Hegel, the absolute can be conceived only in terms of development and mediation. Thus, any language that starts with the immediate or undeveloped must pass beyond itself if it is actually to embody or express the absolute: "Whatever is more than such a word, even the transition (*Übergang*) to a mere proposition, contains a *becoming-other* that has to be taken back, or is a mediation" (PhG 11; 19). Through its rational teleology, self is essentially self-mediation, or reflection of self in other. Only through such mediation does self become *for itself* what it is already *in itself.* The realized self is thoroughly introreflected, and the language of that self, the very body of its existence and development, is the language that passes beyond both the immediate simplicity of the word or name and the nondialectical interpretation of the subject-predicate relation. Dialectically conceived, the subject-predicate relation enacts the self-mediation, self-development, and introreflection of the self.

Now, within the Hegelian framework, the immediate name of God remains empty to the extent that it is not determined in and through the dialectical relation with its essential predicates. In its emptiness, the name of God appears as a "mere" name, a name that initially seems to lack determinate meaning or content. The apparently fixed subject, "God," will assume life and actuality only through the determinations of its predicates, which pass beyond the mere name:

The need to represent [*vorzustellen*] the Absolute as *Subject* has found expression in the propositions [*Sätze*]: God is the eternal, the moral world order, love and so on. In such propositions the True is only posited [*gesetzt*] *immediately* as Subject, but is not presented [*dargestellt*] as the movement of reflecting itself into itself. In a proposition of this kind, one begins with the word "God." This by itself is a meaningless sound, a mere name [*ein sinnloser laut, ein bloßer Name*]; it is only the predicate that says *what God is*, gives Him content and meaning [*ist seine Erfüllung und Bedeutung*]. Only in the end of the proposition does the empty beginning become actual knowledge. (PhG 12; 20)

The "mere" name of God will be meaningfully fulfilled or given content, and thus real knowledge of *what* God is will be actually secured, only in and through the dialectical articulation of those predicates that constitute God's very self-development. Subject and predicates here remain inseparable. Thus, the relation between God's mere name and God's predicates, the subject-predicate relation, must be interpreted in the properly dialectical fashion. Lacking that dialectical interpretation, the subject-predicate relation would fail to convey, or embody, the thoroughly self-developing dynamic and introreflected structure of the absolute; it would fail to express, precisely, the subjectivity of the absolute as spirit.

According to these principles of self-development and introreflection, the "mere name" must pass beyond its initial appearance as conceptually impoverished so as to afford actual knowledge of *what* God is. At the same time, however, such an initial impoverishment is not wholly or simply a deficiency, since it alone allows for the positive freedom of subjective development; indeed, the emptiness of the mere name will serve to indicate the very power and freedom of the absolute as subject. How so?

Having observed that the mere name of God requires the content and meaning that are provided only through those predicates that say *what God is*, Hegel observes that, "this being so, it is not clear why one does not speak merely of the eternal, of the moral world-order, and so on, or, as the ancients did, of pure notions like 'Being,' 'the One,' and so on, in short, of that which gives the meaning without adding the *meaningless* sound as well" (PhG 13; 17). The mere name, the name that is neither a pure notion nor yet developed through any predication, appears initially as a meaningless, empty sound. In this sense, the mere name would resemble a body or vehicle—a letter—that does not yet contain or convey the spiritual or ideal content that gives it its life, meaning, and fulfillment.

But this meaningless sound actually proves significant in its very meaninglessness, significant precisely in that it does *not* yet contain its developed conceptual content, but rather *comes to* its conceptual determination only through its free self-development. The absolute is not simply an immediate, pure notion, nor a fixed point to which attributes might be affixed; rather, it is the self-mediating subject. The meaningless sound, the mere name, thus serves to indicate the subject's freedom for self-determination, for a self-determination that will occur, precisely, through the predicates in which God's name is fulfilled.

The initial difficulty here stems from an as yet insufficiently dialectical interpretation of the subject-predicate relation; thought at first only *anticipates* the dialectical interplay of subject and predicate, and thus, to begin, conceives the subject only as a fixed point and not as a living movement. The "mere name" thus indicates the freedom of the subject but cannot yet fully express or embody it:

> But it is just this word that indicates that what is posited [*gesetzt*] is not a Being or Essence or Universal in general, but rather something that is reflected into itself, a Subject. But at the same time this is only *anticipated*. The Subject is assumed as a fixed point to which, as their support, the predicates are affixed by a movement belonging to the knower of the Subject, and which is not regarded as belonging to the fixed point itself; yet it is only through this movement that the content could be represented [*dargestellt*] as Subject. (PhG 13; 17)

Hegel here confronts the difficulty of answering both the necessity of establishing meaningful content for the meaningless sound ("God") and the necessity of not making the absolute into an inert, fixed point to which a knower, independent of the absolute, would attach "meaningful" predicates. In short, this difficulty concerns the expression or articulation of the self-movement and immanent development of the absolute.

Such immanent movement is inadequately expressed in the propositional form of the judgment, S is P, and yet such a form, at least initially, is necessary to present the content of an otherwise meaningless sound. At issue here, ultimately, are the relation and transition between the logic of the judgment, which proves necessary but finally inadequate, and the logic of the syllogism, which alone adequately articulates the rational self-development of the absolute. Hegel address these two logics in the

Phenomenology, but they receive their full elaboration only in the *Science of Logic*—specifically, in the Subjective Logic, or the Doctrine of the Concept. A brief exposition of the Judgment and the Syllogism will illuminate the relation in Hegel between the name and the concept.

The Judgment and the Syllogism

Hegel defines the judgment as "the self-determination of the Concept (*das Bestimmen des Begriffes durch sich selbst*)" (SL 258; 71) wherein the individual subject assumes meaning in its predicates, which express the universal. According to this definition, the name within the judgment is initially both empty and arbitrary:

> But only the predicate furnishes the Concept, or at least the essence and the universal in general, and it is this that is asked for within the meaning of the Judgment.—As subject of a Judgment, therefore, God, Spirit, Nature, or whatever else it may be is only the name: what such a subject is according to the Concept is given only in the predicate. (SL 259; 73)

While the being of this subject is determined only through the relation of universal predicates to the initially empty name, within the language of the judgment the initially empty name already implies such predicates. That is, the "mere" name—which, significantly, Hegel will associate with the image or representation, *die bloße Vorstellung*—is already determined by its concept. Or, in other words, there simply is no name or representation that remains outside of an at least implicit conceptual determination.

This determination of the name by the significance of the concept is presupposed but, initially, not yet accomplished by the judgment. Thus, the essential movement of the judgment is that between an initially empty name, on the one hand, and the presupposed conceptual determination of that name, on the other. Or, in other words, the subjectivity of the name awaits its determination in the movement of the judgment:

> If the predicate proper to such a subject is looked for, then a Concept must already be implied to furnish a ground for judgment; but it is only the predicate that expresses this Concept. Really therefore the mere image [*die bloße Vorstellung*] constitutes the presupposed significance of the subject and leads to a declaration of name [*Nah-*

menerklärung]; and what is or is not understood by a name is a historical fact, and contingent. Many controversies whether a predicate is proper or not to a certain subject are therefore no more than verbal disputes, because they begin from this form; that which lies at the bottom (*subjectum*, ὑποκείμενον) is as yet no more than the name. (SL 260; 73–74)

The implicit conceptual unity contained in the judgment is not yet comprehended by representational thinking (*die Vorstellung*), which takes the related terms of the judgment—subject and predicate—to be independent elements that persist externally to one another. So long as the related terms are not comprehended in their essential interrelation, the subjectivity of the subject has not been conceived adequately: "In this subjective consideration, then, subject and predicate are each considered as complete by itself apart from the other: the subject as an object which would exist even if it had not this predicate; and the predicate as a general determination which would exist even if it did not belong to this subject" (SL 260; 74). When the judgment is understood in this way, as the connection of two independent elements, the terms of the judgment prove to be merely "determinations of imagination (*Vorstellungs-Bestimmungen*)" (SL 261; 76), determinations that have not been grasped conceptually in their essential relation.

Now, while the inner conceptual unity of these terms is not yet comprehended, that inner unity is nevertheless implied by the judgment (*Urtheil*) as such, insofar as it is the "original dividing (*das ursprüngliche Theilen*)" of the essentially unified concept. This "original dividing" constitutes the truth of the earlier forms of transition explicated through the course of the *Logic:*

> In Being there is transition into other and in Essence showing in an other, wherein the *necessary* relation reveals itself. This transition and showing have now passed over into the original dividing [*das ursprüngliche Theilen*] of the Concept, which, leading back the Individual into the Being-in-Self of its Universality, equally determines the Universal as actual. That Individuality is posited in its intro-Reflection, and the Universal as determinate—these two processes are one and the same. (SL 262–63; 78)

The identity of these two movements—the determination of the universal in the individual, and the raising of the individual to its universality (the two movements, one should recall, that characterized the "death of

God" above)—can also be read in the reverse direction, such that "the subject may equally well be taken as Being-in-Self, and the predicate as Determinate Being" (SL 263; 78). Taken together, these two readings express the conceptual unity implied by the judgment. Within that unity, subject and predicate would not stand independently of one another, but realize themselves only through one another.

However, in the form of the judgment as taken externally, the two sides still maintain an apparent independence from one another; the unity that is implicit in the judgment has not yet attained the explicit realization that will be achieved in the syllogism:

> But in the judgment this identity has not yet been posited; the cop-
> ula exists as the relation (as yet indeterminate) of Being in general:
> A is B; for the independence of the determinatenesses of the Con-
> cept, or of the extremes, is, in the Judgment, the *reality* which the
> Concept has at this point. If the "is" of the copula were already pos-
> ited as this determinate and completed unity of subject and predi-
> cate, or as their Concept, then it would already be Syllogism. (SL
> 264–65; 80)

Already grounded in the unity of which it is the original dividing, the judgment is not yet the complete, determinate expression of that unity. Here arises the crucial transition to the syllogism, which for Hegel is the rational itself, for "whatever is reasonable is a syllogism" (SL 301; 132).

The syllogism is distinguished from the judgment whose truth it is in this way: the concept-determinations that are posited within the judgment as separate and independent are posited within the syllogism in their explicit unity. Through this determinate unity, the syllogism brings to light what is actually rational in the objects of reason (e.g., God, freedom, the infinite, etc.):

> It is this:—that their infinite element is not empty abstraction from
> the finite, nor universality without content or determination: it is
> filled universality, the Concept which is determinate, and contains
> its determinateness in this verifiable manner, that it distinguishes
> itself in itself and exists as the unity of these its rational and determi-
> nate distinctions. (SL 302; 133–34)

The syllogism consists in the twofold, unified movement of the universal into the individual and of the individual up to the universal; each implies the other such that any appearance of their independence is overcome. The syllogism is thus the movement of the absolute itself, the "movement of the universal through determination to individuality, as also the reverse movement from individuality through superseded individuality, or through determination, to the universal" (PhG 480; 423). At the level of language, the subject, taken either as the universal or the determinate, and the predicate, taken either as the determinate or the universal, are realized here in their completed unity.

In this way, the syllogism expresses the rational concept itself as fully actualized, and the actualized concept constitutes a thoroughly mediated immediacy:

> The Syllogism is mediation—the complete Concept in its positedness. Its movement is the transcendence of this mediation, in which nothing is in and for itself, but each term is only through the mediation of another. Consequently the result is an immediacy which has emerged through the transcendence of mediation, a Being which is equally identical with mediation, and is the Concept which has constructed itself out of and in its otherness. (SL 342; 191)

As the truth of the judgment, the syllogism brings the concept to its rational realization. The determinate being and the meaning of the concept are inextricably unified in the syllogism. There, the concept lives as self-identical negativity that determines itself in and as its own otherness. Characterized by such mediation, the concept is the absolute. By transcending the relativity of subject to predicate through the realization of their mediated identity, the syllogism expresses or actualizes the negative logic of the absolute, thus providing the logic and the language of ab-solvence.

Critique of Propositional and Representational Language

The absoluteness of the concept in Hegel demands that the language of the concept be ab-solvent. Insofar as the concept and its language govern the interpretation of the absolute (or vice versa), the naming of God in Hegel's philosophy will be inextricably bound with the syllogistic formulation of the concept. That naming of God, of course, would be related essentially to the movement of time that I analyzed in chapter 2, since time is for Hegel, precisely, "the existent Concept itself" (PhG 26–27; 34). The logic and language of the syllogism would correspond to the temporal unfolding of the absolute by giving the only fully adequate expression of its truth. Here in the Hegelian concept, then, time and language are essentially tied. The language of the concept must accommodate, or embody, the "sheer unrest," the "life," and the "absolute distinction" of the concept (PhG 26–27; 34). Given this requirement, Hegel will critique all forms of thinking and all forms of language that remain external or inessential and therefore cannot embody the essential, inner life and movement of the concept. Two stand out and illuminate one another as opposite extremes of the same deficiency.

On the one hand, Hegel indicates that the external, inessential character of the thought evident, for example, in mathematics, can mark also, more generally, all forms of thought that proceed through propositional argumentation: "[T]he way of asserting a proposition (*Satz*), adducing reasons (*Gründe*) for it, and in the same way refuting its opposites by reasons, is not the form in which truth can appear. Truth is its own self-movement, whereas the method just described is the mode of cognition that remains external to its material" (PhG 28; 35). Hegel associates this external mode of cognition, characteristic of the understanding (*Verstand*), not only with mathematics but also with the predicative form of language: "Even when the specific determinateness [. . .] is in itself concrete or real, the Understanding degrades it into something lifeless, merely predicating it of another existent thing, rather than cognizing it as the immanent life of the thing" (PhG 32; 39). The language of speculative thought must pass beyond the externality of that predication which merely attaches attributes to a subject as if from outside of it. Truly speculative language, rather, will express the wholly inward, immanent development of the subject.

On the other hand, much like the argumentation that Hegel criticizes, the thought-language relation that characterizes representation or picture-thinking (*Vorstellung*) also proves resistant and finally inadequate to the movement of the concept (as I indicated in chaps. 1 and 2). While the propositional argumentation of the understanding proves overly formalistic and thus empty of any real conceptual content, representational thinking proves overly involved in its material and thus unable to rise above it:

> The habit of picture-thinking, when it is interrupted by the Concept, finds it just as irksome as does formalistic thinking that argues back and forth in thoughts that have no actuality. That habit should be called material thinking, a contingent consciousness that is absorbed only in material stuff, and therefore finds it hard work to lift the [thinking] self clear of such matter, and to be with itself alone.

At the opposite extreme, argumentation is freedom from all content, and a sense of vanity towards it. (PhG 35; 41)[6]

The insufficiencies both of (overly formal) propositional argumentation and of (overly material) representational thinking concern the central relation between subject and predicate. Both the back and forth movement of argumentation and the material thought of representation take the subject as a fixed point to which predicates would be attached (or not), thus leaving subject and predicates in an external, inessential relation. To this, Hegel opposes the speculative or conceptual mode of thinking according to which the predicate is not an accidental property but rather the substantial realization of the subject:

> This Subject [from the point of view of argumentation] constitutes the basis to which the content is attached, and upon which the movement runs back and forth. Speculative [begreifendes] thinking behaves in a different way. Since the Concept is the object's own self, which presents itself as the coming-to-be of the object, it is not a passive Subject inertly supporting the Accidents; it is, on the contrary, the self-moving Concept which takes its determinations back into itself. (PhG 37; 42)

In Hegel's speculative interpretation of predication, as can be seen in the syllogism, predicates are not attached externally to a subject that would persist independently of such predicates, as accidents would be attached to a substance,[7] but rather they express and embody the self-development of the subject itself. Likewise, the subject of consciousness does not simply receive its objects as if from an independent exterior but rather actualizes itself in and through the otherness of its own objects.

---

6. These opposite extremes of resistance to speculative thinking—the overly formal and the overly material—are reflected in Enlightenment thought and religious faith: "Pure insight has, therefore, in the first instance, no content of its own, because it is negative being-for-self; to faith, on the other hand, there belongs a content, but without insight" (PhG 324; 288–89).

7. In Aristotle, the interpretation of consciousness as receptive of the forms is paralleled by the interpretation of the grammatical subject (substance) as receptive of its predicates (accidents). It is precisely this interpretation of predication and consciousness that Hegel opposes: "Hegel sees the Aristotelian notion of predication as strictly paralleling this receptivity [of the forms by the soul]: Predicates are externally and 'passively' received by the grammatical subject, which seems to play no role in the development of the determinations themselves" (SUR 215).

Thus, as opposed to the external and abstract understanding of consciousness and language operative in argumentation or representational thought, consciousness and language together must be conceived in terms of the essential identity of substance and subject.

When the content of predicative language is no longer understood as accident but is rather conceived as the very substance of the subject, representation or picture-thinking must be overcome or sublated:

> Picture-thinking [*das vorstellende Denken*], whose nature it is to run through the Accidents or Predicates and which, because they are nothing more than Predicates and Accidents, rightly goes beyond them, is checked in its progress, since that which has the form of a Predicate in a proposition is the Substance itself. [. . .] it finds that, since the Predicate is really the Substance, the Subject has passed over [*übergegangen*] into the Predicate, and, by this very fact, has been sublated [*aufgehoben*]. (PhG 37; 43)

This "passing-over" of the subject into the predicate, which occurs through the double negation of the *Aufhebung*—and which representational thought cannot conceive fully, but only figure externally—characterizes the movement analyzed above (chap. 1) in the death of God: the "decline" or kenotic movement of the divine into its otherness (creation, incarnation, death). Such a passing-over grounds the Hegelian onto-theology of history. Within that onto-theology, just as God passes kenotically outward into history in order there to be realized concretely, so the name of God passes over into its predicates there to be conceptually determined. This passing-over would constitute the path whereby the mere, empty name is fulfilled—and thus overcome.

The Mere Name and Representational Thinking

The fulfillment and overcoming of the empty name by its conceptual determination and the properly syllogistic language of that determination prove essential to the sublation of representational thinking—that is, the form of thinking in which the name and concept of God are first announced. Already an expression of the absolute, the religious form of representation, because burdened with an insufficiently dialectical conception of the subject-predicate relation, would, according to Hegel, name God in a manner that is not yet wholly adequate. The overcoming of representational thinking, as seen above, occurs within the movement of the divine (its decline or passing-over) through the very forms of that thinking. Overcoming is at the same time fulfillment, and fulfillment is achieved only insofar as representation is overcome.

This overcoming-fulfillment of the representational form within Hegel's speculative philosophy occurs in conjunction with the speculative destruction of the common forms of judgment or proposition. That destruction, I have shown, is effected through the development of the speculative proposition whose logic I outlined, a development that demands and commands the conceptual passage beyond the empty or mere name. The critique of representation in Hegel, then, would be related essentially to the critique of the name that remains insufficiently determined by conceptual content.

In a summary passage leading to a discussion of the name of God, Hegel will set the ground for relating the true naming of God, on the one hand, to the "destruction" of the judgment or proposition, on the other: "Formally what has been said can be expressed thus: the general nature of the judgment or proposition, which involves the distinction of Subject and Predicate, is destroyed by the speculative proposition, and the proposition of identity which the former becomes contains the counter-thrust against that subject-predicate relationship" (PhG 38; 43). Likening the conflict between the judgment or proposition, on the one hand, and the expression of the concept in the speculative proposition, on the other, to the dynamic of rhythm, Hegel indicates that the destruction of the proposition does not entirely efface the distinction between subject and predicate, but rather establishes an essential unity-in-difference. The "accent" of the proposition corresponds to the determinate sense conveyed by the predicate in the propositional form, while the unity or "harmony" corresponds to the fact "that the predicate expresses the Substance, and that the Subject itself falls into the universal" (PhG 38; 44).

As an "illustration," of this unity-in-difference of the speculative proposition, Hegel chooses the onto-theological statement par excellence: "God is being (*Gott ist das Sein*)" (PhG 38; 44). This proposition illustrates the manner in which, within truly conceptual thought, the predicate is not merely tacked on to a fixed, preestablished subject, but rather constitutes the very substance of the subject: "'Being' is here meant to be not a Predicate, but rather the essence; it seems, consequently, that God ceases to be what he is from his position in the proposition, viz. a fixed Subject" (PhG 38; 44). Nonspeculative thought blocks comprehension of the predicate as a realization of the subject's being or essence because such thought takes subject and predicate one-sidedly, as

if in an external relation to one another. Through the destruction of the
proposition, nonspeculative thought is destabilized; its one-sidedness is
undone, and it enters into the true interplay of subject and predicate:
"Thinking therefore loses the firm objective basis it had in the subject
when, in the predicate, it is thrown back on to the subject, and when, in
the predicate, it does not return into itself, but into the subject of the
content" (PhG 39; 44).

In his commentary on this illustration, Surber identifies, within the
to-and-fro movement from subject into predicate and from predicate
back into subject, two moments, a metaphysical and an ontological, the
unity of which would constitute the speculative. That unity depends on
a dialectical interpretation of the copula such that the proposition reads:
1) metaphysically: "God (receives the determination of his essential nature in) Being" and 2) ontologically: "God (is the ground for predicating)
Being" (SUR 225–26). According to the metaphysical moment, the subject, God, is lost in the predicate, Being, while according to the ontological moment, the predicate is thrust back toward the subject, where it
finds its ground.

Through a modification in terminology, one can identify in this
scheme the fundamental ambiguity of onto-theology's twofold ground
as explicated by Heidegger. Surber's metaphysical moment would correspond to what Heidegger calls "ontologic" while Surber's ontological
moment would indicate what Heidegger names "theo-logic": onto-logic
is that thought in which Being appears as the ground common to all
beings (including the highest being, God), while theo-logic is that
thought in which beings as a whole (and thus Being as such) are thought
with respect to their cause in the highest being, God (see ID 70–71;
63).

In light of this correspondence between the schemes of Surber and
Heidegger, the dialectical interpretation of the copula within the speculative proposition can be seen in its onto-theological determination. According to that dialectical interpretation, the name of God is fulfilled
only on the basis of the thought and language of Being (which are the
thought and language of the concept) wherein the abstract "is" is thoroughly developed into *ground*.[8] For Heidegger, the significance of Hegel's speculative sentence consists in precisely this:

8. This occurs at the logical transition from judgment to syllogism. See SL 299;
129–30.

I arrive at the speculative sentence when the predicate of the sentence (*Sein*) is made subject, becomes subject. Thus: *das Sein ist Gott* [Being is God]. [. . .] *Das Sein ist Gott* now understood speculatively means: *das Sein "istet" Gott, d.h., das Sein lässt Gott Gott sein* ["Being 'ises' God, i.e., Being lets God be God"]. *Ist* is transitive and active. It is only *Being* as unfolded (in the sense that it is in the *Logic*) which (in a speculative rebound) makes being-God possible.[9]

Within the determination of God on the basis of Being, and the determination of Being in terms of God, the name of God will be conceptually fulfilled in such a way that the "mere" name of God is overcome.

At the conclusion of his prefatory comments on the role and status of predication, Hegel comes again to the "mere" name of God in order to indicate its positive role within the movement that would pass beyond it. He reaffirms his point that it might seem expedient to avoid the empty, proper name insofar as it carries no inherent concept, and he thereby contrasts the proper and the conceptual name so as to stress the emptiness of the former and the fullness of the latter. Again, the mere name is likened in its emptiness to the self that is only sensuously intuited or represented (*dem sinnlich angeschauten oder vorgestellten Selbst* [PhG 40; 45]). The likeness of the mere name and the sensuously intuited self consists in the fact that both serve to designate the as yet undeveloped subject, or the emptiness out of which the subject will become itself:

> Apart from the self that is sensuously intuited or represented, it is above all the name as name that designates the pure Subject, the empty unit without thought-content. For this reason it may be expedient [*dienlich*], e.g., to avoid [*vermeiden*] the name "God," since this word is not immediately also a Concept [*Begriff*], but rather the proper name [*der eigentliche Name*], the fixed point of rest of the underlying Subject; whereas, on the other hand, e.g. "Being" or "the One," "Singularity," "the Subject," etc. themselves at once suggest concepts. (PhG 40; 45–46)

The difficulty indicated here concerning the proper name is this: it can be determined and filled with conceptual content only by passing through the propositional form, but the propositional form itself finally

9. Martin Heidegger, "A Heidegger Seminar on Hegel's *Differenzschrift*," trans. William Lovitt, *Southwestern Journal of Philosophy*, vol. 11, no. 3 (Fall 1980): 38.

proves inadequate to the rationality of the concept. Within that form, the name appears as a fixed point to which predicates are then attached, thus indicating that the subject "is present merely in the form of a passive subject" (PhG 40–41; 46); the external attachment to a passive subject of predicates whose content "lacks the immanent Concept" (PhG 40; 46) because it lacks the dialectical form constantly risks falling into "the form of mere edification" (PhG 41; 46). Speculative philosophy seeks, on the contrary, to understand the absolute as immanent movement and self-development. The speculative content of philosophy therefore must be maintained in and through a dialectical form of language, the form of the concept.

This difficulty accounts for the ambiguity of Hegel's remarks on the avoidance of the name. While he suggests that it might be expedient (*kann es . . . dienlich sein*) to avoid the name "God," in fact he does not avoid it. Indeed, it pervades his thought. This is due to the unique capacity of the name to indicate the freedom of the subject. The proper name of God—in contrast to such conceptual names as Being, One, Eternal, and so on—initially appears impoverished with regard to conceptual content; this initial poverty, however, in fact serves to indicate the freedom of the subject that develops, out of emptiness, through its own self-mediation. While Hegel suggests that it might be useful to avoid the name God insofar as it lacks an immediate concept, he adopts the name insofar as the freedom of the subject springs out of such an initial lack.

And yet, this subject that will be reflected into itself, the subject indicated by the proper name, is "only anticipated" (PhG 13; 21):

> But it is just this word [i.e., the "meaningless sound," "God"] that indicates that what is posited is not a being [i.e., something that merely *is*], or essence, or a universal in general, but rather something that is reflected into itself, a Subject. But at the same time this is only anticipated. The Subject is assumed as a fixed point to which, as their support, the predicates are affixed by a movement belonging to the knower of this Subject, and which is not regarded as belonging to the fixed point itself; *yet it is only through this movement that the content could be represented as Subject.* (PhG 13; 21; emphasis added)

What serves to indicate the freedom of the subject, the proper name, also resists the true expression of that freedom by making of the subject a passive, fixed point to which predicates are attached, as by one who knows it externally; but such an external relation is contrary to the concept, whose actuality is the immanent movement of self-knowledge. The propositional form, which presents its content through the external distinction of a subject and predicate that are independent of one another, remains inadequate to the speculative predicate. The name of God, then, must be rendered in the form appropriate to its speculative, conceptual content. In his discussion of this name, Hegel pronounces a guiding principle for the whole of his philosophy: "In keeping with our insight into the nature of speculation, the exposition (*Darstellung*) should preserve the dialectical form, and should admit nothing except in so far as it is comprehended (*in so fern es begriffen wird*) and is the Concept (*und der Begriff ist*)" (PhG 41; 46).

In setting down these principles for the properly philosophical form of expression, the concern with the appropriateness of form to content might seem to render expedient the avoidance of the mere name, the proper name, of God. At the same time, it is that proper name which indicates, from out of its initial emptiness and in a way that the immediately conceptual name cannot, the freedom and self-development of the subject. The initial emptiness of the name proves to be at one and the same time an emptiness necessary to the freedom of the subject and an emptiness whose purpose is met only to the degree that the emptiness is negated, filled, and thus overcome.

The Naming of God and the Dialectic of the "This"

Hegel likens the mere, empty name of God that is not yet conceptually determined to the sensuous self not yet comprehended as subject—which means that the mere name of God would need to be overcome much in the way that the sensuous existence of the Christ must be overcome in the realm of religious representation: both must be raised to the conceptual level. Both the overcoming of the name and the overcoming of the sensuous Christ would concern at bottom an overcoming of the singularity that cannot be raised to the universality of the concept. The significance of such overcoming or annulment of the singular appears within the *Phenomenology*'s earliest exposition of the *Aufhebung*—within the analyses of sense-certainty and the dialectic of the "This."

The significance of the "This" in Hegel could not be overestimated. Indeed, the meaning and utterance of the This set the *Phenomenology* as a whole into motion and bring to light, together with the basic character of language, the fundamental dynamic of the *Aufhebung* in its double negativity. As Giorgio Agamben indicates in his study of Hegel and Heidegger, *Language and Death: The Place of Negativity*, "it is in relation to this *Wahrnehmung* of the *This* that Hegel articulates completely for the first time in the *Phenomenology* the explanation of the dialectical significance of the term *Aufhebung*."[10]

Within the analysis of sense-certainty that opens the *Phenomenology*, the movement of the *Aufhebung* accounts for the conceptual universalization, through language, of a meaning that would initially appear singular. While on a given occasion I might well mean to indicate a singular, sensible *this*, I can think and utter only the universal. This insistence of the universal first appears through a movement that begins with the utterance of the "This."

Hegel attacks the assumption of natural consciousness that what seems most immediate—that is, what is sensibly certain—is therefore also most knowable and true. He argues, to the contrary, that the most immediate proves in fact to be the most empty and abstract, for it involves nothing other than sheer Being—the certainty *that* what is is, without any determination or comprehension of *what* it is: "this very certainty proves itself to be the most abstract and poorest truth. All that it says about what it knows is just that it *is;* and its truth contains nothing but the sheer Being (*Sein*) of the thing (*Sache*)" (PhG 58; 63).

Hegel argues that in the seemingly immediate certainty of what merely *is*, in the certainty of sheer Being, mediation is in fact always already at work: a division is always already made, at least implicitly, between the conscious I, on the one hand, and that of which the I is conscious in its certainty, on the other. Thus, the division of the I and its object signals an essential mediation that operates already in every encounter with a "This." The I and the object of sense certainty both prove to be universals whose truth consists in their mediation through one another:

10. Giorgio Agamben, *Language and Death: The Place of Negativity*, trans. Karen E. Pinkus with Michael Hardt (Minneapolis: University of Minneapolis Press, 1991), p. 14. Agamben develops an analogy between "taking the this" in Hegel and "being the there" in Heidegger so as to illuminate the negative ground of metaphysics, according to which the capacity for language and the capacity for death would be inextricably bound. Agamben begins his analysis by noting the morphological and semantic connection between the *Da* of Dasein and the demonstrative pronoun *diese*. In light of that connection, Agamben develops the possibility of an analogy "between the experience of death in *Sein und Zeit* that discloses for Being-there the authentic possibility of its *there*, its *here*, and the Hegelian experience of 'This-taking'" (p. 5). It is from the analysis of the This in Hegel that "negativity springs forth" (p. 5). Agamben's fascinating analyses leave me wondering whether he does justice to the significant differences between the

> An actual sense-certainty is not merely this pure immediacy, but an instance of it. Among the countless differences cropping up here we find in every case that the crucial one is that, in sense-certainty, pure being at once splits up into what we have called the two "Thises," one "This" as "I," and the other "This" as object. When we reflect on this difference, we find that neither one nor the other is only immediately present in sense-certainty, but each is at the same time mediated: I have this certainty through something else, viz. the thing; and it, similarly, is in sense-certainty through something else, viz. through the "I." (PhG 59; 64)

According to Hegel's analysis, what is given within any sense certainty is not an immediate singularity, but rather a mediated instance; the object is mediated through the I and the I through the object. Every case of meaning within sense certainty is thus already an exemplification, an instance of the mediated or the universal.

Hegel seeks to show that the self-contradiction inherent in natural consciousness's assumption that sense certainty is the truest knowledge appears straightaway in the attempt to indicate or express the immediate or what merely *is*. Such indication or expression can occur only in language, which itself, on Hegel's interpretation, can speak only the universal—that is, that which remains self-identical in and through its own negation: "A simple thing of this kind which is through negation, which is neither This nor That, a not-This, and is with equal indifference This as well as That—such a thing we call a universal. So it is in fact the universal that is the true [content] of sense-certainty" (PhG 60; 65). For Hegel, it is the universal that constitutes the truth of sense-certainty (which according to that truth will be raised to perception), and this truth comes to expression or realization in language.

What one *means* to say, then, namely, the immediate, sensuous, particular "This" (spatially as the "Here," temporally as the "Now"), does not in fact reach language. In this sense, meaning and truth stand at odds, and in language truth will prevail:

> It is as a universal too that we utter what the sensuous [content] is. What we say is: "This," i.e. the universal This; or "it is," i.e. Being in general. Of course, we do not envisage the universal This or Be-

---

Hegelian and Heideggerian interpretations of negativity—an issue clearly central to the present work.

ing in general, but we utter the universal; in other words, we do not strictly say what in this sense-certainty we mean to say. But language, as we see, is the more truthful; in it, we ourselves directly refute what we mean to say, and since the universal is the true [content] of sense-certainty and language expresses this true [content] alone, it is just not possible for us to say, or express in words, a sensuous being that we mean. (PhG 60; 65)

The force and truth of language negate and pass beyond the singularity of the meant, a sheer sensuous Being, and thus raise it to the conceptual universality of the uttered or expressed. Language will thus annul the singularity that meaning intends to express with it.

Now, this movement of language, as a movement of negativity, implies a very specific conception of time, to which I pointed in chapters 1 and 2. Within the expression of truth by language, the universal asserts or reveals itself according to a movement of time that becomes an essentially historical movement—that is, a time articulated and comprehended within the recollection of consciousness. The conception of time operative here, then, privileges the "having-been" as the essence of time; what "has been" is recuperated within the negative movement of historical consciousness. When time is articulated in terms of recollection, that recollection functions by taking up, sustaining, and indeed rendering productive, the negativity that grounds the being of the universal. Once pointed out or expressed, the This, the Here, and the Now have always already passed. They *are* only in the mode of *having been*. Thus, they are insofar as they also are "not." In this manner, as Heidegger glosses, what is meant or intended in sense certainty "is something of the nature of a *nothing* (*Nichtiges*). What sense certainty intends (*meint*) in exemplification, what sense certainty takes as a being by intending it, is a *non-being*, that which 'does not continue existing'" (HPS 63; 89–90). The *true* Being of sense certainty is the Being that persists, precisely, through this negativity or this "nothing." It is the Being that is realized through the negation of negation.

In a substantial passage where Hegel summarizes the dialectic of the Now, one can see the crucial interplay between temporality and the negativity of the meant as that negativity operates within the double negation that secures the universality of language's truth:

> In this pointing-out [*in diesem Aufzeigen*], then, we see merely a movement which takes the following course: 1) I point out the "Now," and it is asserted to be the truth. I point it out, however, as

something that has been [*als gewesenes*], or as something that has been superseded [*als ein aufgehobenes*]; I set aside the first truth. 2) I now assert as the second truth that it has been, that it is superseded. 3) But what has been is not; I set aside the second truth, its having been, its supersession, and thereby negate the negation of the "Now," and thus return to the first assertion that the "Now" is. The "Now," and pointing out the "Now," are thus so constituted that neither the one nor the other is something immediate and simple, but a movement which contains various moments. A This is posited; but it is rather an other that is posited, or the This is superseded: and this otherness, or the setting-aside of the first, is itself in turn set aside, and so has returned into the first. However, this first, thus reflected into itself, is not exactly the same as it was to begin with, viz. something immediate; on the contrary, it is something that is reflected into itself, or a simple entity which, in its otherness, remains what it is: A Now which is an absolute plurality of Nows. (PhG 63–64; 67–68)

Within this summary explication of the Now, the fundamental structure and temporality of dialectic as double negation and recollection come to light. The double negation that recollects operates within a temporality whose essence lies in the having-been. The universal is the introreflected being of that which *is* in and through the otherness of its *not* being. In the dialectic of the This, consciousness learns by experience the movement and truth of the universal, which consists in the self-identity secured through the negation of negation. Consciousness means to point out the immediate, the sensuous, the singular, but in that very pointing out, it learns that its own language, its own essence, is in truth the universal. That universal is not an immediate, abstract and empty universal, but rather a universal that contains concretely the negative moments of its self-mediation.

Making its way through double negation and reflection into self, consciousness arrives at the mediated simplicity of the universal. The universal truth of consciousness comes to light only when the movement of consciousness itself comes to consciousness. It is precisely the comprehension *by* consciousness *of* consciousness's own temporal movement that determines experience as historical: "it is clear that the dialectic of sense-certainty is nothing else but the simple history (*Geschichte*) of its movement or of its experience, and sense-certainty itself is nothing else but just this history" (PhG 64; 68). In the very ground of its experience,

consciousness is essentially historical; that ground sustains the movement of negativity that is taken up within, carried along by, made productive for, the power of recollection or memory. In and through such
memory, negativity—even that of death itself—becomes productive.[11]

Now, within this exposition of sense-certainty, an essential aspect
of the tie between consciousness and language has come to light. The
conception of language developed in the dialectic of sense certainty involves an articulation and final negation of the singular, which in this
framework proves to be "ineffable." The particular *This* that consciousness means or intends cannot in truth be said: "This that is meant cannot
be reached by language, which belongs to consciousness, i.e., to that
which is inherently universal. In the actual attempt to say it, it would
therefore crumble away" (PhG 66; 70). The force of the universal imposes itself in the very experience of consciousness and its expression;
that force effects the sublation of the sensuous, immediate particular into
its truth, which is the essentially mediated, the spiritual. That which
eludes the universality of speech eludes reason itself: "Consequently,
what is called the unutterable is nothing else than the untrue, the irrational, what is merely meant" (PhG 66; 70). What is "merely meant" is
not said and cannot be said—and it is this fundamental ineffability that
indicates the characteristic reversal effected by what Hegel calls the "divine nature (*die göttliche Natur*)" of language.

What Hegel means by this "divine nature" of language—and no
doubt by the "divine" as such—can be thought only in terms of the universality of spirit, which on Hegel's account is and must be that which is
fully spoken or expressed:

> But if I want to help out language—which has the divine nature
> of directly reversing the meaning of what is said, of making it into
> something else, and thus not letting what is meant *get into words* at
> all—by *pointing out* this bit of paper, experience teaches me what the
> truth of sense-certainty in fact is: I point it out as a "Here," which
> is a Here of other Heres, or is in its own self a "simple togetherness
> of many Heres"; i.e. it is a universal. (PhG 66; 70)

Hegel's interpretation of the singular as the ineffable, and of the ineffable
as the irrational, an interpretation integral to his conception of the divine

11. Such a power and activity will be integral to Hegel's conception of the death
of the sensuous Christ and the life of Spirit in the Christian community, which is the
resurrected—i.e., spiritualized—body of Christ.

nature of language, is inextricably bound with his conception of God as the absolute. Heidegger brings this out nicely: "Language has a divine, absolute essence. Language has in it something of the essence of God, the absolute—what is non-relative—the absolute or the absolvent. Language is divine because language is absolvent, because language detaches us from one-sidedness and allows us to state what is universal and true" (HPS, 64; 90–91). It is from within his conception of the absolvence of the absolute that Hegel interprets the ineffability of the meant as irrational and untrue. This interpretation would confirm Jean Hyppolite's suggestion that the movement of philosophical consciousness in Hegel's philosophy constitutes a "refutation of the ineffable," which goes in hand with the "exorcism of non-knowledge."[12]

Hegel's refutation of the ineffable pertains both to the overcoming of the "mere" name of God through that name's wholly conceptual determination and to the elevation of the sensuous Christ to the universality of spirit. In both cases, the Hegelian conception of language and representation commands an annulment of the singular "this" that would resist the universality of the concept. That annulment of singularity occurs through the double negation that renders negativity positive, the finite infinite. That same double negation, I argued above, fills death itself with meaningful content. It is according to the same logic that death is rendered productive, that the individual, sensuous Christ is raised to universal spirit, and that the mere name of God is filled with determinate conceptual content. The annulment of finitude that I analyzed in chapters 1 and 2 thus appears here to determine Hegel's naming of God. If Hegel's onto-theology is characterized by the annulment of finitude both at the level of temporal consciousness and at the level of the language that would articulate the truth of such consciousness, then the attempt to read apophatic theologies against or outside of such an onto-theology might well imply an attempt to reassess the question of

12. Hyppolite, *Logique et existence*, p. 13. See chap. 1, "L'Ineffable." In my reading of Hegel, through Hyppolite, on the "refutation of the ineffable" and the "exorcism of nonknowledge," I am in strong agreement with Cyril O'Regan's assessment in *The Heterodox Hegel* (Albany: State University of New York Press, 1994) that while Hegel engages the thought of apophatic mystics, he does so only while also carrying out an "apophatic erasure" (p. 43) ". . . whereby apophatic vocabulary, and thus the implications of such a vocabulary, are excised from a religious or theological proposal [. . .]. Practically this means that Hegel relates positively to such mystics as Boehme and Eckhart only to the degree to which he ignores, or better, systematically represses, the apophatic vocabulary and the suggested limits of cognition" (p. 382). For further discussion, see esp. chap. 1, sec. 1.1, "Against Negative Theology."

finitude. The indispensable horizon for such attempts today, I believe, remains that of Heidegger.

Thus, in the next chapter, I turn to the Heideggerian thinking in which the singularity of factical existence remains insurmountable, finitude remains radical, and death without content.

FOUR

*The Mortal Difference: Death
and the Possibility of Existence
in Heidegger*

*I*n both the temporal experience of consciousness and the speculative language conceived by Hegel, the finite is sublated so as to erase the singular—and that erasure goes hand in hand with the Hegelian overcoming of death in and through death, an overcoming whereby death is elevated into the meaning of universal spirit. Heidegger will resist Hegelian thinking—and more broadly, the modern metaphysics it embodies—precisely on the question of finitude, and for Heidegger that question relates necessarily to the singularity of existence which is itself given by death. I aim in this chapter, then, to understand, by contrast to Hegel, the singularity of finite existence with regard specifically to death and to the insurmountable nullity of death for the being that thinks and speaks. Having established such an alternative conception of finitude, where death remains empty and thus the language of mortal existence radically open, I will be able in the next chapter to establish, correlatively, an alternative naming of God where the fullness of language fails.

As seen above, in his encounter with Hegel, Heidegger formulates the question of finitude largely in terms of the ontological difference. However, the question of finitude in Heidegger predates the explicit development of the ontological difference, constituting as it does a central theme within the existential analysis of Dasein carried out by *Being and Time* (1927).[1] Having touched on Heidegger's response to Hegel in terms of ontological difference, I should now tie that response back to the earlier analyses of finitude—and death—in *Being and Time*.

Already in 1927, in his summer course *The Basic Problems of Phenomenology*, Heidegger articulates the tie between ontological difference and Dasein more explicitly than in *Being and Time*:

> Somehow Dasein knows about something like Being. Since it exists, Dasein understands Being and comports itself toward beings. The distinction between Being and beings *is there [ist da]*, latent in Dasein and its existence, even if not in explicit awareness. The distinction *is there, ist da* [i.e., exists]; that is to say, it has the mode of being of

---

1. For a thorough analysis of the status of ontological difference within *Sein und Zeit*, see chap. 4 in Jean-Luc Marion's *Reduction and Givenness: Investigations of Husserl, Heidegger, and Phenomenology*, trans. Thomas A. Carlson (Evanston, Illinois: Northwestern University Press, 1998).

Dasein: it belongs to existence. Existence means, as it were, "to be in the performance of this distinction."[2]

For Heidegger, the ontological difference belongs to existence; to exist is to distinguish between beings and Being, and vice versa—which means, Heidegger goes on to suggest in § 22 of *Basic Problems*, that the ontological difference belongs to the temporality that defines Dasein's projective existence. "The *distinction between Being and beings is temporalized in the temporalizing of temporality*"[3]—but that temporality, as Heidegger makes clear in *Being and Time*, is a radically finite temporality, the temporality of a mortal existence that is "toward death." What, then, is the relation between the ontological difference and death?

Well after the foundational works of 1927, Heidegger explicitly relates the difference between beings and Being to mortality, to the "relation to death" (*Bezug zum Tode*) that constitutes the horizon of Dasein's temporal finitude within *Being and Time*. The ontological difference developed in Heidegger's later writings is a difference made only by that being, Dasein, which orients itself fundamentally with regard to death. The ontological difference, then, implies what Jean-François Courtine has termed the "mortal difference." The formulation of this "mortal difference" can be discerned in a passage from Heidegger's *Zollikoner Seminare* (1968):

> The difference of Being and beings belongs to the reference that relates to Being. But to experience this difference implies experiencing what is not beings [what is nothing of beings]. The fundamental experience of this "not being" [*Nicht das Seiende*] is given in the stroke that relates to death [*Bezug zum Tode*], in mortality, if it is true that death is the dis-cease of beings [*Abschied von Seiendem*].[4]

Beings stand in their difference from Being only insofar as Being itself is not a being or beings, insofar as it is no thing among beings, or is "nothing of beings." The "experience" of that difference, which would imply a reference or relation to the Being that is no-thing among beings,

---

2. Martin Heidegger, *Basic Problems of Phenomenology*, trans. Albert Hofstadter (Bloomington: Indiana University Press, 1982), p. 319 (translation slightly modified).

3. Ibid. (translation slightly modified).

4. Martin Heidegger, *Zollikoner Seminare*, ed. Medard Boss (Frankfurt am Main: Vittorio Klostermann, 1987), p. 230; quoted in Jean-François Courtine's fine study "Voice of Conscience and Call of Being," in Connor, Cadava, and Nancy, eds., *Who Comes after the Subject?* (New York: Routledge, 1991), p. 91.

is given proximally in the phenomenon of anxiety and ultimately in death, insofar as death marks the limit at which Dasein simply cannot be, and thus the border of its departure from beings. I will relate here, then, the difference of Being and beings to the mortal difference of finitude as explicated in *Being and Time*, where Dasein's finite existence is situated within the fundamental horizon of temporality. Against the difference of consciousness whose overcoming marks the annulment of time and the death of death through the infinite Being of an absolute subjectivity, the "mortal difference" and its temporality determine singular existence in its radical finitude.

The Significance of Dasein as Being-in-the-World

Especially in his later writings, Heidegger will highlight the intimate tie between the capacity for death and the capacity for language, and such a tie proves crucial to such major twentieth century writers as Georges Bataille, Maurice Blanchot, and Jacques Derrida. A decisive basis for this connection between death and language, it seems to me, must be located in the 1927 definition of Dasein in terms of "significance."

In *Being and Time*, Heidegger defines finite human existence, or Dasein, as "Being-in-the world" (*In-der-Welt-Sein*) and he defines the worldhood of that world (without which Dasein simply is not, and vice versa) as a primordial totality of referential relations that constitute the "significance" (*Bedeutsamkeit*) in terms of which Dasein's existential possibility is constituted and appropriated understandingly. Dasein is at bottom a being that deals in significance, and precisely this involvement in significance confers Dasein's ontic-ontological distinctiveness—for through such involvement alone can Dasein's very Being be an issue for Dasein. Dasein is distinguished as that being in whose Being that Being itself is an issue, and it is in this sense that Heidegger defines Dasein's Being as "care" (*Sorge*). Dasein can care about its own Being, its Being can be an issue for Dasein, only in the measure that Dasein deals in significance. Significance and care thus go hand in hand, naming two essential aspects of the same Being-in-the-world. This connection calls for explication.

Heidegger understands the world and its significance to consist in a referential totality of "equipment" (*Zeug*), which amounts to a context wherein the beings that we daily encounter and manipulate refer or relate to one another primordially in their various interrelations or "involvements" (*Bewandtnisse*). Significance issues in terms of precisely those involvements, for they open Dasein's basic "potentiality-for-Being" (*Sein-können*) and so its understanding of Being as such: "In its familiarity with these [relations of involvement that are constitutive of a world], Dasein 'signifies' to itself: in a primordial manner it gives itself both its Being and its potentiality-for-Being as something which it is to understand with regard to its Being-in-the-world. [. . .] The relational totality of this signifying we call '*significance*'" (SZ 120; H 87). "Significance," then, names the total referential context that makes up a world and that, in doing so, articulates the range of potentiality for Dasein's ability to be. That context comes to light in the interrelation of the various forms of "equipment" that Dasein always already manipulates—*understandingly*—within its day-to-day dealings.

Indeed, it is only and precisely insofar as Dasein *understands* "significance" that beings, as equipmentally involved, come to light. In other words, the total structure of significance, and Dasein's understanding of significance, precede and render possible the appearance of any beings whatsoever (which means, in a sense, that phenomenology in Heidegger is ever already hermeneutical). Beings appear to Dasein only as already significant, assigned, involved—in short, contextualized: "the world-hood of the world [i.e., the 'system of Relations' constitutive of worldhood] provides the basis on which such beings [i.e., those ready-to-hand within-the-world] can for the first time be discovered" (SZ 122; H 88). Each element of worldly "equipment" refers indissolubly to the whole system of worldly significance and is encountered only according to Dasein's understanding manipulation of equipment within that system.

Dasein's definitive situation within worldly significance indicates an essentially passive or submissive aspect of Dasein, which can never be converted wholly into activity. Such passivity must not be forgotten in the interpretation of Dasein's basic traits. Insofar as Dasein always already finds itself in a world, it is always already handed over to that world and thus to itself: "[Significance] is what makes up the structure of the world—the structure of that wherein Dasein as such already is. [. . .] Dasein, in so far as it *is*, has always submitted itself (*hat sich . . . angewiesen*) already to a 'world' which it encounters, and this *submission* (*Angewiesenheit*) belongs essentially to Dasein" (SZ 121; H 87). Significance, as that to which Dasein is always already given over, assigned, or submitted, constitutes the worldhood of the world. Dasein does not found that world, nor does it simply come upon it as something independent of and external to itself. Rather, Dasein always finds both itself and its world together in a totality of significance.

Precisely such significance, such a system of referential relations, opens up the "space" of the world; as Heidegger will insist, space becomes possible only within a world—and not the reverse. The spatiality of the world is precisely what defines Da-sein as Being-*there*, in the world. The fact that Dasein *is* its there, that Dasein is fundamentally Being-*in*-the-world, determines the manner in which Dasein maintains access to its characteristic understanding of Being, for through this fact that Dasein is its *there*, two essential traits of Dasein come to light: its "facticity," and hence its essential nullity or lack of ground, and its "existence," its standing-out into its own possibility, which arises only against the ultimate horizon of Being-toward-death.

The Radical Possibility of "Being the There": State-of-Mind and Understanding

How, then, does Dasein find itself to be its own *there*? Heidegger identifies two basic ways of "Being the there": "state-of-mind" (*Befindlichkeit*) and "understanding" (*Verstehen*).

He begins his description of the existential constitution of the "there" with an analysis of "state-of-mind," or *Befindlichkeit*, which is a term by which he indicates that, as radically situated in its world, Dasein always *finds* itself in one mood (*Stimmung*) or another and is thus brought before its own facticity (*Faktizität*), before the pure fact *that* it is situated in a definite manner and will always already have found itself to be situated—without any answer to the question "why?" The "that-it-is" of Dasein's "there" "stares it in the face with the inexorability of an enigma" (SZ 175; H 136).

The moods to which Dasein is inescapably subject thus mark a fundamental, primordial aspect of existence "in which Dasein is disclosed to itself *prior to* all cognition and volition (*vor allem Erkennen und Wollen*), and *beyond* their range of disclosure" (SZ 175; H 136). Such a priority indicates that Dasein will always and ever lag "behind" itself in a fundamental way: Dasein can never precede the pure fact of its own Being so as to ground or master that fact through knowing or willing; it cannot have been present to accept or reject the pure fact *that* it is.

This manner in which Dasein is radically given over to its moods, the manner in which Dasein thus *finds* itself as *already* in its Being, points to Dasein's essential *"thrownness"* (*Geworfenheit*), and thrownness, wherein the pure *that* of Dasein's *there* is disclosed without any clear indication of its "whence" or "whither" and without any initiative on Dasein's part, indicates in turn Dasein's definitive "facticity" (*Faktizität*): "This characteristic of Dasein's Being—this 'that it is'—is veiled in its 'whence' and 'whither,' yet disclosed in itself all the more unveiledly; we call it the *'thrownness'* of this being into its 'there'; indeed, it is thrown in such a way that, as a Being-in-the-world, it is the 'there.' The expression 'thrownness' is meant to suggest the *facticity of its being delivered over* (*die Faktizität der Überantwortung*)" (SZ 174; H 135). The facticity of Dasein's "Being-delivered-over" (*Überantwortetsein*) indicates that Dasein is always given (prior to knowledge or will) in "answer" or response to the pure fact of its Being—and in this givenness one can discern an irreducible margin of passivity; as "thrown," Dasein cannot achieve the kind of self-grounding or self-transparency that would orient the modern conception of a purely spontaneous or autonomous subject. Delivered over to the pure "that it is," Dasein does not posit or ground its Being but rather suffers it, takes it up in the irreducible opacity that issues from a margin of passivity that remains insurmountable.

Now, the fact that Heidegger develops the characteristic thrownness and facticity of Dasein in terms of "state-of-mind" and "mood" does not indicate that his analysis moves within the realm of psychology. To the contrary, the fundamental significance of state-of-mind and mood issues not from any possible psychological explication of the human mind or soul, but from the *hermeneutic* analysis of Dasein as that being whose Being is articulated fundamentally in terms of "significance." In other words, state-of-mind and mood concern not states or processes of a psyche (which would be distinct from the "external world") but the meaning of Being-in-the-world as such, which must be approached hermeneutically.[5] The state-of-mind implied by Dasein's moods concerns primarily the fact that Dasein exists as a being who understands and interprets.

Such understanding (*Verstehen*) constitutes the second basic way of Being the "there," for state-of-mind is not an unthinking, brute moodiness but rather "always has its understanding," just as understanding "al-

---

5. As Heidegger points out, "it is not an accident that the earliest systematic Interpretation of affects [the term under which philosophy has treated the modes of state-of-mind] that has come down to us is not treated in the framework of 'psychology.' Aristotle investigates the πάθη [affects] in the second book of his *Rhetoric*," and the *Rhetoric*, on Heidegger's view, "must be taken as the first systematic hermeneutic of the everydayness of Being with one another" (SZ 178; H 138).

ways has its mood" (SZ 182; H 142–43). State-of-mind and understanding are "equiprimordial." While state-of-mind signals the thrownness and facticity of Dasein, the pure fact that it is without first having known or willed its Being, understanding concerns the essentially related ability of Dasein *to be*, the potentiality that defines the existence of Dasein:

> The kind of Being which Dasein has, as potentiality-for-Being [*Sein-können*], lies existentially in understanding [*Verstehen*]. Dasein is not something present-at-hand which possesses its competence for something by way of an extra; it is primarily Being-possible [*Möglichsein*]. Dasein is in every case what it can be, and in the way in which it is its possibility [*Möglichkeit*]. (SZ 183; H 143)

As Being-in-the-world, Dasein finds itself always "with" others and "alongside" the entities that appear within the world, and in its dealings with such others and such entities, Dasein always acts in some way "toward itself," or for the sake of itself. This means not that Dasein always returns to itself like absolute subjectivity in Hegel but rather that Dasein is that being for whom, in existing, its own Being is always at issue. The "for the sake of itself" (SZ 183; H 143) does not close Dasein in on itself, but indeed occurs only within the open context of significance that renders possible the various ways in which Dasein can be. That context is inhabited or enacted by Dasein in terms of understanding.

The fact that Dasein finds itself in the context of its world through understanding means that Dasein has always, if only implicitly, interpreted itself according to the possible ways in which it can be:

> Dasein is such that in every case it has understood (or alternatively, not understood) that it is to be thus or thus. As such it "knows" *what* it is capable of—that is, what its potentiality-for-Being is capable of. This "knowing" does not first arise from an immanent self-perception, but belongs to the Being of the "there," which is essentially understanding. (SZ 184; H 144)

Dasein, then, *is* its *there* only by understanding the range of its potentiality-for-Being, by understanding its situated existence in terms of what and how it can be. That range of potentiality, the can-be of Dasein's defining to-be, involves possibilities that are determined by the fact of Dasein's being thrown into its there—which is both finite and radically open. Thus, Dasein's *understanding*, or its manner of Being toward its possibilities, relates back inextricably to Dasein's *state-of-mind*, or the manner in which it is given over to itself, thrown into its existence and thus into a definite range of possibility.

The fact of Dasein's thrownness, the fact that Dasein cannot get "behind" its Being so as to ground it, constitutes the source and indicates the character of Dasein's potentiality-for-Being. Dasein's possibility is *thrown* possibility, which implies a *lack* of autonomy in Dasein's existence, a passivity that disallows Dasein's self-grounding even while, at the same time, it constitutes the very condition of possibility for Dasein's ability-to-be, the condition of possibility for its freedom: "In every case Dasein, as essentially having a state-of-mind, has already got itself into definite possibilities. [...] But this means that Dasein is Being-possible which has been delivered over to itself—*thrown possibility* through and through. Dasein is the possibility of Being-free *for* its ownmost potentiality-for-Being" (SZ 183; H 144). Understanding is thus Dasein's mode of Being in its potentiality-for-Being, and that potentiality-for-Being is "based" or "grounded" on Dasein's having been thrown (without any ground) into its range of possibilities. The possibility of Being free for such possibilities depends on the facticity that Dasein never masters.

Now, just as the thrownness signaled by state-of-mind is never present as an experienced event, or present-at-hand like a being, so the possibility that issues in conjunction with thrownness is never wholly reducible to a specific ontic plan of action, to a projected state of affairs that would be actualized or made definitely present through the efficient causality of an agent. The potentiality-for-Being that is as understanding "is never something still outstanding as not yet present-at-hand, but which, as something which is essentially never present-at-hand, '*is*' with the Being of Dasein, in the sense of existence" (SZ 183–84; H 144). The understanding existence of Dasein is oriented according to a possibility that is never simply the possibility of something that becomes "actual" in the sense of "ontically present-at-hand."

Here I would distinguish between existential, ontological possibility and ontic, existentiell possibili*ties*. The latter, which can be actualized as present-at-hand, would be founded on the former, which cannot. This possibility that is not oriented toward ontic actuality, but rather constitutes its "ground" or condition of possibility, maintains a decisively "forward" orientation that comes to light in the relation between thrownness and "*projection*" (*der Entwurf*).

Precisely as thrown, Dasein is also always already projecting, pressing "forward into possibilities" (SZ 184–85; H 145) that it takes up understandingly. Thus, "understanding has in itself the existential structure which we call '*projection*'" (SZ 183–84). Like thrownness, which was and is never ontically present in an experienced event, so projection does not concern primarily the prediction or planning of future ontic occurrences, actions, events. Projection is a matter first of existential possibility, not existentiell, ontical possibilities. It is not a function of cognition or volition so much as it is a structure of existence in which Dasein always already is without first having known, willed, or intended it: "as thrown, Dasein is thrown into the kind of Being which we call 'projecting.' Projecting has nothing to do with comporting oneself towards a plan that has been thought out, and in accordance with which Dasein arranges its Being. On the contrary, any Dasein has, as Dasein, already projected itself; and as long as it is, it is projecting" (SZ 185; H 145). To say that Dasein has ever already projected, and is ever already projecting, itself is not to say that Dasein is fundamentally active. Indeed, the fact that Dasein is *thrown* into projecting, the fact that Dasein inhabits a projecting that is ever already under way, would indicate that, in a fundamental sense, Dasein has not itself grounded that projecting or actively initiated it. Dasein *finds* itself projecting, in a projecting that fundamentally "precedes" it. Just as it finds itself "behind itself" as always already thrown, so Dasein ever finds itself "ahead" of itself, projecting forward in terms of what or how it might be. This structure of existence in which Dasein always already is without having known, willed, or intended it indicates the radical character of possibility in Heidegger, and that radical possibility issues on the "basis" of Dasein's irreducible passivity.

Possibility, then, indicates not first the possibility of this or that eventual actuality, but rather the possibility of possibility itself, the possibility of Dasein's "to be," in terms of which Dasein has always already understood itself:

> As long as it is, Dasein always has understood itself and always will understand itself in terms of possibilities. Furthermore, the character of understanding as projection is such that the understanding does not grasp thematically that upon which it projects—that is to say, possibilities. Grasping it in such a manner would take away from what is projected its very character as a possibility, and would reduce it to the given contents which we have in mind; whereas projection, in throwing, throws before itself the possibility as possibility, and lets it *be* as such.(SZ 185; H 145)

That Dasein is always already thrown into its projecting indicates that its radical possibility, the possibility that it *is* (its "to be"), issues from the nullity or groundlessness according to which Dasein is essentially thrown. Dasein carries along the nullity of its thrownness within the projection of its possibility. In such projection, possibility remains radical; it cannot be reduced to or exhausted by eventual actualization; it has, finally, no determinate content.

This radical possibility, then, implies the nullity or negativity of an irreducible "*not yet*," for in its defining possibility, Dasein is constitutively "not yet" what it can or might be. This "not yet" inherent to Dasein's possibility, this lack or emptiness in its Being, this gap between what or how it is actually and what or how it might ever yet be—all of this indicates the manner in which Dasein *exceeds* itself (or, equally, lags behind itself) in its possibility: "Dasein is constantly 'more' than it factually is" (SZ 185; H 145).[6] The "more" here issues in the "not yet"—and so, in fact, in the "less"—and it indicates the irreducibility of possibility to an actual content, to "something-at-hand." As Being-possible, Dasein "*is* existentially that which, in its potentiality-for-Being, it is *not yet*. Only because the Being of the 'there' receives its Constitution through understanding and through the character of understanding as projection, only because it *is* what it becomes (or alternatively, does not become), can it say to itself 'Become what you are,' and say this with understanding" (SZ 185–86; H 145). As distinct from the becoming of the absolute in Hegel, where the negativity or difference that drives becoming is overcome in the measure that consciousness fully conceives itself, becoming in Heidegger depends on the irreducible negativity of Dasein's thrownness—which appears or returns in the radical possibility of its projecting. In other words, while the *not yet* in Hegel is overcome by or reduced to the *already* (i.e., while the difference of consciousness is not a radical difference but a provisional one), the *already* in Heidegger (thrownness) indicates the absolute irreducibility of the *not yet* (possibility, projection). For as long as Dasein is, its radical possibility is *not yet* reduced to actuality.

In sum, then, Heidegger identifies in state-of-mind and understand-

---

6. One might remember here the significance of the *Mehrmeinung* in Husserl's understanding of horizon, and Levinas's appropriation and transformation of that *Mehrmeinung* to indicate that which radically overflows the intention of the "I." For a definition of the *Mehrmeinung* in Husserl, see *Cartesianische Meditationen, Husserliana* (The Hague: Martinus Nijhoff, 1963), 1:84 (Eng. trans. Dorion Cairns [The Hague: Martinus Nijhoff, 1960], p. 46). For Levinas's interpretation, see *Totality and Infinity*, trans. Alphonso Lingis (Pittsburgh: Duquesne University Press, 1979), p. 28, and "La Ruine de la représentation," in *En Découvrant l'existence avec Husserl et Heidegger* (Paris: Vrin, 1988), pp. 125–35.

ing two basic modes of Dasein's Being-the-there, two existential elements that open the world of all Dasein's possibility, the world of Dasein's existence as "thrown projection."[7] Having explicated these elements in the constitution of Dasein's Being the "there," which Dasein confronts as an "enigma," Heidegger goes on to work out these *existentialia* concretely.

Such a concrete working-out leads to his analysis of the circularity of *interpretation*, which constitutes the development or unfolding of understanding, wherein alone Dasein *is* Being-possible. Insofar as interpretation is based on understanding, I would emphasize, it is tied inextricably to the radical possibility that characterizes understanding, the possibility in which the *not yet* remains irreducible. For this reason, the circularity involved in the hermeneutic Being of Dasein will not, and cannot, constitute the return of consciousness to itself (as in Hegel) but will mark, rather, the impossibility of any such return.[8] The radical possibility (and so the nullity) on which the circularity of Dasein's hermeneutical Being is "based" would demand a circularity "without return." To develop the sense in which Dasein remains circular "without return," one must turn to the issue of interpretation.

Interpretation

Interpretation (*Auslegung*), according to Heidegger, is "the working-out (*Ausarbeitung*) of possibilities projected in understanding" (SZ 189; H 148), and it is thus based on the understanding wherein we implicitly take beings *as* something within their appearance (primordially as ready-to-hand). Interpretation makes explicit the "as" structure that underlies understanding. According to the priority of existential understanding, existent Dasein has always already understood beings that appear to it *as* something or other, for it has always already taken those beings up within

---

7. See summary, SZ 188; H 148.
8. In this respect I will be closer to David Krell, who insists on the gap between Hegelian onto-theology and Heideggerian hermeneutics (see pp. 31–40 of "Hegel, Heidegger, Heraclitus," in John Sallis and Kenneth Maly, eds., *Heraclitean Fragments* [University: University of Alabama Press, 1980]), than to Jacques Taminiaux, for whom it is "conceivable that the hermeneutical circle is the result of a *Wiederholung* of the speculative circle" ("From One Fundamental Ontology to the Other: The Double Reading of Hegel," p. 159, in Taminiaux, *Heidegger and the Project of Fundamental Ontology*, trans. and ed. by Michael Gendre [Albany: State University of New York Press, 1991], pp. 144–59).

the projection of its own potentiality—itself opened by the significance structure of the world. This means that Dasein always has some preconception of beings in their Being, that beings have always already been articulated (if not clarified and thematized) in the potential meaning of their Being.

In light of this priority of articulation, the circularity of Dasein's relation to Being appears. "That which is understood gets Articulated when the being to be understood is brought close interpretatively by taking as our clue the 'something as something'; and this Articulation lies *before* (*liegt* vor) our making any thematic assertion about it" (SZ 190; H 149). Understanding is based on the *as* structure that goes presupposed but largely unnoticed in our ontic dealings, but "if the 'as' is ontically unexpressed, this must not seduce us into overlooking it as a constitutive state for understanding, existential and *a priori*" (SZ 190; H 149). This existential a priori, which for Heidegger precedes both intuition and conceptual thinking, points us to the "fore-" structure within which Dasein's fundamental circularity issues. According to the circularity of Dasein's "fore-" structure, Dasein is always already within the realm of significance; it always already has a preconception of the Being of beings. In other words, beings come to light in their Being only on the basis of significance.

Interpretation, therefore, is not primarily a process of imposing significance, but of uncovering and explicating it. Because every being that we encounter "already has an involvement which is disclosed in our understanding of the world" (SZ 190; H 150), because it appears only in and through such involvement, the significance of that being, its range of possible meaning, has already been given to us. *Before* we explicitly interpret, we have an understanding of the meaning of the beings that we manipulate and so encounter. We have that understanding through the ways that, in our potentiality-for-Being, we can fore-see beings in their significance. On the basis of such fore-having and fore-sight, we develop certain fore-conceptions that determine possible (as well as impossible) paths of interpretation. To interpret, on this view, is to appropriate explicitly that understanding which, in our potentiality, we *already* have, see, and conceive implicitly. Because interpretation is always based in such a "fore-" structure, which itself is a fundamental characteristic of Dasein's existence, it always moves within the realm of *presupposition* (*Voraussetzung*) or *assumption* (*Vormeinung*). "An interpretation," quite simply, "is never a presuppositionless apprehending of something presented to us (*eines Vorgegebenen*)" (SZ 191–92; H 150).

The totality of presuppositions belonging to the fore-structure of Dasein Heidegger calls, precisely, the "hermeneutical Situation" (SZ 275; H 232). As distinct from the "presupposition of the absolute" in Hegel, which is finally assumed and "retrospectively" grounded by the subject who returns to itself in self-consciousness, the presupposition that determines the circularity of Dasein's Being-as-understanding can never be fully assumed or grounded by Dasein itself. Dasein always negotiates that circularity without ever closing or completing it. The irreducibility of such negotiation, the radical openness or incompletion of the circle, relates to the structure of possibility in light of which meaning comes to light for Dasein.

As seen above, possibility for Heidegger is understood in terms of "thrown projection." That being (Dasein) who ever finds itself thrown in its world and who, therefore, never gets behind its own Being so as to ground it (through will, knowledge, etc.), has, accordingly, always already projected itself in its possibility upon the horizon of its world, its context of significance. "Meaning" (Sinn) for Heidegger must be understood precisely in terms of this projection and possibility. Meaning is fundamentally existential, a function of Dasein's Being:

> In the projecting of the understanding, entities are disclosed in their possibility. [. . .] Beings within-the-world generally are projected upon the world—that is, upon a whole of significance, to whose reference-relations concern, as Being-in-the-world, has been tied up in advance. [. . .] *Meaning is the "upon-which" of a projection in terms of which something becomes intelligible as something; it gets its structure from a fore-having, a fore-sight, and a fore-conception.* In so far as understanding and interpretation make up the existential state of Being of the "there," "meaning" must be conceived as the formal-existential framework of the disclosedness which belongs to understanding. Meaning is an *existentiale* of Dasein, not a property attaching to entities, lying "behind" them, or floating somewhere as an "intermediate domain." (SZ 192–93; H 151)

Thus, meaning (and therefore also, in a derivative mode, "meaninglessness") belongs to Dasein as a fundamental character of its existence; meaning is not simply inherent to beings or to the "world" as a simple collection of beings. As the "upon-which" of a projection, meaning is related essentially to the function of *possibility* in Dasein's Being—which means that meaning always issues in relation to the radical "not yet" of Dasein. In this respect, I would argue that the condition of possibility of

meaning (projection according to possibility, which involves an insurmountable nullity) also constitutes the condition of impossibility of
meaning's closure.

Having thus indicated the essential traits of understanding in terms
of the "existential *fore-structure* of Dasein itself" (SZ 195; H 153), Heidegger insists that the circularity of Dasein's understanding is irreducible
and so not to be avoided. "The 'circle' in understanding belongs to the
structure of meaning, and the latter phenomenon is rooted in the existential constitution of Dasein—that is, in the understanding which interprets. A being for which, as Being-in-the-world, its Being is itself an
issue, has, ontologically, a circular structure" (SZ 195; H 153). Such circularity would imply neither empty tautology nor dialectical fulfillment;
it would constitute neither the pure absence of meaning nor its full ac-
complishment. Rather, it would signal the excess of meaning within that
existence whose possibility is based on an insurmountable nullity. Because this circularity characterizes Dasein's very existence, "what is decisive is not to get out of the circle but to come into it in the right way"
(SZ 195; H 153), and to enter the circle "in the right way" requires an
understanding of *language* (*die Sprache*), wherein interpretation occurs,
and of *discourse* (*die Rede*), which Heidegger identifies as language's "exis-
tential-ontological foundation" (SZ 203; H 160–61).

Discourse and Language

Along with state-of-mind and understanding, "discourse" marks a third
essential element of Dasein's Being the "there." "The intelligibility of
something," Heidegger writes, "has always been articulated, even before
there is any appropriative interpretation of it. Discourse is the Articulation of intelligibility" (SZ 203–204; H 161). Discourse gives that which
interpretation will or will not appropriate. In light of the discourse that
defines Dasein, Heidegger reframes the classic understanding of human
being as the ζῷον λόγον ἔχον. Within that reframing, this Greek formulation would indicate not (primarily) that human being is (first) a living
being who (then) "has" reason or language, but rather that human being
(as Dasein) is a being that *is* discursive, a being that *is* only in and through
discourse. In other words, Dasein shows itself "as the being which talks"
(SZ 208; H 165).

Now, importantly, that which is proper to Dasein, that in which its
"authenticity" might consist—namely, its discursivity—is at the same
time that which can "dispossess" Dasein and render it "inauthentic." The

fact that Dasein has the kind of Being that is understood and gets interpreted, the fact that Dasein is therefore discursive, means that individual
Dasein might or might not appropriate and make its own the ways in
which it and its Being get interpreted:

> For the most part, discourse is expressed by being spoken out, and
> has always been so expressed; it is language. But in that case under-
> standing and interpretation already lie in what has thus been ex-
> pressed. In language, as a way things have been expressed or spoken
> out [*Ausgesprochenheit*], there is hidden a way in which the under-
> standing of Dasein has been interpreted. [. . .] Proximally, and with
> certain limits, Dasein is constantly delivered over to this interpret-
> edness, which controls and distributes the possibilities of average
> understanding and of the state-of-mind belonging to it. (SZ 211;
> H 167–68)

Precisely because it is delivered over to a certain range of interpretation,
a certain distribution of the possibilities of average understanding, Dasein can become absorbed by and lose itself in the averageness of everyday interpretation, an averageness determined by the vague but powerful
force of the "they" (*das Man*).

The "they," which to some degree or other every Dasein is, is a self
(*Man-selbst*) to which all belong, a self that, in this very measure, is actually "no one" in particular. The discourse of the they-self determines the
predominant modes in which "Reality" gets interpreted in daily life, the
possible ranges of meaning available to interpretation, and that discourse
(*Rede*) can take the form of "idle talk" (*Gerede*), which is the kind of talk
that gets passed along anonymously in such a way that all accept it (to
some degree or other) but no one explicitly authorizes or owns it.
"They" say what no one in particular has said, what all in general simply
accept or "know."

It is this anonymity of idle talk that constitutes what Heidegger will
identify as its "groundlessness," but such groundlessness does not endan-
ger idle talk's pervasive strength; it reinforces it:

> The groundlessness of idle talk is no obstacle to its becoming public;
> instead it encourages this. Idle talk is the possibility of understand-
> ing everything without previously making the thing one's own [. . .];
> it not only releases one from the task of genuinely understanding,
> but develops an undifferentiated kind of intelligibility, for which
> nothing is closed off any longer. (SZ 213; H 169)

When in this way "nothing" is closed off, because "everything" is "understood" in an undifferentiated and ungenuine way, the true character of Dasein's disclosedness (*Erschlossenheit*) is covered over. Dasein does not make understanding its own, but rather takes over the dominant—anonymous—interpretations of reality that are available to it within the sway of idle talk.[9] Idle talk, therefore, "is the kind of Being which belongs to Dasein's understanding when that understanding has been uprooted" (SZ 214; H 170). In accepting the self-evidence of the they-self's ways of interpreting, Dasein is in fact "cut off" from the primordial ways in which the world opens up to it (SZ 214; H 170).

When "cut off" in this way, according to Heidegger, Dasein is "uprooted," and such an uprooting of Dasein indicates an uncanniness (*Unheimlichkeit*), or a "homelessness," that remains hidden to Dasein insofar as it remains under the sway of idle talk. Such uncanniness, in which Dasein is, paradoxically, most "comfortable," becomes significant here to the degree that it will be disrupted by another, qualitatively different and more fundamental uncanniness or groundlessness that operates in the mood of anxiety. In the groundlessness involved in idle talk, Dasein would "cover over" or "flee from" the more fundamental groundlessness and primordial thrownness of Dasein—a more fundamental groundlessness that comes to light proximally in anxiety and ultimately in Being-toward-death. In anxiety and Being-toward-death, the truly fundamental nullity of Dasein comes to light, a nullity more fundamental than the nullity of the they-self. While the groundlessness of the they-self allows Dasein not to own itself individually, to absorb itself in the anonymity of all and none, the groundlessness of thrown Being-toward-death individualizes Dasein radically, throwing it up against itself and itself alone. In order to gain insight into this second groundlessness and its characteristic negativity, one must explicate the basic Being of Dasein as *care* and the phenomenon in which care becomes evident—anxiety.

Anxiety

As just seen, the nullity of the they-self appears in the inauthenticity characteristic of "falling," which belongs essentially to Dasein's everyday

9. Heidegger distinguishes between the world (no quotation marks) as the structural totality in terms of which Dasein must be interpreted and the "world," which signifies the ontologically insufficient interpretation that takes the world as a collection of entities present-at-hand. What becomes "available" to everyone in the idle talk of the

Being. In falling, Dasein becomes absorbed in the "world" of its concern as that world is determined by the they-self. By falling in this way, Dasein takes over the various given interpretations provided by the they-self and thus avoids having itself to choose its own "potentiality for Being its Self" (SZ 229; H 175). Importantly, these two modes of Being, falling and choosing oneself, belong to Dasein equally.

In falling, Dasein falls away from itself (as individual) into itself (as anonymous). The difference between these two selves concerns the manner in which Dasein negotiates its potentiality for Being. In falling, Dasein is "inauthentic" in the sense that it does not take over its individual potentiality for Being as its own—but rather accepts unknowingly or unquestioningly a range of possibilities that are ready-made and sustained by the they-self, a range taken as secure and self-evident. However, while this falling into the "world" along with the they-self is, to be sure, a possibility of Dasein and Dasein alone, that possibility depends on the fact that Dasein has the potentiality for choosing possibilities more fundamentally its "own": "This downward plunge into and within the groundlessness of the inauthentic Being of the 'they' has a kind of motion which constantly tears the understanding away from the projecting of authentic possibilities, into the tranquilized supposition that it possesses everything, that everything is within its reach" (SZ 223, H 178). This groundlessness and nullity into and within which Dasein falls deprive Dasein of its ownmost individuality and lead it to suppose that *everything* is within its reach.

By contrast, another form of groundlessness and nullity will utterly individualize Dasein by removing or undoing precisely every-thing; it will show Dasein that *not* everything is available—or that everything can fall under the nullity implied by the *not*. This other groundlessness leaves Dasein on its own, leaves it literally *nothing* against which to fall, nothing to grasp or possess, nothing to project—nothing other than its ownmost self. This other groundlessness and nullity appear to Dasein in anxiety.

Having reached the crucial point at which he will attempt to define the Being of Dasein not only in each of its aspects but as a whole (the *Seinsganzheit des Daseins*), Heidegger turns to an analysis of *anxiety* (*Angst*), a "basic state-of-mind" that will grant phenomenological access to the Being of Dasein as *care* (*Sorge*) (SZ 227; H 182). The significance of anxiety becomes clear only against the background of falling.

---

they-self is an understanding of the "world" or of a "Reality" that is understood according to the ontology of the present-at-hand.

In falling, where Dasein flees in face of itself, Dasein flees in face of a being that is not simply a being within-the-world, a being either ready-to-hand or present-at-hand. Indeed, in falling Dasein falls up against, becomes absorbed in, precisely such beings within-the-world. Fleeing *itself*, Dasein flees not a being within-the-world, but Being-in-the-world as such.

This fleeing, Heidegger suggests, is both occasioned and disrupted by anxiety. As distinct from fear, which is indeed fear of some-thing, some definite being or object in the world, anxiety has no object; it can be traced back to no one being within-the-world, it can be traced back to no-thing.[10] That no-thing-ness in the face of which Dasein has anxiety is the *"Being-in-the-world as such"* which "is a basic state of Dasein" (SZ 230; H 186). Being-in-the-world as such as a whole constitutes the no-thing that engenders anxiety because it is a Being that cannot be reduced to an ontic entity that might be feared.

The fact that that in the face of which Dasein has anxiety is no thing and thus "completely indefinite" indicates a dismissal or disqualification of beings (they are "not 'relevant' at all") and the collapse or suspension of the significance relations in which beings usually appear to Dasein:

> Nothing which is ready-to-hand or present-at-hand within the world functions as that in the face of which anxiety is anxious. Here the totality of involvements of the ready-to-hand and the present-at-hand discovered within-the-world, is, as such, of no consequence; it collapses into itself; the world has the character of completely lacking significance. (SZ 231; H 186)

Just as that in the face of which anxiety is anxious constitutes no thing within-the-world, so it is "nowhere" in the world, even as it presses close, constricting or choking the one in anxiety (from ἄγχω, "*to press tight*, esp. the throat: *to strangle, throttle, hang*").

Now, when the "cause" of anxiety presses close (all the while coming from nowhere and nothing within-the-world) and the significance of beings within the world collapses, the world does not simply disappear. Indeed, somewhat paradoxically, the collapse of worldly significance brings the worldhood of the world more clearly to light: "The utter in-

---

10. Heidegger remains indebted to Kierkegaard perhaps nowhere more than in his definition of anxiety according to the "nothing." On this, see esp. Kierkegaard's *Concept of Anxiety*, trans. Reidar Thomte (Princeton, New Jersey: Princeton University Press, 1980). A similar distinction between fear and anxiety can be found also in Freud.

significance which makes itself known in the 'nothing and nowhere,' does not signify that the world is absent, but tells us that entities within-the-world are of so little importance in themselves that on the basis of this *insignificance* of what is within the world, the world in its worldhood is all that still obtrudes itself" (SZ 231; H 187). What "oppresses" or chokes me in anxiety is not "this or that" being but rather "the *possibility* of the ready-to-hand in general; that is to say, it is the world itself" (SZ 231; H 187). This *possibility*—the world itself—is itself the no-thing that "causes" anxiety.

Here again, I want to stress, possibility comes to light as irreducible to *this or that* possibility, *this or that* particular ontic state of affairs which one might envision, will, or actualize. Possibility refers to the ontological structure of the world as such. In this sense, "the 'nothing' of readiness-to-hand is grounded in the most primordial 'something'—in the *world*" (SZ 232; H 187). That world, again, appears only there where Dasein exists as Being-in-the-world. "So if the 'nothing'—that is, the world as such—exhibits itself as that in the face of which one has anxiety, this means that *Being-in-the-world itself is that in the face of which anxiety is anxious*" (SZ 232; H 187). Insofar as anxiety reveals Being-in-the-world as such to be that in the face of which one has anxiety, the "world" recedes or disappears, and vice versa. In this way, anxiety deprives Dasein of that into or against which it falls in its falling.

As so deprived of the support for its falling or fleeing, Dasein, as Being-in-the-world, finds itself alone, utterly individualized, torn out of its absorption in the public "world": "[A]s Dasein falls, anxiety brings it back from its absorption in the 'world.' Everyday familiarity collapses. Dasein has been individualized *as* Being-in-the-world" (SZ 233; H 189). In anxiety, then, Dasein is thrown back upon itself—upon the nothing or nullity of which it is the "basis." That "nothing" comes to light essentially in terms of the *possibility* that Dasein in each case *is*—the possibility of Being-in-the-world as such. Being-in-the-world *is* Being-possible, and the nullity of possibility is precisely that which provokes anxiety: "Therefore, with that which it is anxious about, anxiety discloses Dasein as *Being-possible*" (SZ 232; H 187–88).[11]

11. As I conclude this discussion of anxiety with the "nothing" that occasions it, I should stress that Heidegger himself will note the significance of anxiety in relation to theological thinking. While, according to Heidegger, genuine attempts to interpret anxiety are in fact historically rare—due first to the "general neglect of the existential analytic of Dasein" and then more specifically to "a failure to recognize the phenomenon of state-of-mind" (SZ 235; H 190)—the primary frameworks where anxiety *has* been

Care

The "nothing" of the "primordial something" that emerges in the phenomenon of anxiety signals the ultimate horizon of Dasein's Being, Being-toward-death, and the analysis of Being-toward-death opens and
guides the second division of *Being and Time*, where Heidegger repeats
the analysis of Dasein's existential structures (Division I) according to
their fundamental temporal modes. Before considering Being-toward-
death, however, I should summarize those structures—the totality of
which, coming to light in the analysis of anxiety, are understood in terms
of care, which has three basic elements: "Thus the entire phenomenon
of anxiety shows Dasein as factically existing Being-in-the-world. The
fundamental ontological characteristics of this being are existentiality,
facticity, and Being-fallen" (SZ 235; H 191). These fundamental structural characteristics, which make up the whole of Dasein, indicate the
three aspects of Dasein that will be correlated in Division II with the
three basic temporal modes or ecstases of "pastness" (facticity), "futurity" (existentiality), and the "present" (falling).

Now, to say that Dasein's total Being is fundamentally "care" is to
indicate that "Dasein is a being for which, in its Being, that Being is an
issue" (SZ 236; H 191), and Dasein's Being "is an issue" insofar as it exists
understandingly "as self-projective Being towards its ownmost potentiality-for-Being. This potentiality is that for the sake of which any Dasein
is as it is" (SZ 236; H 191). Dasein's Being, then, must be understood in
terms of the potentiality according to which Dasein, insofar as it is, is
essentially *ahead of itself*: "ontologically, Being towards one's ownmost
potentiality-for-Being means that in each case Dasein is already *ahead* of
itself (*ihm selbst . . . vorweg*) in its Being. Dasein is always 'beyond itself'
(*über sich hinaus*), not as a way of behaving towards other entities which
it is *not*, but as Being towards the potentiality-for-Being which it is itself"
(SZ 236; H 191–92).

---

interpreted are frameworks concerning the Being of human being toward God (*Sein des
Menschen zu Gott*). Thinkers taking up the issue include, from Heidegger's perspective,
Paul, Augustine, Luther, Pascal, and Kierkegaard (see SZ 492; H 190, n. 4, and the
recent work of van Buren, esp. pp. 172–76). Likewise, regarding death, Heidegger will
note that "in its interpretation of 'life,' the anthropology worked out in Christian theology—from Paul right up to Calvin's *meditatio futurae vitae*—has always kept death in
mind" (SZ 494; H 249). I note this here in order to signal that the problem of the
"nothing" as it relates to anxiety and Being-toward-death has both historical and conceptual ties to the question of human beings' Being-toward-God.

The potentiality for Being that characterizes Dasein issues precisely in the gap indicated by this "ahead of itself." By contrast to the experience of consciousness in Hegel, where consciousness overcomes its self-difference, the "ahead of itself" of Dasein is irreducible, for it belongs to Dasein's constitutive potentiality-for-Being, which Dasein neither grounds nor closes. The "ahead of itself" in Dasein remains irreducibly open precisely because it arises only in conjunction with the radical "already" that marks the facticity of Dasein. The being that exists as "ahead of itself" is Being-in-the-world and therefore includes "the fact that it has been delivered over to itself—that it has in each case already been thrown *into a world*" (SZ 236; H 192).

The "*already in*" in conjunction with which the "ahead of itself" arises signals the passivity essential to Dasein's potentiality. Dasein finds its potentiality-for-Being, its "Being ahead of itself," on the "basis" of its always having been thrown into the world. Dasein is ahead of itself in its potentiality not as a self-grounding, self-positing being, but rather as an insurmountably passive being characterized by the "already" of its facticity. "Being ahead" thus means "*ahead-of-itself-in-already-being-in-a-world*" (SZ 236; H 192). Or, in other words: "Existentiality is determined by facticity" (SZ 236; H 192).

As seen above, in addition to being an existentiality determined by facticity (that is, thrown potentiality-for-Being), Dasein also becomes "absorbed in the world of its concern" (SZ 237; H 192)—Dasein is as falling. Indeed, Dasein falls into the "world" and flees itself precisely insofar as thrown projection, or factical existence, is related essentially to anxiety. As "ahead-of-itself-Being-already-in-a-world," Dasein also falls so as to be "alongside" the things with which it concerns itself. The totality of Dasein's ontological structure thus comes to light: "the Being of Dasein means ahead-of-itself-Being-already-in(-the-world) as Being-alongside (entities encountered within-the-world). This Being fills in the term '*care*' (*Sorge*), which is used in a purely ontologico-existential manner" (SZ 237; H 192).

As the existential a priori of Dasein, "care" names the total "fore-" structure of Dasein's Being and characterizes specifically the nature of the "presupposition" without which Dasein is not. "As a primordial structural totality" care "lies 'before' (*vor*) every factical 'attitude' and 'situation' of Dasein, and it does so existentially *a priori*" (SZ 238; H 193). Philosophically, one might presuppose a worldless subject, the distinction between reality and consciousness, outside and inside, and so on (all of which come to play especially in Heidegger's engagement with

Kant and the problem of skepticism),[12] but any such presupposition would depend on the more fundamental presupposition indicated in the total structure of care: "'Earlier' than any presupposition which Dasein makes, or any of its ways of behaving, is the '*a priori*' character of its state of Being as one whose kind of Being is care" (SZ 249; H 206). With care, the classic epistemological problem of the "external world" and the presupposition of a "worldless subject" on which that problem is based simply no longer hold. The a priori of care, then, arises in conjunction with the Heideggerian interpretation of truth in terms of disclosure—an interpretation essential to the circularity of Dasein.

Interpreting truth not in the terms of adequation or correspondence between assertion or judgment and "reality" (SZ 257; H 214), but rather in terms of the disclosure or unveiling (ἀλήθεια) that first makes possible any notion of correspondence (or noncorrespondence), Heidegger insists that truth and Dasein presuppose one another: "Dasein, as constituted by disclosedness (*Erschlossenheit*), is essentially in the truth. Disclosedness is a kind of Being which is essential to Dasein. '*There is*' *truth only in so far as Dasein is and as long as Dasein is.* Entities are uncovered only *when* Dasein *is*" (SZ 269; H 226). As the uncovering of beings in their Being, truth is given only so long as Dasein—the being whose very Being consists in disclosing—*is*. Heidegger is not here promoting a radical subjectivism, but rather a "relativism" that holds simply that truth *is* at all only *for* a being that can meaningfully encounter truth: "*Because the kind of Being that is essential to truth is of the character of Dasein, all truth is relative to Dasein's Being*" (SZ 270; H 227).

In this relation between Dasein and truth, the radical nature of "presupposing" comes out. For Heidegger, radical presupposition concerns the fact that Dasein is already in its Being, and so in the truth, in such a way that, precisely, it never fully catches up with itself or grounds the truth of its Being; presupposition, then, would differ radically here from the presupposition of the absolute in Hegel, according to which absolute subjectivity consists in the infinitude of self-grounding Being: "In Dasein's state-of-Being as care, in Being-ahead-of-itself, lies the most primordial 'presupposing.' *Because this presupposing of itself belongs to Dasein's Being, 'we' must also presuppose 'ourselves' as having the attribute of disclosedness*" (SZ 271; H 228). The presupposition of disclosedness—and so of truth—is inherent to the very Being of Dasein. In this sense, it is an irreducible presupposition, a presupposition that Dasein cannot

12. On this see § 43, esp. H 202 ff.

ground or account for in the manner that Hegelian consciousness might be grounded in, or accounted for by, self-consciousness.

The role of passivity here indicates the manner in which Dasein differs fundamentally from any self-grounding, autonomous subject. The presupposition of truth, the "always already" of disclosedness, is a presupposition in which Dasein radically *finds* itself—always after the fact. The presupposition of truth "belongs to Dasein's essential thrownness into the world. *Has Dasein as itself ever decided freely whether it wants to come into 'Dasein' or not, and will it ever be able to make such a decision?"* (SZ 271; H 228). No: Dasein as such is always already decided in its Being, without having itself made any decision that would precede the primordial presupposition of its truth.

Heidegger's reflections here on the nature of presupposition sustain his rejection of any "ideal subject," "pure I," or "consciousness in general" (SZ 272; H 229). The radical a priori to be taken up by philosophy is the a priori of Dasein's existence as facticity. Truth and Being "are" only so long as Dasein is. The Being that "is to be distinguished from every being" (SZ 272; H 230) appears in its meaning only in conjunction with that being, Dasein, whose Being consists in existence, facticity, and falling—in short, care.

At this point in Heidegger's analysis, which has established the presupposition of care as the existential a priori, the differentiated elements of care still need to be taken into view as a whole, and the horizon on which that whole arises is Being-toward-death.

Limit without Measure: Being-toward-Death and the Primacy of the Negative

The significance of Being-toward-death emerges within Heidegger's recapitulation of the structures of care according to the modes of time, for "in terms of temporality, the articulated structural totality of Dasein's Being as care first becomes existentially intelligible" (SZ 277; H 234). In and through this recapitulation of ontological structures according to temporal modes, the finitude of the temporality that defines Dasein's Being as a whole comes to light.

Taking Dasein as a whole into view requires considering its "potentiality-for-Being-a-whole," and that potentiality immediately implies the question of death; death marks the limit without which Dasein's wholeness cannot be accounted for. The consideration of Dasein's "potentiality-for-being-a-whole" thus requires "an ontologically adequate conception of death" insofar as death marks the outstanding "end" which closes all of Dasein's "can be and will be" (SZ 276–77; H 233–34). Death marks Dasein's "end" insofar as it closes (even as it opens) the potentiality that defines Dasein's existence. The "can be" of Dasein's "to be" reaches its limit in death, where Dasein is simply no longer to be, where it can no longer be its "to be." At the same time, death itself remains a possibility of Dasein, and indeed a possibility of Dasein alone, which relates fundamentally to Dasein's possibility as such.

As noted above, Dasein is, as care, always "ahead of itself," which indicates that its potentiality-for-Being always maintains itself *as potentiality.* The openness of that potentiality makes the question of "wholeness" a difficult one. In every moment that it is, Dasein is always also yet "to be"—and so is always in some respect "not yet." As long as it is, Dasein is not all that it can be, has not exhausted its possibility, is *not yet* what it remains to be. These characteristics of Dasein's potentiality-for-Being, the "ahead of itself" and the "not yet," might seem to indicate an essential lack of wholeness, the impossibility of Dasein's ever Being a whole, for "as soon as Dasein 'exists' in such a way that absolutely nothing more is still outstanding in it, then it has already for this very reason become 'no-longer-Being-there' (*Nicht-mehr-da-sein*)" (SZ 280; H 236). The Being-there of Dasein involves this irreducible "not yet" in such a way that Dasein *is* only so long as it is *not yet* all that it is to be. To achieve any such completion is for Dasein to lose its "there." If death closes Dasein as a whole, if it marks the point at which Dasein is no longer "ahead of itself," the point at which Dasein is absolutely no longer "to be"— that is, no longer characterized by its potentiality for Being—then death signals the loss of Dasein's "there," which means the loss of Dasein itself.

Such a loss marks the ultimate limit of Dasein's experience, for only a being that has the significance structure of care, the structure of potentiality, can "have" experience. Insofar as I am Dasein, my ultimate possibility—death—marks the *end* of my possibility in such a way that it wholly eludes experience: "When Dasein reaches its wholeness in death, it simultaneously loses the Being of its 'there.' By its transition to no-longer-Dasein (*Nichtmehr-dasein*), it gets lifted right out of the possibility of experiencing this transition and of understanding it as something experienced" (SZ 281; H 237). The structures of significance that constitute the "there" of Dasein, where Dasein understandingly appropriates its potentiality-for-Being, collapse absolutely in the transition marked by death. That absolute collapse is signaled in a relative manner through the experience of anxiety—where Dasein encounters the collapse of significance while nevertheless remaining in the world. As distinct from the collapse of significance in anxiety, the collapse of significance in death is irrevocable; the world and the being defined by its Being-in-the-world would simply no longer hold. Such a collapse disallows that death be experienced at all; death cannot present itself as an event or occurrence to that being who has the capacity for meaningful experience.

To be sure, one can say that "death" might be observed in the demise of animals or in the decease of other Dasein, but such death is never individual Dasein's own dying. As Dasein, I cannot exist toward my *own* end by observing the end of another living being. In this sense, my death is singular, or radically my own, and for this reason death presents an insurmountable limit to substitution or representation: no one can take my place in dying my death, nor can I take the place of another. I and I alone can be toward my death—and yet, at the same time, I myself can never be present to experience the death that is my own.

"Not yet" at its end, Dasein "will be" in death there where it cannot be—where the "there" no longer holds. In this sense, Dasein cannot be *at* its end—for that end marks the end of all "Being-there." Rather, Dasein ever exists *toward* its end, toward that which it cannot realize in or as actual experience. Thus, the "not yet" of death remains irreducible; it indicates the ultimate potentiality that never becomes an actuality: "The 'not-yet' which belongs to Dasein, however, is not just something which is provisionally and occasionally inaccessible to one's own experience or even to that of a stranger; it 'is' not yet 'actual' at all" (SZ 287; H 243).

Dasein, then, *is* only in terms of this "not yet." It carries that negativity in its very Being. Death does not represent some purely future event that will someday befall Dasein; it belongs inherently to the constitution of Dasein's Being. Dasein always already *is* its "not yet." As distinct from the Hegelian subject of historical consciousness, which is not yet (explicitly) that which it always already is (implicitly—i.e., the absolute, self-conscious subject), Dasein is always already that which it is not yet: "[J]ust as Dasein *is* already its 'not yet' and is its 'not yet' constantly as long as it is, it *is* already its end too. The 'ending' which we have in view when we speak of death does not signify Dasein's Being-at-an-end (*Zu-Ende-sein*), but a *Being-towards-the-end* (*Sein zum Ende*) of this being. Death is a way to be, which Dasein takes over as soon as it is" (SZ 289; H 245). This "way to be" can rightly be understood only so long as Dasein and its death are not understood as a being present-at-hand. As the ultimate "not yet" toward which Dasein always already *is*, death is ever impending and yet never present.

As so impending and never present, death renders each Dasein singular or irreplaceable, for it gives to each Dasein that which belongs to it alone. Paradoxically, however, Dasein cannot actually possess that which most belongs to it, precisely because death is never present as such. The "belonging" of death to Dasein, then, is a curious one, for the death that in each case is my own alone is that which, precisely, undoes me of my "there," and so dispossesses me of the Being-in-the-world that I am. Death therefore both gives and takes away what is my ownmost: always only my own, my death is also that wherein I can no longer be myself, that wherein I can no longer be or have anything at all.

Because my death cannot be shared, furthermore, it is absolutely nonrelational, and this nonrelationality, according to which I am fully and singularly given over to my uttermost possibility, is essential to the "authenticity" that comes to light in Being-toward-death:

> With death, Dasein stands before itself in its ownmost potentiality-for-Being. This is a possibility in which the issue is nothing less than Dasein's Being-in-the-world. Its death is the possibility of no-longer-being-able-to-be-there [*Nicht-mehr-dasein-können*]. If Dasein stands before itself as this possibility, it has been *fully* assigned to its ownmost potentiality-for-Being. When it stands before itself in this way, all its relations to any other Dasein have been undone. This ownmost non-relational possibility is at the same time the uttermost one. (SZ 294; H 250)

As my uttermost possibility, the one that assigns me most to myself even as it undoes me, death cuts me off from all relation with others (a major point of objection for Levinas)—and it does so with the force of death's *certainty*, for the possibility of death is utterly certain, even in the irreducible *indefiniteness* of its "when" (SZ 302; H 258).

Now, the much debated distinction between authenticity and inauthenticity in Heidegger arises insofar as the radical singularity and indefinite certainty of death can be covered over in the falling of Dasein's average everydayness, which tries to confer "definiteness" upon death (SZ 302; H 258) and deprive it of its singularity in such a way that "one"—and thus finally "no one" in particular—dies: "'Dying' is leveled off to an occurrence which reaches Dasein, to be sure, but belongs to nobody in particular" (SZ 297; H 253).

In such covering-over, Dasein seeks to ignore the radical character of the possibility signaled in Being-toward-death. From this perspective, the distinction in Heidegger between authentic and inauthentic Being-

toward-death would concern the distinction between a radical and a derivative sense of possibility. To be authentically would be to confront
radical possibility. To be inauthentically would be to reduce the radical
possibility of death—which as singular and certain in its indefiniteness
resists calculation and eludes actualization—to a particular ontic possibility that might be actualized and manipulated:

> "Being-towards" a possibility—that is to say, towards something
> possible—may signify "Being out for" something possible, as in
> concerning ourselves with its actualization. Such possibilities are
> constantly encountered in the field of what is ready-to-hand and
> present-at-hand—what is attainable, controllable, practicable, and
> the like. In concernfully Being out for something possible, there is
> a tendency to *annihilate the possibility* of the possible by making it
> available to us. (SZ 305; H 261)

By making possibility available as some thing with whose actualization I
might concern myself, I annihilate the fundamental *possibility* of the possible; I reduce possibility—in all of its incalculability—to a simple actuality in reserve, an actuality whose availability would render it suscept-
ible to calculation, manipulation, or even mastery. But, precisely, the
possibility of death gives Dasein nothing that Dasein as such might actualize. In this "nothing" that death gives, the most radical, incalculable
possibility emerges—that of Dasein's absolute impossibility.

The radical possibility of Dasein's impossibility, a possibility not sus-
ceptible to actualization or experience, and so finally resistant to calculation or manipulation, must thus be distinguished from "something possible." As distinct from something possible, this radical possibility resists
any expecting (*Erwarten*) or awaiting (*Warten*), for these already seek to
reduce possibility to the (eventually) actual—and so they ignore possibility *as* possibility:

> To expect something possible is always to understand it and to
> "have" it with regard to whether and when and how it will be actu-
> ally present-at-hand. [. . .] Even in expecting one leaps away from
> the possible and gets a foothold in the actual. It is for its actuality
> that what is expected is expected. By the very nature of expecting,
> the possible is drawn into the actual, arising out of the actual and
> returning to it. (SZ 306; H 262)

If expecting draws the possible into the actual, if what is expected is expected "for actuality," then death, which Dasein cannot actualize as such,

cannot be expected. Death resists absolutely any expectation in which I would "have" death as something actually present at hand, something calculable as to its whether and when and how.

Rather than expect death, then, I would stand toward death in a relation of "anticipation" (*Vorlaufen*), which, instead of reducing possibility to an actuality in reserve, *maintains* the possibility of the possible: "In this kind of coming close [i.e., anticipation] [. . .] one does not tend towards concernfully making available something actual; but as one comes closer understandingly, the possibility of the possible just becomes 'greater.' *The closest closeness which one may have in Being towards death as a possibility, is as far as possible from anything actual*" (SZ 306–7; H 262). In the anticipation of death, the possibility of the possible just becomes "greater" because the possibility concerned constantly proves incommensurate with the actual. Death is a possibility, and indeed a certain possibility, but it is a possibility that, even as it opens all possibility, finally ends all possibility, for it is "*the possibility of the impossibility of any existence at all*" (SZ 307; H 262).

According to Heidegger, the possibility of death, this possibility of the impossibility of existence, takes away all possibility (as well as all actuality) even as it *gives*. "What" does death give? Strictly speaking, it gives no-thing, for "Death, as possibility, gives nothing to be 'actualized,' nothing which Dasein, as actual, could itself *be*" (SZ 307; H 262). Giving nothing that Dasein could be, death gives a "beyond" of Being, and that beyond, which "is" Dasein's ownmost possibility, signals nothing that Dasein might have or possess. Insofar as death undoes Dasein of all Being or having, Dasein's "ownmost" possibility in fact dispossesses.

Such a dispossession goes hand in hand with a most remarkable characteristic of death: its lack of measure. Death gives itself in such a way that it dispossesses absolutely. It is thus a measureless giving that, at one and the same time, gives Dasein its ownmost possibility and deprives Dasein of all possibility whatsoever. Limitless deprivation and limitless giving here coincide, for "in the anticipation of this possibility it becomes 'greater and greater'; that is to say, the possibility reveals itself to be such that it knows no measure at all, no more or less, but signifies the possibility of the measureless impossibility of existence" (SZ 307; H 262). Like the excess of an absolute giving, the possibility of death knows no measure. Like "all" or like "nothing," it recognizes no difference between more and less. What is given in the possibility of death is nothing—and yet death can indeed mean everything, for its horizon gives Dasein all that it might ever have or be. The possibility of death signals the measureless or the absolute—the absolute impossibility of existence, which knows no measure.

Like an absolute gift (whose paradoxes occupy chap. 6), death is unforeseeable in its when (even as it is certain), irreducible to presence at hand, and nonrepeatable. In its measurelessness, the possibility of death resists or undoes all intention and representation: "In accordance with its essence, this possibility offers no support for becoming intent on something, 'picturing' to oneself the actuality which is possible, and so forgetting its possibility. Being-towards-death, as anticipation of possibility, is what first *makes* this possibility *possible*, and sets it free as possibility" (SZ 307; H 262). Now, while the possibility of death resists all intention or representation, while the possibility of death gives without measure and to that very extent deprives absolutely, the possibility of death nevertheless delivers Dasein over to itself, to its ownmost Being, its authenticity. I should briefly consider, therefore, the relation between the radical possibility of death, which undoes representational thought and, indeed, dispossesses absolutely, and authenticity, or the notion of Dasein's "ownmost." In that relation, the "nothing" common to death and anxiety becomes central.

Death delivers Dasein over to its "ownmost" or authentic existence insofar as it individualizes Dasein by tearing it away from the they-self:

> The ownmost possibility is *non-relational*. Anticipation allows Dasein to understand that the potentiality-for-being in which its Being is an issue, must be taken over by Dasein alone. Death does not just "belong" to one's Dasein in an undifferentiated way; death *lays claim* to it as an *individual* Dasein. The non-relational character of death, as understood in anticipation, individualizes Dasein down to itself. (SZ 308; H 263)

In and through this individualizing, death deprives Dasein of the support that it might seek in confronting the possibility of death. As in anxiety, no beings within-the-world will offer Dasein any support in its anticipation of death: "This individualizing is a way in which the 'there' is disclosed for existence. It makes manifest that all Being-alongside the things with which we concern ourselves, and all Being-with-Others, will fail us when our ownmost potentiality-for-Being is the issue" (SZ 308; H 263).

Insofar as it is deprived of any beings within the world that might "support" it in its Being-toward-death, Dasein is utterly individualized or singularized. As we saw, the state-of-mind that accompanies such singularity is anxiety, whose "object" is nothing. The proximity of death and anxiety depends on precisely that nothing; the anxiety of death is anxiety in the face of the nothing toward which I inevitably exist:

> In [anxiety], Dasein finds itself *face to face* with the "nothing" of the possible impossibility of its existence. Anxiety is anxious *about* the potentiality-for-Being of the being so destined [*des so bestimmten Seienden*], and in this way it discloses the uttermost possibility. Anticipation utterly individualizes Dasein, and allows it, in this individualization of itself, to become certain of the totality of its potentiality-for-Being. For this reason, anxiety as a basic state-of-mind belongs to such a self-understanding of Dasein on the basis of Dasein itself. Being-towards-death is essentially anxiety. (SZ 310; H 266)

Being-toward-death is essentially anxiety in that both give Dasein nothing to project or intend, nothing to represent or objectify, nothing to calculate or realize. But in that "giving" of nothing, Being-toward-death and its basic state-of-mind, anxiety, also give to Dasein *all* that it might be—the whole of Dasein in its ownmost individuality. The possibility of Dasein's own impossibility thus constitutes the ultimate horizon of all Dasein's possible Being. In other words, Dasein is radically finite; the utter individualization of Dasein in the anxiety of Being-toward-death frees Dasein for its ownmost possibilities, "which are determined by the *end* and so are understood as *finite (endliche)*" (SZ 308; H 264).

Now, the nothing common to anxiety and Being-toward-death—which for Heidegger is attested in the "call of conscience" where Dasein knows an ineradicable guilt—is essential to Dasein's authentic potentiality-for-Being and signals a depth of negativity in Dasein that is insurmountable because primordial. Heidegger interprets the Being-guilty known through conscience not at the level of specific debts incurred or of specific boundaries transgressed. Rather, he interprets it at the level of Dasein's primordial nullity: guilt can speak its negative pronouncement ("Guilty!") only to a being who exists on the "basis" of such a nullity. Guilt thus signals the lack or negativity inherent to Dasein's Being: "Hence we define the formally existential idea of the 'Guilty!' as 'Being-the-basis for a Being which has been defined by a "not"'—that is to say, as *'Being-the-basis of a nullity'*" (SZ 329; H 283). The "not" of Being-guilty *precedes* any particular instance of transgression or debt and would constitute the "basis" of these.

To say, as Heidegger does, that Being-guilty is "primordial" and that in it lies the character of the "*not*" is to say that negation is not secondary but primary, that lack or negativity is primal and not the privation of any plenitude or positivity that would have preceded it. This primordial negativity or nullity is inherent to the very Being of Dasein as care, where it appears especially in terms of Dasein's thrownness and the projection of that thrownness:

> Dasein's Being is care. It comprises in itself facticity (thrownness), existence (projection), and falling. As being, Dasein is something that has been thrown; it has been brought into its "there," but *not* on its own [*nicht von ihm selbst*]. As being, it has taken the definite form of a potentiality-for-Being that has heard itself and yet has given itself to itself [*sich zu eigen gegeben hat*] but *not* as itself. (SZ 329–30; H 284)

What does Heidegger mean here when he indicates that Dasein, as care, is determined as potentiality-for-Being that has heard itself and *given itself to itself but not as itself?* He means to indicate the paradox of Dasein's thrownness: Dasein is always already decided in the finitude of its Being, it is given over to itself, without ever having been present "originally" to make any such decision or intentionally to receive any such gift. As so decided or given, Dasein cannot ground itself, for it "receives" itself before being itself. This is the meaning of Dasein's primordial nullity and its radical finitude: "As existent it never comes back behind its thrownness in such a way that it might first release this 'that-it-is-and-has-to-be' from *its Being*-its-Self and lead it into the 'there'" (SZ 330; H 284). As thrown, Dasein has been "called" to be; it has heard that call and been given to itself *before* it could have been present *as itself* to receive such a call or to will such a giving. It always comes to itself as after the fact; it always *finds* itself. How does it find itself? It finds itself always already taking up its possibilities, which it projects existentially.

It is in this way, and this way alone, that Dasein becomes its own "basis." But to become a basis is for Dasein *never* to initiate, command, or master that basis. According to the constitutive "not" of Dasein, Dasein can never wholly assume or command its passivity. Heidegger stresses that even in "Being-a-basis," Dasein *never* has power or control over its own Being:

> In being a basis—that is, in existing as thrown—Dasein constantly lags behind its possibilities. It is never existent *before* its basis, but only *from it* and *as this basis*. Thus "Being-a-basis" means *never* to

have power over one's ownmost Being from the ground up [*Grund-sein besagt demnach, des eigensten Seins von Grund auf nie mächtig sein*]. This "*not*" belongs to the existential meaning of "thrownness." It itself, being a basis, *is* a nullity of itself. "Nullity" does not signify anything like not-Being-present-at-hand or not-subsisting; what one has in view here is rather a "not" which is constitutive for this *Being* of Dasein—its thrownness. (SZ 330; H 284)

This constitutive "not" or nullity of Dasein shows itself in the temporality of Dasein—where Dasein fundamentally lags with respect to itself. Only on the basis of that lag does Dasein take up its potentiality-for-Being. Thus, that "assumption"—which means "becoming a basis"—will *never* master or annul the nullity out of which it arises, for Dasein never fully catches up with itself. The "reception" of thrownness in and through projection, therefore, is never a full conversion of passivity into activity.

It is precisely the irreducibility of this lag that differentiates it radically from the lag of consciousness within Hegel's difference of consciousness—a lag that is always implicitly and finally explicitly overcome so as even to "annul" time. The lag of Dasein remains irreducible, by contrast, precisely to the degree that the temporality wherein it issues is a radically finite temporality, a temporality that cannot be annulled, overcome, or sublated through the recollection of the infinite. The overcoming or annulment of time in Hegel, then, indicates from a Heideggerian perspective an insufficiently radical conception of negativity. To close, I should briefly lay out the Heideggerian conception of finite temporality and some key differences between it and the Hegelian conception of time.

Finite and Ecstatic: The Temporality of Dasein

Having unfolded the existential structure of Dasein as care, Heidegger proceeds to define the temporal ground of that structure. Within that definition, the three equiprimordial elements of care—facticity (thrownness), falling, and existence (projection)—are correlated with three equiprimordial aspects of temporality—having-been, the present, and futurity. Seeking a more primordial understanding of time than is given in common understanding (or in the history of philosophy), Heidegger focuses in his analyses of time on Dasein's "anticipatory resoluteness" (*vorlaufende Entschlossenheit*): "*Temporality gets experienced in a phenomenally primordial way in Dasein's authentic Being-a-whole, in the phenomenon of anticipatory resoluteness*" (SZ 351; H 304).

Anticipatory resoluteness, and thus primordial temporality, relates fundamentally to the nullity of Dasein in its Being-guilty and in its Being-toward-death, which mark two of the three essentially interconnected elements within the interpretation of primordial time:

> When Dasein is resolute, it takes over authentically in its existence the fact that it *is* the null basis of its own nullity. We have conceived death existentially as what we have characterized as the possibility of the *im*possibility of existence—that is to say, as the utter nullity of Dasein. Death is not "added on" to Dasein at its "end"; but Dasein, as care, is the thrown (that is, null) basis for its death. The nullity by which Dasein's Being is dominated primordially through and through, is revealed to Dasein itself in authentic Being-towards-death. Only on the basis of Dasein's *whole* Being does anticipation make Being-guilty manifest. Care harbors in itself both death and guilt equiprimordially. Only anticipatory resoluteness understands the potentiality-for-Being-guilty *authentically and wholly*—that is to say, *primordially.* (SZ 354; H 306)

In saying that death and guilt are equiprimordial, Heidegger indicates two aspects of the fundamental role played by nullity in the Being of Dasein as care. Anticipation makes manifest precisely that nullity, precisely that which disallows that Dasein ever gain control over its ownmost Being (*eigenstes Sein*) "from the ground up." The anticipation of death, which cannot have an object as would awaiting or expecting, but is rather an anticipation of the *im*possibility or nullity of my existence, makes fundamentally manifest that upon which such anticipation itself would be based: the nullity of my thrownness, or my Being-guilty. Thrownness and Being-toward-death go together essentially; abandoned to itself, Dasein is "thrownness into death" (SZ 356; H 308). The nullity in which I find myself as thrown is projected "authentically" within my Being-toward-death without that authenticity ever indicating a mastery.

The radical priority of my thrownness—which "precedes" and constitutes me in such a way that I could never get behind or before it to will, intend, or ground it—comes to light only in the radical futurity of my death, which, as a future that never becomes present in actuality or experience, nevertheless manifests the "whole" of my Being. If Dasein's nullity or Being-guilty becomes manifest only on the basis of Dasein's "whole" Being, that "wholeness" proves, precisely at that point, to be radically *open*. The past that never was in the sense of being present in any presence (in short, my thrownness) returns—or first appears—in the future that never arrives (the impossible death that is nevertheless my own). Temporality stretches Dasein out between its thrownness (which it always carries along with itself) and its projection against the ultimate horizon of Being-toward-death (death being not a future event but a constitutive mode of Dasein as such); in doing so, it holds together the overall ec-static structure of Dasein: Dasein "stands" (*sistit*) "out" (*ex*) from itself in its very existence—out from the nullity of its past and toward the nullity of its future.

While temporality in this way holds together the three equiprimordial ecstases of Dasein according to three equiprimordial temporal modes, the futurity of Being-toward-death does hold a certain privilege insofar as it alone brings the three ecstases and temporal modes together as a whole. The ultimate "upon which" where the whole of Dasein's Being will be projected consists in that ultimate possibility, death, which frees all possibilities. In the temporal mode of that projection, the futural, Dasein exists, or stands out from itself, as "coming toward" itself: "Being-towards-death is possible only as something *futural* (*als* zukünftiges) [. . .]. By the term 'futural,' we do not here have in view a 'now' which has *not yet* become 'actual' and which sometime *will be* for the first time. We have in view the coming (*Kunft*) in which Dasein, in its ownmost potentiality-for-Being, comes towards itself" (SZ 373; H 325). Dasein comes toward itself futurally in terms of that possibility which is "based" on the nullity of its thrownness.

In existing, then, or in projecting, Dasein "assumes" or "takes over" futurally the nullity of its own thrownness. Dasein projects all possibilities within the horizon of its ultimate possibility, which is the nullity of death, and the projection of such nullity issues from the "basis" of the nullity of thrownness. As thrown projection, Dasein is thrown into death. Temporally, this means that the futural mode of projection upon the horizon of Being-toward-death is tied inextricably to the "having-been" inherent to thrownness: "Only in so far as Dasein *is* as an 'I-*am*-as-having-been' (*ich bin gewesen*), can Dasein come towards itself futurally in such a way that it comes *back*. As authentically futural, Dasein *is* authentically as '*having been*.' Anticipation of one's uttermost and ownmost possibility is coming back understandingly to one's ownmost 'been'" (SZ 373; H 326).

As distinct from Hegel, for whom the "having-been" is essentially recollected, through double negation, in the self-presence of absolute self-consciousness, the "having-been" in Heidegger marks an insurmountable limit to recollection and self-presence. That is, the having-been in Heidegger appears futurally in the death that Dasein anticipates but cannot expect or await or make present to experience. The radical basis of the having-been "is" as never having been present; it therefore cannot be recollected or represented. Likewise, the radical future of Dasein's possible "to be" cannot be rendered present in experience, for it is nothing other than the forward aspect, the future return, of having-been. Dasein exists ecstatically in the *between* of these two nullities.

Indeed, while Heidegger here undoubtedly privileges the futural (see SZ 373; H 326), he nevertheless insists on the inextricable tie among the basic temporal modes, and in and through the tie between the futural and the having-been emerges the third essential temporal mode: Dasein's "present." The "present" of Dasein's primordial temporality differs fundamentally from the presence of a "now" that would pass between future and past. It concerns more primordially the manner in which the resoluteness of Dasein "makes present." When this "making-present" is brought together with the futural and the having-been, the three fundamental "ecstases" of primordial temporality, the three basic ways Dasein "stands out" from itself in and through time, can be seen in their essential interplay:

> Coming back to itself futurally, resoluteness brings itself into the Situation by making present. The character of "having been" arises from the future, and in such a way that the future which "has been" (or better, which "is in the process of having been") releases from itself the Present. This phenomenon has the unity of a future which makes present in the process of having been; we designate it as "*temporality*." (SZ 374; H 326)

According to its primordial temporality, Dasein exists, or "stands out" in three fundamental ways. The three fundamental ecstases of primordial temporality (the futural, the having-been, the present) give the primordial meaning of care (existence, facticity, falling).

Thus, "*temporality reveals itself as the meaning of authentic care*" (SZ 374; H 326) insofar as the three elements of care find their movement and unity in the three inextricable modes of temporality. Dasein is existentially "ahead of itself" (i.e., it is characterized by existence) insofar as it is temporally futural; Dasein is existentially "already-in" (i.e., it is characterized by facticity) insofar as it is temporally as "having been";

Dasein is existentially "alongside" (i.e., it is characterized by falling) insofar as it is temporally as making-present (see SZ 375–76; H 327–28). The ecstatic structure of care is essentially unified just as the basic modes of temporality are inextricably bound: "Temporality makes possible the unity of existence, facticity and falling, and in this way constitutes primordially the totality of the structure of care" (SZ 376; H 328).

Now, through this phenomenon of primordial temporality emerges the fundamental finitude of Being, and that finitude must be interpreted in terms of the ecstatic movement that defines temporality. The temporalizing of temporality is a unified movement in which each of the three differentiated temporal modes "stands out" as an "ecstasis" in a particular way: "The future, the character of having been, and the Present, show the phenomenal characteristics of the 'towards-oneself,' the 'back-to,' and the 'letting oneself be encountered by.' The phenomena of the 'towards . . . ,' the 'to . . . ,' and the 'alongside . . . ,' make temporality manifest as the ἐκστατικόν pure and simple. *Temporality is the primordial 'outside-of-itself' in and for itself*" (SZ 377; H 328–29). Outside of itself *in and for itself*, temporality determines the ecstatic Being of Dasein in its three basic and unified dimensions.

While the temporal ecstases do not arise sequentially, but rather equiprimordially, they do nevertheless temporalize in different modes, and in conjunction with the decisive role of Being-toward-death within the structure of care, the futural mode of temporalizing is decisive for primordial and authentic temporality: "Primordial and authentic temporality temporalizes itself in terms of the authentic future and in such a way that in having been futurally, it first of all awakens the Present. *The primary phenomenon of primordial and authentic temporality is the future*" (SZ 378; H 329). Heidegger's motivation for privileging the future here concerns the primary element within his understanding of care. While care consists indissolubly of existence, thrownness, and falling, the first, which in the end occurs only in terms of Being-toward-death, comes to dominate the whole.

Indeed, it dominates in such a way that Heidegger can ultimately equate the whole of care with this one element within it: "Care is Being-towards-death" (SZ 378; H 329). Heidegger can make this equation to the extent that Being-toward-death alone gives care its character of totality (which, again, remains open); the manifold structure of care becomes a whole only against the horizon of Being-toward-death, which utterly individualizes Dasein and so gives Dasein wholly to itself alone.

This means that the being whose Being is defined as care is a being

whose Being proves radically finite. Being finite does not mean that Dasein "is" and then, at some later point, "ends." It means that Dasein is,
in the very way of its Being, finite; it exists finitely. Finitude operates
adverbially, not adjectivally: "Care is Being-towards-death. We have defined 'anticipatory resoluteness' as authentic Being towards the possibility which we have characterized as Dasein's utter impossibility. In such
Being-towards-its end, Dasein exists in a way which is authentically
whole as that being which it can be when 'thrown into death.' This being
does not have an end at which it just stops, but it *exists finitely*" (SZ 378;
H 329). To say that Dasein exists finitely is to say that primordial temporality itself is finite. More specifically, the futurity that dominates the
temporalizing of primordial temporality—the future that constitutes
the horizon of Dasein's Being-toward-death—is itself essentially finite.
The finitude of primordial temporality must be understood first in terms
of the finitude of the future, a finitude that becomes apparent in Being-
toward-death. The finitude of primordial temporality does not mean
that "after" Dasein "dies" time ceases or does not "go on"; it means
rather that time is temporalized in an essentially finite way; time emerges
only within the finite structures and modes of Dasein's primordial temporality.

Within those modes and structures, Dasein exists toward (and starting from) its own nullity, a nullity into which it is as thrown, a nullity
that gives Dasein to itself even as it closes Dasein absolutely:

> [Primordial temporality's] finitude does not amount to a stopping,
> but is a characteristic of temporalization itself. The primordial and
> authentic future is the "towards-oneself" (to *oneself!*), existing as the
> possibility of nullity, the possibility which is not to be outstripped.
> The ecstatical character of the primordial future lies precisely in the
> fact that the future closes one's potentiality-for-Being; that is to say,
> the future is closed to one, and as such it makes possible the resolute
> existentiell understanding of nullity. Primordial and authentic com-
> ing-towards-oneself is the meaning of existing in one's ownmost
> nullity. (SZ 379; H 330)

This finitude, I insist, does not mark simply a closure of Dasein, but
indeed the very condition of its radical openness. Radically open to the
possibility that Dasein never actualizes, Dasein's existence is temporalized finitely. Dasein is *open* to (or through) possibility precisely because
time is not infinite but finite, not endless but ending—that is, ever yet
to be closed by the nullity that also opens it. The "closure" of the future

alone opens Dasein, alone allows Dasein to exist toward that radical, null possibility that it never actualizes.

This essentially finite temporality finally means that Dasein exists always and only as a radical *between*. The temporality dominated by the futurity of Being-toward-death is a temporality determined equally by the other "end" of Dasein—its beginning or birth. Ecstatic Being is thus ever in the midst. "Only that being which is 'between' birth and death presents the whole which we have been seeking" (SZ 425; H 373). Neither birth nor death constitutes an event that was or will be simply present (or past). Rather, both birth and death indicate *ways* in which Dasein as such always already exists:

> The "between" which relates birth and death already lies *in the Being* of Dasein. [. . .] Understood existentially, birth is not and never is something no longer present-at-hand; and death is just as far from having the kind of Being of something still outstanding, not yet present-at-hand but coming along. Factical Dasein exists as born; and as born, it is already dying, in the sense of Being-towards-death. As long as Dasein factically exists, both "ends" and their "between" *are*, and they *are* in the only way which is possible on the basis of Dasein's Being as *care*. (SZ 426; H 374)

Dasein *is* the very between of its birth and death—and that between would constitute an essentially mortal difference. The primordial, ecstatic temporality that articulates such a between alone opens the possibility of Dasein's being historical. Historical being, which is possible only for a being determined by temporality, is therefore essentially finite. As distinct from the Hegelian conception of history wherein spirit through history annuls the time into which spirit has fallen, the Heideggerian conception of history will be founded on that temporality in which the between—and thus the movement of difference—remains irreducible. Existing not *in* time but *as* temporality, which is radically finite, Dasein remains ever between its birth and its death. Only in that between does the meaning of Being arise, for only in that between does there arise a being who can experience the nothingness of beings and so make the difference between beings and Being. The meaning of Being arises only for that being who can encounter the nullity of beings—proximally in anxiety and conscience and ultimately in Being-toward-death. In this sense, the difference between beings and Being, which Dasein alone makes, would necessarily imply the mortal difference.

FIVE

Transcending Negation:
The Causal Nothing and Ecstatic
Being in Pseudo-Dionysius's
Theology

*H*aving situated the question of finite, mortal existence with respect to the Heideggerian critique of onto-theology and its modern "completion," I turn now to the indispensable historical background for contemporary post-Heideggerian discussions of the apophatic traditions: the enigmatic, early sixth-century theologian, Dionysius the Areopagite, or Pseudo-Dionysius, who more than any other figure founds the Christian apophatic traditions and provides the center of discussion today. Because the motivations for such a shift from nineteenth- and twentieth-century thought to the early sixth century might not be immediately evident, I should briefly situate Dionysius historically and indicate his relevance for the contemporary context I seek to address.

This early sixth-century figure was a pseudonymous writer who presented himself—and was long accepted—as an Athenian convert of Saint Paul appearing in Acts 17:34.[1] His writings were viewed in the Middle Ages as having an authority whose antiquity was surpassed only by that of the Bible itself.[2] Judging from the style and substance of his writings, however, modern scholars agree that Dionysius was most likely a Syrian monk who wrote sometime between 480 and 510 c.e. Little more is actually known of the person, but his writings themselves had an extensive influence on medieval thought and spirituality. Indeed, on the basis of Dionysius's substantial legacy to the medieval world, a scholar such as Hans Urs von Balthasar can maintain that the influence of Dionysius's theology is "scarcely less than that of Augustine" himself and that "one can see virtually all medieval philosophy up to the Aristotelian renaissance and the whole of theology up to Thomas as derived from the fecundity of these two."[3]

1. Bearing out suspicions raised already by certain Renaissance humanists, in the late nineteenth century J. Stiglmayr and H. Koch demonstrated, independently of one another, Dionysius's dependence on Proclus and thus the impossibility of his having been an actual convert of Paul. On Dionysius's debt to Proclus, see esp. Henri-Dominique Saffrey's "New Objective Links between the Pseudo-Dionysius and Proclus," in Dominic J. O'Meara, ed., *Neoplatonism and Christian Thought* (Albany: State University of New York Press, 1982).
2. As Paul Rorem, among others, indicates, in *Pseudo-Dionysius: A Commentary on the Texts and an Introduction to Their Influence* (Oxford: Oxford University Press, 1993), p. 239.
3. Hans Urs von Balthasar, *Glory of the Lord*, trans. Andrew Louth, Francis McDonagh, and Brian McNeil (New York: Crossroad, 1984), 2:148; hereafter cited parenthetically as GL.

Pivotal points within this diverse and extensive Dionysian legacy would include Maximus Confessor's influential reinterpretation and appropriation of Dionysian thought and spirituality in the seventh century;[4] the crucial ninth-century translation of both the Dionysian corpus and the Dionysian conceptuality into the Latin language and thought-world by the Carolingian philosopher and theologian John Scotus Eriugena;[5] the great scholastic theologies of Albert the Great and his student Thomas Aquinas, who both take up the central Dionysian question of theological language;[6] the Franciscan spirituality of Bonaventure, a major synthesis of Dionysian and Augustinian thought; and the mysticism of Meister Eckhart (and of his followers such as Johannes Tauler and Henry Suso), whose dialectic is grounded in a deeply Dionysian apophaticism. Into the late Middle Ages and beyond, one can trace Dionysian modes of thought and language in figures and ideas from Nicholas of Cusa's fifteenth-century "learned ignorance," through Angelus Silesius's seventeenth-century apophatic poetry. Some scholars have also suggested the possible influence of Dionysian thought, through such intermediaries as Eriugena or Jacob Boehme, in German idealism.[7]

---

4. As Jaroslav Pelikan notes, Maximus played a major role in transmitting Dionysian thought to orthodox theology and spirituality, but he did so not so much through his *scholia*, which have been "conflated (and confused) in the transmission of the literary tradition with those of John of Scythopolis," but rather "through his orthodox restatement and reinterpretation of the Dionysian structure both in his theology and even more in his spirituality" (introduction, *Maximus Confessor: Selected Writings* [New York: Paulist Press, 1985], p. 6).

5. As Bernard McGinn points out, "If John Scottus Eriugena had done nothing more than translate the *corpus dionysiacum* into Latin, he still would have been accorded a place of merit in the history of Western mysticism. But Eriugena did even more for the history of both Dionysianism and mysticism, writing his own commentary on the *Celestial Hierarchy* and explaining so many passages from the *Divine Names* in the *Periphyseon* that the thirteenth-century compilers of the glossed Dionysian corpus used at Paris incorporated a virtual Eriugenian commentary into this important source of mystical theology" (*The Growth of Mysticism*, vol. 2 of *The Presence of God: A History of Western Christian Mysticism* [New York: Crossroad, 1994], p. 90).

6. See esp. Albert's commentary on the *Mystical Theology*, available in the English translation of Simon Tugwell (New York: Paulist Press, 1988). Tugwell's introduction to the Paulist Press edition also contains a very helpful section entitled "Albert and the Dionysian Tradition" (pp. 39–95). Dionysius is crucial to Aquinas, of course, not only in the commentary on the *Divine Names*, but indeed in the very first section of the *Summa Theologica*, where the question of naming God is an essential element in the doctrine of God.

7. See, e.g., Rorem, and the work in which Werner Beierwaltes has indicated possible connections (as well as necessary distinctions) between Neoplatonism (both pagan

In light of this diverse and far-reaching influence, how might one characterize its overall character? While Dionysius's influence clearly extends within the Middle Ages to several areas,[8] two in particular stand out. First, especially in his treatises on the *Celestial Hierarchy* and the *Ecclesiastical Hierarchy*, Dionysius conveys to the medieval world its deeply Neoplatonic, dialectical, and fundamentally hierarchical conception of reality as a movement of divine "procession and return." The term "hierarchy," in fact, first appears in Dionysius (along with the related term, "thearchy," which did not enjoy equal success), and, of course, the concept proves decisive for the conception of reality—and authority—in the Middle Ages and beyond. Second, especially in his treatises on the *Divine Names* and on *Mystical Theology*, Dionysius establishes what will become a classic scheme of three modes for theological language—namely, the affirmative or "kataphatic" mode, the negative or "apophatic" mode, and finally the mystical mode. The term "mystical theology" itself originates with Dionysius, and his apophatic approach to "mystical unknowing" decisively shapes the course of much subsequent mysticism. In sum, the Dionysian writings inform fundamental medieval (and later) approaches to the interplay between the divine and the cosmos in which human being finds itself, and, correlatively, they establish a classic theological language and method through which that interplay can be articulated.

But how precisely do these Dionysian understandings of theological thought and language, so crucial in the Middle Ages, become important to the late twentieth-century, post-Heideggerian thinkers who would reread Dionysius today? As I indicated in the introduction, and as I will develop further in the next chapter and in the conclusion, two predominant concerns within this contemporary context tend to motivate the rereading of Dionysius.

First, post-Heideggerian thinkers invariably find themselves confronted with the "death of God" (Hegelian and/or Nietzschean) and thus in a situation where thought and language surrounding God tend to be

---

and Christian) and German idealism (*Platonismus und Idealismus* [Frankfurt am Main: V. Klostermann, 1972]).

8. Foremost among those themes would be, in addition to the conception of hierarchy and the systematic definition of the modes of theological language, the related description and ordering of the angelic ranks and functions (a fundamental source for medieval "angelology"); the definition and interpretation of liturgical and biblical symbolism; and the ordering of spiritual and ecclesial practices along the path to God (especially the threefold scheme of "purification," "illumination," and "perfection").

deeply negative. As early as Christos Yannaras's study in 1967, attempts have been made to relate the "absence and unknowability" of God that follows from the "death of God" to the "absence and unknowability" of God as articulated within the classic theologies stemming back to Dionysius's apophatic mysticism. More recently, in a manner reminiscent of Yannaras, Jean-Luc Marion has argued that the death of God involves nothing more than a destruction of the rational idols of metaphysics; such a destruction, on Marion's account, actually clears the way for a truer thought of God's incomprehensibility and a truer language of God's ineffability than were possible within metaphysics' rational conception and expression of God.

Second, and correlatively, a thought of the "unthinkable" has been developed within recent post-Heideggerian discussion according to the notion of absolute gift, or of giving "without return." As I'll show in the next chapter, for Marion the thought of an absolute giving, at least in its theological form, finds a decisive formulation in the Dionysian notion of the "Good beyond Being." For others, like Jacques Derrida, Dionysius represents less an unqualified success and more an important test case for the difficulties involved in realizing or sustaining both a thought of unthinkable giving and a radically apophatic or "unsaying" form of language that would correspond to such a thought. No matter whether one embraces Dionysius outright or approaches him with greater reservation, however, the case remains that he represents a most decisive historical figure in whom one confronts the interplay between negative language (in this case the doubly negative language of apophatic and mystical theology) and an attempted thought of absolute giving. If contemporary approaches to these two issues and their interrelation are to have substantial historical ground and significance, then such approaches should necessarily engage Dionysius and his legacy.

Thus, from the contemporary perspective through which I am attempting to approach Dionysius, my two primary and interconnected concerns are, on the one hand, the function of "negative" language in Dionysian theology and, on the other hand, the thought of an inconceivable Goodness to which such negative language would answer. In order to establish and develop such a contemporary perspective, however, one needs first to understand as thoroughly as possible the Dionysian system on its own terms. For this reason, the analysis in this chapter will be primarily internal to the Dionysian texts themselves, while making reference also to the pertinent secondary literature within modern Dionysian scholarship.

Through such an approach, this chapter seeks to illuminate in particular the double function of negation within Dionysius's irreducibly threefold theological method. As I will show, that method, consisting in the "kataphatic" or affirmative, "apophatic" or negative, and "mystical" modes of theology, itself corresponds to Dionysius's hierarchical conception of reality. I will unfold and clarify the precise nature of that correspondence within the course of the chapter.

From the outset, however, I should lay out the basic approach: within Dionysius's fundamentally threefold theological language, the structure of the cosmos and the movement of the soul therein prove to be essentially ecstatic, driven as they are by the erotic dynamism of the divine. Within this framework, kataphatic language corresponds primarily to the procession of the divine "out" of itself into the cosmos, and in this sense such language signals an ecstasy of the divine;[9] apophatic language articulates and promotes the return movement of the created soul beyond itself toward the transcendence of the divine, and in this sense it corresponds to an ecstasy of the creature; finally, the mystical mode of language (embodied in the "hyper-" terms that I address below) articulates the ineffable consummation of a reunion in which the created being would have abandoned itself in the God beyond Being, thus signaling the moment where the divine ecstasy that calls all created beings to be and the human ecstasy that answers to such a call would finally and most fully meet.

Within this scheme, all created beings exist, and so stand "outside" of themselves, by straining dynamically between the nothingness from which they are called (by the ecstatic generosity of the divine Good) and the God for whom they yearn (who remains inconceivably transcendent in his Goodness). As "source" of the call that brings all beings into the yearning that characterizes their existence, God functions primarily as Cause. He is the unique and divine αἰτία, or that without which beings simply are not because they are not called to be. The divine Cause marks

---

9. On the notion of divine ecstasy (in both pagan and Christian contexts) and its relation esp. to Dionysius's central understanding of God as "eros," see Bernard McGinn's "God as Eros: Metaphysical Foundations of Christian Mysticism," in *Historical Theology and the Unity of the Church: Essays in Honor of John Meyendorff* (Grand Rapids: William B. Eerdmans Publishing Company, 1995). Also very helpful on the role of divine ecstasy in Dionysius (as well as in his predecessors Plotinus and Gregory of Nyssa) is Kevin Corrigan's "Ecstasy and Ectasy in Some Early Pagan and Christian Mystical Writings," in *Greek and Medieval Studies in Honor of Leo Sweeney, S.J.* (New York: Peter Lang, 1994), pp. 27–38.

the central term around which the ecstatic being of created beings circles, the transcendent term toward and around which created beings ever turn. This divine Cause, therefore, thoroughly determines Dionysius's threefold theological method, for that method articulates the ecstatic being of world and soul as they relate to the divine, causal transcendence that ecstatically gives itself through creation.

Within that threefold method the role of conceptual and linguistic negation proves decisive, for Dionysius seeks to think and express a transcendence that remains, by definition, inconceivable and ineffable. Negation in Dionysius, however, does not simply constitute a one-sided reversal of affirmation. Rather, a twofold, "redoubled" negation, or a "hyper-negation,"[10] answers to the God who is the Cause of all things and yet itself no thing among things, the source of all beings and yet itself wholly beyond both beings and nonbeings. This chapter seeks to illuminate Dionysius's articulation of ecstatic being, its relation to the God who, as Cause, is no thing, and the double role of negation in the thought and language that answer to such a God. It seeks furthermore to suggest that if such a naming of the unnameable in Dionysius is determined in relation to the hierarchical structure and movement whose source and norm prove christological, then a certain notion of death—represented in the Christ—operates at least implicitly in the Dionysian understanding of negativity. The significance of such a tie between death and negativity, I believe, can be traced in subsequent mysticism, where negative theologies often imply an essentially related negative anthropology that is figured in terms of a "death" or annihilation of the soul.

Hierarchy and Ecstasy

Being in Dionysius is fundamentally ecstatic, and the ecstasy of being moves in two interrelated directions: all being at once issues from and returns to the transcendent Cause, "for, as the sacred Word says," and as Dionysius indicates in opening his *Celestial Hierarchy*, "'from him and to him are all things'" (CH 121A). On the one hand, the hierarchical structure of reality embodies the thearchic movement of the divine proces-

10. I borrow the term "redoubled negation" from Michel Corbin, whose interpretation of negation and transcendence in Dionysius I will take up below. My thanks to Bernard McGinn for suggesting the term "hyper-negation" to indicate the second form of negation in Dionysius that passes beyond the mere reversal of affirmation without constituting a double negation (i.e., an affirmation) of the Hegelian type.

sion, or πρόοδος. Through the movement of procession, the divine stands ecstatically outside of itself and into the realm of creation. On the other hand, the same structure can be understood according to the corresponding return movement of reversion or conversion—ἐπιστροφή. The turning-about of all created being toward its source effects the characteristic ecstasy of created being. The ecstasy of the created human soul, which Dionysius's theology seeks both to articulate and to promote, indicates the manner in which created, human being stands constitutively or essentially "outside" of itself. In response to the ecstatic movement of divine procession, the created soul turns or re-turns ecstatically toward its transcendent source, ever tending or straining beyond itself toward the God who abides transcendently in himself even as he most fully gives himself.

While the functions of negative thought and language regarding the divine source perhaps find their most decisive formulations in Dionysius's *Divine Names* and *Mystical Theology*, one must, in order to situate those treatises, explicate Dionysius's conception of the hierarchical structure of reality as it embodies the causal activity of the triune God, or Thearchy. As René Roques demonstrates both in his articles and in his decisive study, *L'Univers dionysien: Structure hiérarchique du monde selon le Pseudo-Denys*,[11] the Dionysian universe is constituted according to the structure and dynamic of hierarchy, in and through which the triune God or Thearchy makes himself manifest and known to all intelligent creatures, all the while remaining wholly concealed and unknown.

The hierarchical world of Dionysius operates according to the fundamental principle of "dissimilar similarity," which means that all beings both manifest and conceal God in one and the same movement. Bernard McGinn nicely articulates this dynamic of the hierarchical world and indicates its essential relation to Dionysian method: "All things both reveal and conceal God. The 'dissimilar similarity' that constitutes every created manifestation of God is both a similarity to be affirmed and a dissimilarity to be denied. Therefore, the universe is both necessary as an image and impossible as a representation of the God for whom there is no adequate representation."[12] Within his discussion of Dionysius's

---

11. René Roques, *L'Univers dionysien: Structure hiérarchique du monde selon le Pseudo-Denys* (1954; Paris: Editions du Cerf, 1983). See also Roques's article regarding Dionysius ("Denys l'Aréopagite") in the *Dictionnaire de spiritualité*.

12. Bernard McGinn, *The Foundations of Mysticism*, vol. 1 of *The Presence of God: A History of Western Christian Mysticism* (New York: Crossroad, 1991), p. 174; hereafter cited parenthetically as FM.

symbolic theology, Hans Urs von Balthasar stresses that the doctrine of
God operative within this Dionysian articulation of manifestation and
concealment, similarity and dissimilarity, relates also directly to the
(largely implicit) Dionysian doctrine of human being:

> the whole tension between cataphatic and apophatic theology runs
> right through symbolic theology, as Denys continually emphasizes.
> For in the sensible symbol, in its necessity and impossibility, there
> is exposed not only the dialectic of the doctrine of God, for God is
> and must be both all in all and nothing in anything, but also the
> doctrine of man, for man is "indivisible" as regards his soul and "di-
> visible" as regards his body, and a divine revelation to him therefore
> naturally needs both levels [. . .]. It is the greatness of man and his
> tragedy to embrace both without being able to bring them into a
> final synthesis: to be immersed in the aesthetics of the world of im-
> ages and at the same time to have irresistibly to dissolve all images
> in the light of the unimaginable. (GL 179)

Just as God moves incomprehensibly between self-presentation and self-
withdrawal, so human being is divided or dynamically suspended between its immersion in the imaginary and its movement toward the un-
imaginable. The self-manifestation and self-concealment of the divine
within the God-world relation thus provide the necessary starting point
for theology. From such a starting point, theology moves—with respect
to God—between, on the one hand, an endless proliferation of images
and names and, on the other hand, the final impossibility of naming or
representation.

   The first to develop the term, Dionysius defines "hierarchy" as "a
sacred order (τάξις ἱερὰ), a state of understanding (ἐπιστήμη), and an
activity (ἐνέργεια) approximating (ἀφομοιουμένη) as closely as possible
to the divine" (CH 164D). Hierarchy articulates the integral interplay
of an order, understanding, and activity that aim at the divinization
(θέωσις) of created beings. The process of divinization consists in becoming like to God, and becoming like to God consists in becoming one
with God (ἕνωσις):

> The goal [σκοπὸς: the mark or object on which one fixes the eye] of
> a hierarchy, then, is to enable beings to be as like as possible to God
> and to be one with him. A hierarchy has God as its leader of all
> understanding and activity. A hierarchy bears in itself the mark of
> God. Hierarchy causes its members to be images of God in all re-

spects, to be clear and spotless mirrors reflecting the glow of primordial light and indeed of God himself. It ensures that when its members have received this full and divine splendor they can then pass on this light generously and in accordance with God's will to beings further down the scale. (CH 165A)

Hierarchy looks toward its goal, which is to reflect the primordial, luminous generosity of God, and that goal determines hierarchy's essential structures and functions. Within those structures and functions, to become one with God (ἕνωσις), is to become as like as possible to God (θέωσις)—that is, to become an image of God's primordial generosity. To become one with God as an image of God, then, would be to overflow *oneself* in the very manner that the primordial light of God overflows so as to be passed along amidst the beings to whom it is given.

On this interpretation, to become an image of, and thus one with, the generosity of God is not to achieve the stasis of any selfsame identity, but to embody the ecstasy of generosity itself. To receive the glow of primordial light is to become an image or mirror of it, to reflect the divine generosity by repeating it, by passing it along within the constitutive movement of hierarchy: "when the first rank has directly and properly received its due understanding of God's Word from the divine goodness itself, then it passes this on, as befits a benevolent hierarchy, to those next in line" (CH 212B–C). If unity or unification (ἕνωσις) with God consists essentially in likeness to God (θέωσις), then such unity must be interpreted *ecstatically*. To be unified with God—and thus made like to him—would be to stand ecstatically out of oneself in a manner reflecting the generous ecstasy, or the ecstatic generosity, of God himself. Von Balthasar rightly points out that the unity of God's ecstasy and unity is inherent to the mystery of creation and the indispensable category of participation: "Just as in God rest in himself and going out from himself are held together, so also with the creature: its movement towards God in ecstasy, a movement that reflects God's movement and answers to it, is held together with its nature as established and complete in itself" (GL 170). On this interpretation, through the coincidence of unity and ecstasy (in God and in the human as a reflection of God), the hierarchical structure and movement in Dionysius would transport souls into knowledge of and likeness to the triune Thearchy.

Now, because the hierarchical function is oriented toward a God who is triune, the hierarchical structures and movements will themselves be trinitarian. Like the God whom they image, and to whom they lead thereby, the hierarchies must somehow be both one and three. The trinitarian framework in Dionysius remains, of course, deeply influenced by pagan Neoplatonic, and especially Proclean, trinitarian thought, but Dionysius transforms such thinking in a fundamental manner. Unlike the pagan Neoplatonic schemes of emanation, wherein each level of emanation constitutes a principle in itself, the Dionysian conception of hierarchy requires that each hierarchical level *receive* the whole of its activity from the triune Thearchy, which is "a Monad and a tri-hypostatic Unity" (CH 212C; see also DN 592A, EH 396D, and EH 533B; McGinn's translation, see FM 163 ff.). As distinct from the pagan Neoplatonic emanations, each level of reality in Dionysius stands in a direct relation of "absolute dependence" on the divine. The significance of such an absolute dependence issues from Dionysius's specifically creationist, Christian reconception of the Neoplatonic framework. McGinn clearly summarizes this major Dionysian transformation of pagan Neoplatonism:

> Although Dionysius does present a hierarchical view of creation that uses the emanational language of late Neoplatonism, and although he does allow for intermediate causality in the way in which the hierarchies interact within their own orders and in relation to each other, the most important thing in his universe is the direct relation of absolute dependence that each individual reality has to the Thearchy that creates all things. From the human perspective, the understanding of the activities of the hierarchies reveals the immediacy of all creatures to divine Eros. This is the heart of Dionysius's distinctive Christian Neoplatonism. (FM 170; see also GL 192)[13]

Within his creationist transformation of the emanational schemes from pagan Neoplatonism, Dionysius establishes a relation of absolute dependence between all beings and their divine source, and that relation proves to be fundamentally erotic. The structures and movements of divine emanation in Dionysius will be structures and movements of loving desire. The absolute dependence of creatures on creator relates essentially to the generous movement of divine eros. Such an absolute dependence is also reflected specifically in Dionysius's understanding of the soul's divinization: effected in and through the structures and movements of hierarchical reality, the divinization of the soul occurs as gift. As con-

---

13. For a more extended discussion of Dionysius's relation to pagan Neoplatonism, see esp. Stephen Gersh, *From Iamblichus to Eriugena: An Investigation of the Prehistory and Evolution of the Pseudo-Dionysian Tradition* (Leiden: Brill, 1978).

trasted with the innately divine soul of the pagan Neoplatonists, the soul in Dionysius is not inherently divine, but rather becomes divine in becoming like to the source on which it wholly depends and toward which it erotically strives.[14]

In keeping with the principle of triunity, the threefold activity of the Thearchy that imparts itself to all hierarchy consists in cathartic or purificative, illuminative, and perfective or unitive functions (this threefold scheme, of course, becomes decisive within medieval thought and spirituality). Each of these functions remains operative at *all* levels of hierarchy, but each level of hierarchy can be characterized predominantly by one function in particular. Here I will indicate only briefly the forms assumed by the threefold thearchic activity within the *Ecclesiastical* and *Celestial Hierarchies.*

The ecclesiastical hierarchy falls midway between the material, legal hierarchy (developed in a treatise that was lost or never written) and the wholly spiritual, celestial hierarchy.[15] Thus, its modes of order, understanding, and activity involve both material and spiritual aspects. As does every hierarchy, the ecclesiastical hierarchy has a triadic structure that includes the initiated, the initiators, and the sacraments or mysteries through which initiation occurs such that souls are led progressively toward God (see EH 5, especially 504A–C). In the ecclesiastical hierarchy, baptism is administered to catechumens by deacons, who purify; the Eucharist (or divine σύναξις) is administered to baptized and confirmed Christians by priests, who illuminate; and finally, anointing (μύρον) is administered to the monastics by bishops or hierarchs, who perfect.

The highest level of the ecclesiastical hierarchy receives its knowledge of the divine as mediated by the lowest level of the celestial hierarchy. This latter hierarchy, of course, also contains three levels, the highest of which enjoys immediate knowledge of God, which is then mediated downward, according to capacity, through all the levels of both the celestial and ecclesiastical hierarchies. As Roques and others point out, the scheme of the *Celestial Hierarchy* is constructed from the givens

14. On the distinction between the innate divinity of the soul, on the one hand, and the divinization of the soul as gift, on the other hand, see McGinn, *Foundations of Mysticism,* p. 178, as well as the passages to which he refers in von Balthasar (GL 2:161–62) and in Roques ("Contemplation, extase et ténèbre mystique chez le Pseudo-Denys," *Dictionnaire de spiritualité* 2:1898).

15. On the Legal Hierarchy and its relation to the Celestial and the Ecclesiastical, see Dionysius, EH 501B–D, and Roques's explications in *Dictionnaire de spiritualité* 3:270 ff., and in *L'Univers dionysien,* pp. 171–74.

of revelation (that is, from the angelic names available in Scripture) as ordered according to a deeply Neoplatonic (again, especially Proclean) triadic structure.

Dionysius's ordered conception of the angelic ranks had an immeasurable impact on medieval reflection and spirituality relating to the angels, and—more important for my present concerns—it conveys a decisive aspect of Dionysius's thought: the ordering of the angelic ranks and the description of their natures and functions offer ground for insisting that the divinizing unification with God (ἕνωσις as θέωσις) is a dynamic process, not an achieved state and, further, that such a process is fueled by a desire that remains strictly endless.

Dionysius arranges the angels in descending order of proximity to God: Seraphim-Cherubim-Thrones, Dominations-Virtues-Powers, Principalities-Archangels-Angels. In the Seraphim one finds the key by which to interpret the meaning of proximity to God within Dionysius's hierarchical world, for the triad within which the Seraphim stand highest is itself "found immediately around God and in a proximity enjoyed by no other" (CH 201A).

On the interpretation that I would advance here, proximity proves to be not a state or position but a movement. Proximity consists, indeed, in a circular and endless movement of excessive love or overflowing heat: "For the designation Seraphim really teaches this—a perennial circling around the divine things, penetrating warmth, the overflowing heat of a movement which never falters and never fails, a capacity to stamp their own image on subordinates by arousing and uplifting in them too a like flame, the same warmth" (CH 205B–C). Proximity to God imposes an excessive transcendence of self—an overflowing of self that moves not only toward God but also toward others.[16] As proximate to God, one shares with others the warmth, illumination, or flame of the divine. To exceed oneself in the movement toward God is also to exceed oneself in

16. In this way, the circling of angels and the soul around God can be seen to occur within a movement that is actually threefold: "The divine intelligences are said to move as follows. First they move in a circle while they are at one with those illuminations which, without beginning and without end, emerge from the Good and the Beautiful. Then they move in a straight line when, out of Providence, they come to offer unerring guidance to all those below them. Finally they move in a spiral, for even while they are providing for those beneath them they continue to remain what they are and they turn unceasingly around the Beautiful and the Good from which all identity comes" (DN 704D–705A).

a movement toward others. Proximity to the Other and proximity to others would in this manner remain inextricably bound.

This ecstatic dynamic of proximity must guide any interpretation of unity with and likeness to God. The first rank of heavenly beings "circles in immediate proximity to God. Simply and ceaselessly it dances around an eternal knowledge of him. [. . .] It is filled with divine nourishment which is abundant, because it comes from the initial stream, and nevertheless single, because the nourishing gifts of God bring oneness in a unity without diversity" (CH 212A). To be in proximity or union with God, to commune with God, is to share in his work (to be σύνεργος), to imitate "the beauty of God's condition and activity (ἐνεργειῶν)" (CH 212 A), which means to share in the ecstasy of his generosity.

That sharing, which passes warmth and illumination downward toward others, thus providing for lower ranks of being, constitutes at the same time a stirring upward toward God. To move upward in the desire for God *is* at the same time to share generously downward in the transmissive enactment of divine providence. Just as God's overflowing generosity remains without measure, so the upward movement toward God remains without end: "The sacred image of [the Seraphim's] six wings signifies an endless, marvelous upward thrust toward God by the first, middle, and lower conceptions" (CH 304D). The Seraphim act, in harmony, "to be like God amid a stirring that [is] ceaseless, exalted, forever (ἐν συμμετρίᾳ τῶν θεομιμήτων ἐνεργειῶν ἀκαταλήκτου καὶ ὑψιπετοῦς ἀεικινησίας)" (CH 305A). Without end, the stirring of beings upward toward God defines their unity with and likeness to him.

The ecstasy of upward stirring, which sustains the "perpetual journey to divine things" (CH 332C), and which offers the reverse side of the divine self-giving or downward overflowing, at the same time constitutes a movement of self-identity, a movement wherein angelic beings "tirelessly circle around their own identity" (CH 333B). Within this perspective, self-identity would be the movement of a circle and not the stasis of a point. Such a movement, while securing both self-identity and unity with or likeness to God, is a movement that ceaselessly overflows, endlessly passes beyond itself—at one and the same time upward toward God and downward in the generous movement of providence. Self-identity, then, would be a process of self-differing through self-giving, and all such movement—all movement of the overflowing circle of self-identity and self-giving—would feed on desire.

Dionysius characterizes this desire by distinguishing it from desire of the flesh, which would be a desire born of fragmentation and lack. The desire of angelic beings (and thus the desire that all created beings desire) is a desire characterized not by fragmentation or absence, but by unity and presence. For Dionysius, true or real desire (ἀληθὴς ἔρως, DN 709C; τοῦ ὄντως ἔρωτος, DN 709B) is not a desire that stems from or grows in the absence of the desired, but rather a desire that arises and expands in the very presence of the desired. Desire feeds on that presence, and rather than being sated by such presence, it grows endlessly in it. Such desire would characterize "that longing felt by the angels in the presence of God (τὴν δὲ αὖ ἐπιθυμίαν εἰς τὸν θεῖον ἔρωτα)" (CH 337B). The desire of the Seraphim, who express the highest intensity of desire, is a desire without fault or end: "For the sacred knowledge characteristic of transcendent beings never falters. Their desire for God never fails" (EH 480C). Eventually I will want to ask whether, according to Dionysius's own approach to the endless end of desire, the distinction between presence and absence, fullness and lack, can be maintained—insofar as such desire undoes the knowing subject who alone could determine or articulate such a distinction. Indeed, I will suggest that desire from excessive presence and desire from excessive lack may well prove indistinguishable. This possible "indiscretion" would be key to my attempt to relate Dionysian unknowing and Heideggerian death. In that attempt, I will take seriously a notion that apophatic and mystical theology can be read to convey: I do not know what I desire—and therefore I cannot say whether it involves the excess of plenitude or of lack. The intensity of excessive desire would blind or devastate me to the point of unknowing—beyond the simple alternative of presence and absence.

Now, for Dionysius the endless desire of the Seraphim expresses itself in "voices that never grow silent, the glorious hymn of the divine praises" (EH 480C). Dionysius learns of these voices and hymns of desire "from the *Hymns of Desire* (ἐκ τῶν ἐρωτικῶν ὕμνων) of the most holy Hierotheus": "When we talk of desire (τὸν ἔρωτα), whether this be in God or an angel, in the mind or in the spirit or in nature, we should think of a unifying and co-mingling power which moves the superior to provide for the subordinate, peer to be in communion with peer, and subordinate to return to the superior and outstanding" (DN 713A–B). In this hymnic description of desire appear the three fundamental movements of Dionysius's ecstatic, hierarchical reality.[17] And again, the ec-

17. One can see in the relations here between superior and subordinate Dionysius's direct dependence on Proclus. See Proclus's commentary on *Alcibiades I:* "So gods

static movements of procession or provision, communion, and conversion or return prove to be *unifying and ecstatic at once.* This coincidence
of ecstasy and unification defines Dionysius's characteristic understanding of desire. Ecstasy grows in the very measure of unification. Just as
the voices that sing divine praises never grow silent, so the desire of those
hymns never comes to any stop or satiety. Desire in Dionysius remains
endless and unsated not because the goal of desire would be empty or
lacking, but because it would be over-present and over-full. But as I'll
suggest, the excess of desire can finally destabilize that very distinction
insofar as such excess carries one into a radical unknowing—and it is
precisely such unknowing that would leave desire ever open.

In the excessive presence of divine enlightenment, the flame of desire flashes and burns. The Seraphim's "numberless faces and many feet
symbolize," for Dionysius, "their outstanding visual capacity when face
to face with the most divine enlightenment. They symbolize an ever
moving (ἀεικινήτου) ever active conception of the divine goodness" (EH
481A). The endlessness of seraphic activity is stoked by the overflow of
divine fire, the fire whence the Seraphim derive their name: "And we
should piously remember that in Hebrew the scripture gives the designation of Seraphim to the holiest of beings in order to convey that these
are fiery-hot and bubbling over forever because of the divine life which
does not cease to bestir them" (EH 481C).

In the activity of the Seraphim, one learns that desire issues in the
super-presence of revelation. Dionysius sees this interplay of desirous
heat and excessive revelation in Ezekiel's wheels of fire, where revolution
and revelation come together:

> For, as the theologian has pointed out, they are called "Gelgel,"
> which in Hebrew signifies both "revolving" and "revealing." Those
> Godlike wheels of fire "revolve" about themselves in their ceaseless
> movement around the Good, and they "reveal" since they expose
> hidden things, and lift up the mind from below and carry the most
> exalted enlightenments down to the lowliest. (CH 337D–340A)

The wheel of fire joins together, on the one hand, the endless circling of
beings around the good, and, on the other, the ecstatic transmission of
divine heat and illumination. This coincidence of revolution, procession,

---

too love gods, the superior their inferiors providentially, and the inferior their superiors,
reflexively," in *Proclus: Alcibiades I. A Translation and Commentary*, by William O'Neill
(The Hague: Martinus Nijhoff, 1965), p. 37.

and return, which Dionysius's hierarchical reality articulates and sustains, characterizes the whole of divine movement, which is endless: "the power to be stretched upward in an ever-returning movement, the capacity unfailingly to turn about oneself while still holding on to one's own special powers, the ability to share in the power of Providence in a procession which shares with successively lower orders—this is surely typical of all heavenly beings" (CH 328B–C).

The Christic Determination of Hierarchy

The endless striving of an immeasurable desire, the divine movement constitutes a circular path of revelation and return through a triadic hierarchical world. A triadic arrangement of elements that are themselves triadic answers to the activity of the triune God or Thearchy. Through that activity, divine illumination is passed along in such a way that superior provides for subordinate, equal has regard for equal, and subordinate looks to superior (see DN 709B–713D). This passage or transmission of divine illumination describes the movement of divine providence according to which every level of being stands ecstatically outward toward every other level of being. Through the ecstatic movements of such providence, contiguous levels of reality communicate directly, while extreme terms communicate by way of mean terms. Now, while the conception of mean terms in Dionysius stems back to Plato's *Timaeus* 31C, and the three modalities of eros depend on Proclus, the movement of hierarchical communication for Dionysius is specifically Christian due to its trinitarian source and its christological function. To develop a christological reading of Dionysius, one needs to make central his claims that Christ is "the source and the being underlying all hierarchy" (EH 372A) and that "every hierarchy ends in Jesus" (EH 505B).[18]

As the source, being, and end of all hierarchy, Christ embodies and enacts the essence of all revelation. The definitive movement of revelation, which was indicated above through the fundamental hierarchical principle of dissimilar similarity, consists in a dynamic of revelation that conceals and of concealment that reveals. A christological reading of Di-

18. Three of the strongest positions arguing in this direction are those of Hans Urs von Balthasar, in *Glory of the Lord*, Jean-Luc Marion, in *L'Idole et la distance* (Paris: Grasset, 1972), and Michel Corbin, who relies on von Balthasar and Marion, in "Négation et transcendance dans l'oeuvre de Denys," *Revue des sciences philosophiques et théologiques* 69 (1985): 41–76.

onysius would bring together the Christic foundation of the hierarchical
principle so understood and the Christic form of revelation as set forth
in Dionysius's third Letter:

> What comes into view, contrary to hope, from previous obscurity,
> is described as "sudden." As for the love of Christ for humanity, the
> Word of God, I believe, uses this term to hint that the transcendent
> has put aside its own hiddenness and has revealed itself to us by
> becoming a human being. But he is hidden even after his revelation,
> or, if I may speak in a more divine fashion, is hidden even amid the
> revelation. For this mystery of Jesus remains hidden and can be
> drawn out by no word or mind. What is to be said of it remains
> unsayable; what is to be understood of it remains unknowable.
> (1069B)

The revelation given in Christ (recalling the incalculability of death)
comes into view outside of—or contrary to—the horizon of human expectation or foresight. In its suddenness, such revelation gives the very
hiddenness of the divine mystery. Contradicting expectation and disrupting every horizon, the transcendent "puts aside its hiddenness" by
showing itself, paradoxically though precisely, *as hidden*. The transcendence of the transcendent gives itself "as such" by withdrawing itself
from all word and mind, all speech and thought. The endless desire of
beings for God would speak or signal this irreducibly secret aspect of
divine manifestation. Desire in the presence of God would thus be desire
in the presence of that which withdraws entirely even as it manifests itself
most fully. The excess of presence comes indiscretely close to the purest absence.

The desire that arises before the manifestation of the hidden would
be not a desire of the flesh, a worldly desire—"partial, physical, and divided" (DN 709B–C)—but a desire that brings death to fleshly desire
and thereby signals truly divine birth, for "the sacred act, after all, is not
of this world" (EH 436A). For Dionysius, real or true desire remains
indifferent to the flesh and to this world; in its truth, it stands unified
against the fragmentation characteristic of fleshly desire, which constitutes "an empty image or, rather, a lapse from real desire" (DN 709C).
Multiplicity of desires and excess of passion indicate, for Dionysius, fall
and dissolution. Indeed, they signal death—or at least one form of death:
"[human nature] turned to the life of the most varied desires, and came
at the end to the catastrophe of death" (EH 440C). To become a child of
the flesh is to "fall to earth unborn, without life, without light" (EH

433A), while "the sign of the cross indicates the renunciation of all the desires of the flesh" (EH 512A). The death of the cross thus signals divine birth and true life. In Christ, one finds the ground for a dying that gives life through sacred rebirth: the hierarch "shows to those able to contemplate it that Jesus in a most glorious and divine descent willingly died on the cross for the sake of our divine birth, that he generously snatches from the old swallowing pit of ruinous death anyone who, as scripture mysteriously expresses it, has been baptized 'into his death' and renews them in an inspired and eternal existence" (EH 484B).

One should note that the turn from God in the "empty" image of desire, or unreal desire, signals dissolution of being, while salvation would function, precisely, to save or preserve being in its specificity.[19] "This divine Righteousness is also praised as the 'Salvation of the world' since it ensures that each being is preserved and maintained in its proper being and order, distinct from everything else. [...] Salvation is that which preserves all things in their proper places, without change, conflict, or collapse toward evil" (DN 896D, 897A). As the keeping or preservation of a being in its Being, salvation implies the affirmation also of finitude or limit: the being of a being that is preserved is determinate, limited being. The loss of being (countered by salvation) is loss of limit, a fall *from* finitude. The fleshly desire that leads to death would do so because it provokes *dissolution* of the "proper being and order," the "distinction" of the properly placed, rightly limited finite being.

Von Balthasar helpfully stresses this "positive significance" to finitude and limit in Dionysius, and he interprets that positive significance in soteriological terms pertaining to creation and resurrection: "Because God is beyond rest and movement, beyond finitude and infinity, there is no direct opposition between him and anything created; and therefore the latter is set forth in its limitedness and finitude, and as such affirmed and sustained" (GL 194). The created realm is sustained insofar as created beings remain existent, standing out in their specific finitude. Such sustaining for von Balthasar offers the very significance of resurrection, for Dionysius "safeguards his cosmos with the theological doctrine of the resurrection, through which the sustaining of individual form is finally

---

19. Thus, it might well be that, for Dionysius at least, the "God without Being" is *not* necessarily answered by an "I without Being," but indeed assures first and foremost the *Being* if not of the "I" then at least of all finite beings. Salvation in Dionysius would assure persistence in Being, even if that salvation comes from a God beyond or without Being.

assured: 'Its whole being will be saved and live forever in fullness' [EH 553A]" (GL 194). From this perspective, the "eternal existence" achieved through baptism into Christ's death is an essentially finite or limited existence. When the "whole conception of the world, the whole sense of being"[20] is interpreted christologically, creation is already salvation:

> The concept *sôzein* takes on with Denys an undreamt-of wealth. God is above all *Soter* already as creator, in that he affirms and safeguards the natures in their particularity and the individuals in their individuality and preserves them as such from destruction, the tendency to blend with others and to yield before the superior power of the all, and protects "each one in the position allotted to it in accordance with its rank and power." (DN 896B)[21]

If one reads desire in Dionysius from the perspective of the creation and resurrection that save or preserve, then one can understand the condemnation of fleshly desire not as an aversion to materiality per se so much as an attempt to maintain finitude and limit.

To die truly, then, and so sacredly to be born (i.e., to remain within the limits of one's finitude), would be to desire truly. While fleshly desire brings dissolution of limit and the lowest death, divine desire, real desire, brings life to the finite through Christic death. Christic death and its real desire would constitute the manner in which we are rightly maintained within our proper limits and at the same time given up to the divine. In this sense, Christ offers the very source and norm of ecstatic being within the order of hierarchy. Finite, hierarchical being now shows itself as a being through which we stand *within* ourselves as *outside* of ourselves—offered up, or given over, in sacrifice:

> The meaning of all this [concerning the sacraments] is to be found beyond heaven and beyond being in that source, that essence, that perfecting power which makes for the workings of all holiness in us. For it is on Jesus himself, our most divine altar, that there is achieved the divine consecration of intelligent beings. In him, as scripture

---

20. The christological conception of reality, on von Balthasar's view, is specifically Chalcedonian: "Here the Chalcedonian concepts press forward powerfully and broaden their range from christology to the whole conception of the world, the whole sense of being. 'Unconfusedly' (*asynchtôs*), 'unchangeably' (*atreptôs*), 'indivisibly' (*adiairetôs*) and 'inseparably' (*achôristôs*): thus was each of the two natures preserved (*sôzetai*) in its individuality in Christ" (GL 2:194–95).

21. Ibid., 2:195.

says, "we have access" to consecration and are mystically offered as
a holocaust. (EH 484D)

To die with Christ (and thus to be saved) is to become an offering
through fire, a burnt sacrifice. The desire that burns within all hierarchical beings is the fire of holocaust, in which those beings are offered ecstatically to their source. Such an offering ignites the true movement
of death, realized first in Christ and offered through Christ for imitation. Christ saves the finite being whose very identity consists in self-
transcendence.

   The Christ in whom death proves true and in whom finitude is saved
is the Christ who embodies the most essential movement of revelation—
namely, to conceal through revelation and to reveal through concealment. Christic manifestation consists in hiddenness revealed, and in this
sense the figure of true death, the salvation of finitude—that is, the
Christ—determines also the "impossible possibility" of naming God.
For the naming of the unnameable God is grounded, precisely, in the
divine paradox of this hiddenness revealed, which is given in the Christ
with and through whom we die true death. The ecstatic, hierarchical
play of Dionysius's world, if interpreted through this Christic source and
norm, thus brings one necessarily to consider the question of form and
method in the naming of God. Indeed, in one of the most thorough
arguments for the christological foundation of Dionysian thought, "Négation et transcendance dans l'oeuvre de Denys," Michel Corbin draws
a powerful equivalence between Christic revelation and the naming
of God:

> The manifestation of Jesus to man is in no way the abolition of his
> superessential "secret," but indeed his manifestation as an ever
> greater secret, in an identity of manifestation and ineffability, of af-
> firmation and of negation according to transcendence, which Denys
> declares "more divine." Nothing of Jesus is hidden through jealousy;
> on the contrary everything is delivered, without the least reserve,
> but the delivery is that of "the Goodness that surpasses all things"
> (CH IV, 1) or, equally, of the distance of the ungraspable freedom
> that dispenses being, life and reason. *In sum, the movement of the event
> of the "superessential" Jesus* (Letter 4, 1072A) *is entirely superimposable
> upon the movement of the naming of God*, and to speak of Jesus is identi-
> cally to speak of God. *Jesus is not a particular case of the naming of God,
> a contingent figure of a naming that would be conceived independently of*

him, but rather it is in and through him that any naming of God occurs. "We see every hierarchy end in Christ." (EH 5:5–505A)[22]

The naming of God would be thoroughly determined by a christology that, as just seen, determines also the Dionysian conception of death. The interpretation of such naming goes to the heart of Dionysian method.

Ecstasy and Theological Method

The ecstatic play of God's self-revelation and self-concealment, and the anagogy of the soul answering to that God, are both articulated through the structure and movement of the hierarchical realities sustained by the Thearchy. Thus, the question of hierarchical reality in Dionysius leads necessarily to a consideration of his threefold theological method. The whole of that method aims to articulate the relation between created beings and the transcendent God who is understood in terms of Cause (αἰτία). Such an articulation oscillates between, on the one hand, an endless naming of God based on the immanence of God to all creation and, on the other hand, a radical anonymity of God imposed by God's excessive transcendence of the created realm. To recognize the divine as transcendent cause is to recognize "that he is all, that he is no thing" (DN 596C). To name God in accordance with this paradox is both to name him with "the names of everything that is" and to accept that "he is rightly nameless" (DN 596C).

Because negation plays such a prominent and decisive role in Dionysius, Dionysian theology is often and incorrectly cast simply or exclusively as "negative theology." Such a characterization, however, remains misguided because one-sided. Dionysius's method in fact involves three essentially interdependent theological modes: the kataphatic, or affirmative mode, which makes predicative affirmations of God; the apophatic, or negative mode, which undoes or removes such predications; and the mystical mode, which operates through a second form of negation— a "redoubled" negation or a "hyper-negation"—that passes beyond the very alternative of affirmation and negation. While these modes each proceed according to their own distinctive operations, no one mode is possible without the other two, and each mode operates in some way at

---

22. Corbin, "Négation et transcendance dans l'oeuvre de Denys," p. 64 (emphasis added).

every level of Dionysius's theology; the affirmative and the negative depend one on the other, and both presuppose the goal of the mystical. I am particularly concerned here with the twofold play of negation within the "implicated" modes of Dionysian theology, but precisely because those modes are mutually implicated, that play of negation must be seen within the whole.

Through this notion of the "implication" of theological methods, René Roques rigorously defines the dynamic interplay and thorough interdependence of the three Dionysian modes of theology.[23] According to Roques's exposition, Dionysian theology operates through both a "horizontal" and a "vertical" implication of methods. Horizontal implication involves the full interdependence of affirmation and negation both at the sensible level and at the conceptual level. That is, the positivity of both sensible and conceptual symbols finds its full meaning only in being negated, but that negation itself depends no less fully on the affirmation of such symbols. The negation of affirmations at the sensible and conceptual levels (horizontal implication) implies in turn a vertical implication: sensible symbols point necessarily to the conceptual level, from which again one passes (through second negation) to the unitive, mystical level beyond all sense and every concept. Vertically implicated, this highest level cannot dispense with the lower levels on which it wholly depends. Von Balthasar interprets this vertical implication of methods such that "the aesthetic transcendence that we know in this world (from the sensible as manifestation to the spiritual as what is manifest) provides the formal schema for understanding theological or mystical transcendence (from world to God)" (GL 168). According to this schema, deeper penetration *into* positive symbols and concepts leads to more sublime transcendence *of* them.

Now, the kataphatic mode of theology, the positive or affirmative mode, concerns primarily the names of God, both symbolic and conceptual, that refer to the divine as cause. According to the thought and language of affirmative theology, the cause of all becomes immanent to all things caused: "He is all things since he is the Cause of all things. The sources and goals of all things are in him and are anticipated in him" (DN 824B). Precisely to the degree that the divine Cause of all stands out into all that he anticipates, the God named as Cause "has the names

---

23. See René Roques, "De l'implication des méthodes théologiques chez le pseudo-Denys," *Revue d'Ascétique et de Mystique*, no. 119 (July 1954).

of everything that is" (DN 596C); "every attribute may be predicated of him" (DN 824B). This positive naming of God occurs through its direct association with the movement of the divine as πρόοδος or procession. The ecstatic procession of the divine, from which all positive names derive, consists in the self-giving of the divine Goodness, and it is primarily in light of such Goodness that the divine Cause must be interpreted. The divine Goodness, or Eros,[24] embodies the creative ecstasy of the God who imparts himself to all creation. As von Balthasar nicely stresses its un-concealing aspect, the movement of procession constitutes "the *manifestation* of the unmanifest" (GL 164). Kataphatic theology, in this relation to *manifestation*, concerns the ineffable and inconceivable God insofar as that God nonetheless speaks and makes himself known to created beings.

This Cause of all things, while "he is in all things" precisely because he is their cause, at the same time and in the same degree "is also superior to them all because he precedes them and is transcendentally above them" (DN 824B). As von Balthasar stresses, this *analogia entis* that undergirds both affirmative and negative theology must be interpreted in its *singularity* and *irreversibility:* "not for a moment is the singularity of the analogy, its irreversibility, forgotten: things are both like God and unlike him, but God is not like things" (GL 168). Thus, while things caused are "like" (and unlike) their divine Cause, that Cause—in its irreducible transcendence—is not like (or unlike?) any thing caused. In this sense, the cause of all things is, in his transcendence, no thing among things. While the kataphatic mode of theology concerns primarily the *manifestation* of the unmanifest, the apophatic mode aims more toward "the manifestation of the *unmanifest*" (GL 164). In other words, apopha-

---

24. McGinn stresses the significance of Dionysius's interpretation of the Good in terms of Eros, calling Dionysius's theory of Eros "one of his most profound contributions to Christian theology"; see *Foundations of Mysticism*, p. 166 and ff. The significance of Eros is highlighted also by Marion (to whom I shall turn in the next chapter) and by von Balthasar, who distinguishes the concern of love from the concerns of knowledge and representation: "Therefore the final meaning of the hierarchies is not, in a Christian context, designated as the knowledge of God, but love: as the 'perpetual love for God' [EH 376A] to which all three functions raise us, but also, in the game of give-and-take between the creatures, the imitation of God in mutual love" (GL 2:200). In light of McGinn's work, as well as that of von Balthasar and Marion, and in light of the Dionysian writings themselves, Vanneste's position that "in this whole system love has been assigned no place" seems untenable. See Jan Vanneste, "Is the Mysticism of Pseudo-Dionysius Genuine?" *International Philosophical Quarterly*, vol. 3, no. 2 (May 1963): 302.

tic theology treats, in reverse direction, the same field treated by kataphatic theology. While the kataphatic mode of theology concerns the
divine procession into manifestation (through causality), the apophatic
mode signals the reversal of that procession (the irreducible transcendence of the cause), and thus the soul's conversion or return (ἐπιστροφή)
to the irreducibly hidden God. While the kataphatic mode makes affirmations of God as *cause* and bases those affirmations on the being of
things caused, apophatic theology removes or negates those affirmations
insofar as the cause of all things is not itself any thing among things.

Of course, the principles that guide the naming of God are bound
intimately with the conditions and limits for knowing God. In both the
naming and the knowing of God, the movement of negation constitutes
a movement of transcendence. Through negative theological thought
and language, the human soul transcends the world of beings in a movement that answers to the transcendence of the divine Cause, which is
no thing:

> We therefore approach that which is beyond all as far as our capaci-
> ties allow us and we pass by way of the denial and the transcendence
> of all things and by way of the cause of all things. God is therefore
> known through and in all things and apart from all things. God is
> known through knowing and through unknowing. Of him there is
> conception, reason, understanding, touch, perception, opinion,
> imagination, name, and many other things. On the other hand, he
> is not thought, nor spoken, nor named. He is not one of the things
> that are [οὐκ ἔστι τι τῶν ὄντων] and he cannot be known in any
> of them. He is all things in all things and he is nothing in nothing
> [καὶ "ἐν πᾶσι πάντα" ἐστὶ καὶ ἐν οὐδενὶ οὐδὲν]. He is known to all
> from all things and he is known to no one from anything [or: he is
> known . . . to no one from nothing—καὶ ἐξ οὐδενὸς οὐδενί]. (DN
> 869D–872A)

In this major summary passage on the knowing and naming of God, Dionysius makes clear the oscillation between, on the one hand, the affirmation and knowledge of God (as cause), which are based in the knowledge of things caused, and, on the other hand, the denial and unknowing
of God, which result from the fact that the cause of all things caused is
itself no thing, or nothing. As transcendent *cause*, God is all in all, while
as *transcendent* cause, God is no thing or (in) nothing. The negative
movement of thought and language that recognizes God as apart from,
or without, all things (χωρὶς πάντων), and thus as no thing (οὐδέν), ef-

fects the soul's transcendence of all beings, beings from which God is known (or unknown) as distinct (or wholly indistinct). The thorough interdependence of the negative and the affirmative modes for knowing and naming God must be seen within this perspective.

The apophatic mode of theology negates the affirmations proffered in the kataphatic mode such that the former lives and moves only on the basis of the latter. In other words, the negative or apophatic expression of the hiddenly transcendent God is articulated in and through the positive self-manifestation of the *hidden as such*. As von Balthasar stresses, "only with Denys did [the relationship between negation and affirmation] receive its balancing counterpoise: in that the tremendous ascending movement of negation, often rising to a pitch of sheer frenzy, which sets the apophatic (rejection of names) over the kataphatic (affirmation of names) is kindled *only*—and ever more brightly—by God's movement of descent as he imparts himself in manifestations" (GL 2:165). The return or conversion through negation to the transcendent God does not eliminate but rather depends on God's manifest immanence in all things.

At the same time, one can read the interdependence of affirmation/manifestation and negation/transcendence in the reverse direction, such that the former is seen also to depend on the latter. Roques makes this move in "De l'implication des méthodes théologiques chez le pseudo-Denys": "This return [via the negations of the anagogical process] will not be the pure and simple negation of the divine manifestation. It will be the condition thereof. It is through the conversion of minds to the One that the divine manifestation remains possible and realizes itself. In other words, ascending dialectic and descending dialectic subsist one through the other and imply one another."[25] According to the implication of theological methods in Dionysius, the positive manifestation of the divine through creation and the divine's negative transcendence over creation (the aim of the soul in its path of conversion to the divine) condition one another through and through. While the movement of negation undoubtedly enjoys a certain privilege, that privilege never comes at the expense of the necessary movement of affirmation. Rather, the negative movement lends the positive "its true significance."[26]

Now, "Goodness" (τὸ ἀγαθόν), which for Dionysius exceeds being,

25. Roques, "De l'implication des méthodes théologiques chez le pseudo-Denys," p. 272; translations my own.
26. Ibid., p. 270.

constitutes the primary term under which Dionysius expresses the immanent transcendence, or the transcendent immanence, of the divine cause which is no thing:

> ... although it is the cause of everything, it is not a thing since it transcends all things in a manner beyond being [ὅτι πάντων μέν ἐστι τῶν ὄντων αἴτιον, αὐτὸ δὲ οὐδὲν ὡς πάντων ὑπερουσίως ἐξῃρημένον]. Hence with regard to the supra-essential being of God—transcendent Goodness transcendently there—no lover of truth which is above all truth will seek to praise it as word or power or mind or life or being. (DN 593C)

"At a total remove" (ὑπεροχικῶς ἀφῃρημένην) from all, the divine Good, at the same time, "by merely being there is the cause of everything" (DN 593D). The denial by which the "remove" of the divine Goodness is signaled indicates divine excess, and radical anonymity constitutes, in this light, the reverse side of endless polyonymy. Or, in other words, "In [the Good], nonbeing is really an excess of being (Καὶ ἐν αὐτῷ μόνῳ καὶ τὸ ἀνούσιον οὐσίας ὑπερβολὴ)" (DN 697A). Much will depend on how one interprets this excess or hyperbole: does the phrase "excess of being" indicate that which stands *beyond being* entirely, that which is cut off from being, preceding it, independent of it, or, on the contrary, does "excess of being" indicate an overabundant presence or possession of being, the character of *being excessively?* I will return to this issue below, but for now the crucial point is this: the divine Goodness, cause of all that is, is not itself any thing among things, or any being among beings. The causality of this Cause that is no thing functions in a very specific way, which I must now examine: working aesthetically, the causal Good constitutes a Beauty (τὸ καλόν) that exerts itself in the form of *call* (κλῆσις, a calling, summons, indictment, invitation, appellation, naming).

The Good, Beauty, and Desire's Limit without End

Dionysius equates the Goodness that is the Cause of all beings, the Cause which through its own ecstatic self-giving brings all beings ecstatically to be, with Beauty: "The Beautiful is therefore the same as the Good, for everything looks to the Beautiful and the Good as the cause of being, and there is nothing in the world without a share of the Beautiful and the Good (καὶ οὐκ ἔστι τι τῶν ὄντων, ὃ μὴ μετέχει τοῦ καλοῦ καὶ ἀγαθοῦ)" (DN 704B). This aesthetic aspect of the Good proves to be, at the same time, erotic. The Beautiful and the Good constitute the source and goal of all desirous longing among beings, and beings come to be precisely through such longing. The call of Beauty gives rise to an essential desire for the Beautiful and the Good, and it is such desire that brings beings to be. Within the Dionysian conception of Beauty as call, or better as pro-vocation, being as such might be understood as pure *response;* in its very essence, being as such would constitute a response of longing, yearning, or desire to the call of the Beautiful and Good beyond Being. "Beauty 'bids' (καλοῦν) all things to itself (whence it is called 'beauty' [κάλλος]) and gathers everything to itself" (DN 701D). The summons or call of beauty provides the very source or "ground" of Being, for "from this beauty comes the Being of everything (ἐκ τοῦ καλοῦ τούτου πᾶσι τοῖς οὖσι τὸ εἶναι)" (DN 704A).

Established in its being by the beauty that calls it forth, all existence constitutes an erotic longing that Dionysius equates with agapic love: "It is the great creating cause which bestirs the world and holds all things in existence by the longing (ἔρωτι) inside them to have beauty. And there it is ahead of all as the goal, as the beloved (ἀγαπητὸν), as the Cause toward which all things move, since it is the longing for beauty which actually brings them into being (τοῦ καλοῦ γὰρ ἕνεκα πάντα γίγνεται)" (DN 704A). The call that brings beings to birth here is the call of a beauty that provokes or instills the longing desire through which beings are as such—in the mode of response. Such a call grounds all the world from beyond the world; it signals a "power for 'being'" that comes "from a power beyond being (τὸ εἶναι δύναμιν εἰς τὸ εἶναι ἔχει παρὰ τῆς ὑπερ-ουσίου δυνάμεως)" (DN 892B), a power that "founds the earth upon nothing (καὶ τὴν γῆν ἐπ᾽ οὐδενὸς ἱδρύει)" (DN 892D). The beings that are in this way called to be stand ecstatically between the nothing out of which they issue or on which they are founded (as called) and that causal power beyond being toward which they longingly tend—their divine *telos* (τελικὸν αἴτιον [DN 704A]) which "is" itself no thing, or a nonbeing: for "nonbeing (τὸ μὴ ὄν), when applied transcendently to God in the sense of a denial (ὅταν ἐν θεῷ κατὰ τὴν πάντων ἀφαίρεσιν ὑπερουσίως ὑμνεῖται), is itself beautiful and good" (DN 704B). The causality in relation to which the positive names of God are established thus operates also, inextricably, with the negative names of God, the denials that remove (while depending on) all positive names. This play of positing and removal, affirmation and denial, characterizes the thought and language of that ecstatic being who ever is, who ever responds, who ever remains, between the nothing from which it is called and the transcendent nonbeing for which it yearns.

Now, the yearning or desire, the eros, that characterizes created beings' mode of being, starting with their mode of coming-to-be, has its
source already in the end toward which it tends or strains. The beauty
that is the origin (ἀρχή) of all things as creating cause, or ποιητικὸν αἴτιον, is at the same time the end of all things—the πέρας πάντων as the
beloved end (ἀγαπητὸν), the final cause, or τελικὸν αἴτιον (DN 704A).
Teleologically oriented toward the divine end, such desire remains nevertheless—precisely as so oriented—endless, for it gives rise to a ceaseless ecstatic play: "Here is the source of all which transcends every
source, here is an ending which transcends completion (καὶ ἔστι πάντων
ἀρχὴ καὶ πέρας ὑπεράρχιον καὶ ὑπερτελές)" (DN 708A). In the
yearning through which it is, being finds itself oriented toward an end
(πέρας) that is without end or beyond completion (ὑπερτελές).
    Such yearning renders that being irreducibly ecstatic and will thus
imply that being's "dispossession"; beings, in the very movement by
which they are, find themselves carried outside or beyond themselves.
Here, in the loving desire for the beyond of being, there appears the true
significance of hierarchy for Dionysius. The hierarchical ordering of beings signals first and foremost the ecstatic interdependence of the orders
of being:

> And so it is that all things must desire, must yearn for, must love, the
> Beautiful and the Good. Because of it and for its sake, subordinate is
> returned to superior, equal keeps company with equal, superior
> turns providentially to subordinate, each bestirs itself and all are
> stirred to do and to will whatever it is they do and will because of
> the yearning for the Beautiful and the Good. (DN 708A; see also
> DN 709D, 712A, 713AB, etc.)

This ecstatic movement of desire is a movement that, in some sense,
remains finally internal to the Good itself, for the Good itself instills
desire, and all desire looks toward the Good: "The divine longing is
Good seeking Good for the sake of the Good" (DN 708B), or as
McGinn translates, "Divine Eros is the Good of the Good and for the
sake of the Good" (FM 167), or as yet again possible, "Divine Eros is
the Good of the Good through the Good (καὶ ἔστι καὶ ὁ θεῖος ἔρως
ἀγαθὸς ἀγαθοῦ διὰ τὸ ἀγαθόν)," where "through" (διὰ) could be taken
to indicate either "throughout" (the all-pervasiveness and over-fullness
of the Good) or "by reason of" (the causality of the Good). Within the
auto-affection of the causal Good, any final decision between (subjective) yearning and the object of yearning breaks down, for "in short, both

the desire and the object of that desire belong to the Beautiful and the Good" (DN 712B). Within the circle of desire that is the causal Good, beings live and move ecstatically—to a point of indiscretion between subject and object (and hence, we might continue, between apophatic theology and apophatic anthropology).

Ecstasy, which structures the whole movement of the erotic circle of the Good, marks, as I have suggested, the "dispossession" of the beings whose very existence it sustains. Thus, while the truth of hierarchy is found in the ecstasy of divine yearning or desire, the meaning conveyed by that truth is dispossession: "This divine desire brings ecstasy so that the lover belongs not to self but to the beloved (ἔστι δὲ καὶ ἐκστατικὸς ὁ θεῖος ἔρως οὐκ ἐῶν ἑαυτῶν εἶναι τοὺς ἐραστάς, ἀλλὰ τῶν ἐρωμένων)" (DN 712A). Within the ecstatically structured circle of the Good, movement between one order of being and the next is a movement of providence or provision (superior providing for subordinate, equal regarding equal, subordinates returning to superiors). Referring to the figure of Saint Paul, Dionysius casts this ecstatic providence—this source, movement, and end of the desire that both provokes and dispossesses beings— in terms that signal a christological dispossession of self:

> This is why the great Paul, swept along by his desire for God and seized of its ecstatic power, had this inspired word to say: "It is no longer I who live, but Christ who lives in me" [Gal. 2:20]. Paul was truly a lover and, as he says, he was beside himself for God [2 Cor. 5:13], possessing not his own life but the life of the One whom he desired, as exceptionally beloved. (DN 712A)

Like Paul, the true lover of God is dispossessed in and through desire for the One, desire for the beloved who is the lover's end—but an end without end or measure. Such a desire, such a love, indicates that Christ lives in and so dispossesses the one who loves, dividing the lover from self, dispossessing the lover of self, setting the lover beside self. In dispossessing, such love at the same time gives life—life not possessed but received, the life of another that lives in and through the one who loves (by receiving). This dispossession of love displayed in Paul's inspired ecstasy is essentially and explicitly related, for Dionysius, to the figure of death, for "the divine Ignatius writes: 'He for whom I yearn has been crucified'" (DN 709B). The love that dispossesses—or that displaces one life for another—also comes to light, then, in the relation of yearning and death. The crucified, the One put to death, becomes the very figure of the beloved, the One yearned for who undoes me.

These considerations of the christological dispossession of the ecstatic human lover relate directly to the ecstatic self-giving of the beloved, divine Cause. The self-giving of the Cause in Christ constitutes
the divine *kenosis* that would ground a christological reading of Dionysius's hierarchical world. Dionysius pursues this interpretation by invoking Philippians 2:7:

> And out of love he has come down to be at our level of nature and
> he has become a being. He, the transcendent God, has taken on the
> name of man. (Such things, beyond mind and beyond words, we
> must praise with all reverence.) In all this he remains what he is—
> supernatural, transcendent—and he has come to join us in what we
> are without himself undergoing any change or confusion.[27] His full-
> ness was unaffected by that inexpressible emptying of self [κενώ-
> σεως], and, most novel of all, amid the things of nature, he remained
> supernatural and amid the things of being he remained beyond be-
> ing [ἐν τοῖς φυσικοῖς ἡμῶν ὑπερφυὴς ἦν ἐν τοῖς κατ'οὐσίαν ὑπερού-
> σιος]. From us he took what was of us and yet he surpassed us here
> too. (DN 648D-649A)

This self-giving of the transcendent God, figured here specifically in the
kenotic movement of Christ, comes to light more generally in terms of
the Beautiful and the Good:

> And, in truth, it must be said too that the very cause of the universe
> in the beautiful, good superabundance of his benign yearning for all
> is also carried outside of himself in the loving care he has for every-
> thing. He is, as it were, beguiled by goodness, by love, and by
> yearning and is enticed away from his transcendent dwelling place
> and comes to abide within all things, and he does so by virtue of his
> supernatural and ecstatic capacity to remain, nevertheless, within
> himself. (DN 712B)

The movement of revealing concealment and concealing revelation here
occurs through goodness, love, or desire. Through the ecstasy of goodness, love, or desire, the transcendent becomes immanent while remaining fully transcendent. The hidden gives itself "as such." To answer
that transcendence, to respond to its self-giving, is to move within the
erotic circle that it provokes and governs. In that circle, lover and beloved ceaselessly exchange places in an endless flow of desire where

27. One should note the reference here to the Chalcedonian formula.

"both the desire and the object of that desire belong to the beautiful and the Good" (DN 712B). According to this circularity of desire, God is called both love and beloved, for "on the one hand he causes, produces, and generates what is being referred to, and, on the other hand, he is the thing itself" (DN 712C). Causing, producing, or generating the desire of beings, God thereby moves immanently through them. Such desire seeks its end continually; the God who constitutes that end remains irreducibly transcendent.

The circularity of love here stands out in its defining characteristic: it is endless. The endlessness of desire's circle goes hand in hand with the endlessness of all teleological orientation to the divine end or goal. The source and end of desire are themselves beyond or without source, beyond or without end: "In this divine yearning shows especially its unbeginning and unending nature traveling in an endless circle through the Good, from the Good, in the Good and to the Good, unerringly turning, ever on the same center, ever in the same direction, always proceeding, always remaining, always being restored to itself" (DN 712D–713A). From this perspective, the dispossession and ecstasy of created being, answering to the ecstasy of the divine cause which is no thing and which remains beyond or without source and end, are a dispossession and ecstasy located "finally" (and "originarily") within the endless, sourceless circle of the divine. Within that circle the divine remains in itself, ever proceeding from itself and ever restoring itself to itself. Through such remaining and restoration, the divine, ecstatic Good constitutes an *endless* giving, but not a giving *without return*. Indeed, the self-giving of the Good would appear here as an incessant process of self-restoration as return. Created being participates in that return through the incessant movement of conversion. But return or restoration (ἀποκατάστασις, reminiscent of Origen) here leads to, or consists in, not satiety but endless, ecstatic longing, which might be taken as a radical expectation (ἐπέκτασις, reminiscent of Gregory of Nyssa).

Negation and the Mystical

This ceaseless play of expectation would relate essentially to the *redoubled* negation, or the *hyper*-negation, operative in Dionysius. As distinct notably from the Hegelian conception of double negation—wherein the negation of negation secures the positivity of the subject's self-knowing self-relation—the negation of negation in Dionysius articulates a logic of "neither . . . nor . . . ," which signals an endlessly expectant desire and

so characterizes the relation, between the soul and God, of mystical unknowing. Within that relation, the soul is "unified" with the ineffable
and inconceivable transcendence of God—in a unity or indiscretion that
marks an endless opening of desire rather than its closure.

Thus, while kataphatic theology primarily concerns God's activity
as cause, which through the movement of procession (πρόοδος) manifests
itself immanently in all beings, and while apophatic theology primarily
concerns the movement of return or conversion (ἐπιστροφή) to God as
distinct from all beings, the third—mystical—mode of theology concerns primarily that very God as he remains or abides transcendently in
himself (μονή).[28] The mystical form of theology will involve three crucial
aspects. First, it concerns the movement of ἕνωσις, or unification,[29] with
the God who—as no thing or nonbeing—is absolutely, simply One. As
suggested above, the unifying movement of ἕνωσις remains equivalent
with θέωσις, the divinization of the soul. Such a unification with the God
who is no thing requires, second, the negative movement of ἀφαίρεσις,
which effects the removal or denial of all images and concepts regarding
the divine; in this sense, the negative movement of mystical theology is
closely associated with the apophatic mode—indeed, I would say it is a
redoubling of the apophatic. Finally, then, approached through apophasis or aphairesis, unification would "occur" only in and through ἀγνωσία, or "unknowing." Unknowing would consist in the abandonment
of all knowledge that remains preoccupied with beings and things (or
with their negation), and it constitutes the most "adequate" knowledge
of the transcendent God who is no thing and nonbeing—or better, the
God who, beyond *both* being *and* its negation, would in that very measure
signal the irreducible *inadequation* of all "knowledge" of him, his ultimate
irreducibility to the very categories of "truth," for as the *Mystical Theology*
will itself conclude, the transcendent divinity is neither error nor truth
(MT 1048A: οὔτε πλάνη, οὔτε ἀλήθεια).

If kataphatic theology operates through affirmations deriving from
caused beings, and if apophatic theology operates through the negation
of such affirmations and a movement beyond the beings on which they

28. This threefold pattern can be discerned in passages throughout Dionysius's
writings. It issues in the oscillation between the radical polyonymy and the final anonymity of the transcendent cause. In addition to the texts I cite below (especially MT
1000B), see, e.g., DN 593C–596A; DN 596C; DN 641A.

29. I translate ἕνωσις as "unification" rather than as "unity" in order to stress the
sense it which it indicates a movement rather than a state, and the sense in which, as
movement, it would remain without end.

depend, mystical theology makes use of "hyper-" (ὑπερ-) terms which, strictly speaking, remain *neither* affirmative *nor* negative but point beyond the alternative between affirmation and negation. This *beyond* of the categorical alternative of affirmation and negation points to that which comes radically *before:* the "beyond," which signals an "endless" end, indicates also the irreducible *priority* of the Cause over all thought and language—over truth itself. From this perspective, at the very outset of his *Mystical Theology*, Dionysius expresses the necessity of transcending the first (apophatic) form of negation:

> What has actually to be said about the cause of everything is this. Since it is the Cause of all beings, we should posit and ascribe to it all the affirmations we make in regard to beings, and, more appropriately,[30] we should negate all these affirmations, since it surpasses all being. Now we should not conclude that the negations are simply the opposites of the affirmations, but rather that the cause of all is considerably prior [πολὺ πρότερον] to this, beyond privations, beyond every denial, beyond every assertion [ὑπὲρ πᾶσαν καὶ ἀφαίρεσιν καὶ θέσιν]. (MT 1000B)

Beyond (ὑπὲρ) *both* affirmation (θέσιν) *and* negation (ἀφαίρεσιν), the second negation indicated here is, paradoxically, *neither* affirmative *nor* negative. Such a "neither . . . nor . . ." would constitute the mystical logic of, precisely, a *hyper*-negation.

The fullest sense of negative thought and language in Dionysius must therefore be located in this second, mystical, form of negation, which is *not* the simple reverse of affirmation, but rather carries out the logic of a "neither . . . nor . . . ," a logic that signals the irreducible priority of the transcendent cause to the binary opposition of the categorical alternative between affirmation and negation. On the role of this negativity within the thought and language that address God's ineffability and inconceivability, Dionysius speaks clearly:

> There is no speaking of it, nor name nor knowledge of it. Darkness and light, error and truth—it is none of these. It is beyond assertion and denial. We make assertions and denials of what is next to it, but never of it, for it is both beyond every assertion [ὑπὲρ πᾶσαν θέσιν], being the perfect and unique cause of all things, and, by virtue of its

---

30. Eventually one should ask how "more and less" appropriate ways of naming God might be determined when God is utterly unknowable and ineffable.

preeminently simple and absolute nature, free of every limitation, beyond every limitation; it is also beyond every denial [ὑπὲρ πᾶσαν ἀφαίρεσιν]. (MT 1048B)

The logic of the "hyper-" terms seeks to articulate the ineffable and inconceivable cause of all beings that itself, beyond truth, "falls neither within the predicate of nonbeing nor of being (οὐδέ τι τῶν οὐκ ὄντων, οὐδέ τι τῶν ὄντων ἐστίν)" (MT 1048A). The cause of all being, for which even nonbeing longs, marks a movement of difference beyond any simple binary logic (either/or).

The logic of redoubled negation or hyper-negation, expressed here in terms of the "neither . . . nor . . ." (assertion/denial, being/nonbeing, light/darkness, truth/error, etc.) concerns not only the language and thought of God, but also the ecstasy and dispossession of self that occur through such language and thought. In the mystical movement of negation, the removal and abandonment of all beings goes hand in hand with the abandonment or dispossession of self. Theological apophasis goes together with an anthropological apophasis. This twofold abandonment and apophasis structures the advice of Dionysius to Timothy which opens the *Mystical Theology:*

> . . . my advice . . . is to leave behind you everything perceived and understood, everything perceptible and understandable, all that is not and all that is, and, with your understanding laid aside, to strive upward as much as you can toward unification with him who is beyond all being and knowledge. By an undivided and absolute abandonment of yourself and everything, shedding all and freed from all, you will be uplifted to the ray of the divine shadow which is above everything that is. (MT 997B–1000A)

The self here abandons itself in and through the denial and transcendence of beings. Such denial and transcendence are to be kept secret from those not properly disposed to them—which means from those not capable of thinking beyond the beings that constitute the immediate world, "those caught up with the things of this world, who imagine that there is nothing beyond instances of individual being and who think that by their own intellectual resources they can have a direct knowledge of him who has made the shadows his hiding place" (MT 1000A). The apophatic transcendence of beings renders possible an apophatic abandonment of self, and vice versa; those not able to transcend the beings of the world remain bound also to "their own intellectual resources," and those bound to their own intellectual resources can (not) imagine nothing beyond things—the instances of individual being in this world. By contrast, the transcendence of beings through their denial and the inextricably related abandonment of self will alone render possible the impossible unknowing of a God who remains beyond being and thus beyond knowledge.

Such an impossible knowing defines the unknowing, abandonment, and dispossession that occur in mystical theology, the summit of theology, which Dionysius indicates through the figure of Moses on Sinai:

> But then he [Moses] breaks free . . . , away from what sees and is seen, and he plunges into the truly mysterious darkness of unknowing. Here, renouncing all that the mind may conceive, wrapped entirely in the intangible and the invisible, he belongs completely to him who is beyond everything. Here, being *neither oneself nor someone else*, one is supremely united by a completely unknowing inactivity of all knowledge, and knows beyond the mind by knowing nothing. (MT 1001A; emphasis added)

The transcendence and abandonment of self would occur in and through the denial or removal—in thought and in language—of all beings. Like the death that is mine alone and yet never experienced by me as present in consciousness or knowing, in language or expression, the mystical unknowing of a God who is nothing, indeed of a God "without truth," throws me into that unity where I am neither myself nor another—beyond all knowing or language. The hyperbolic movements of denial and removal, of transcendence and abandonment, would lead the dispossessed soul into unknowing knowledge of God, and such knowledge knows truly by knowing nothing. In the mystical unknowing of the radically unknowable, and in the mystical naming of the radically unnameable, the self is thoroughly dispossessed—to a point of indiscretion. Neither oneself nor another, one knows the Other beyond mind by knowing nothing. Transcending negation, a redoubled negation or hyper-negation through which self is dispossessed of itself, attains its indiscrete sense in knowing, or unknowing, nothing.

In the next chapter, I investigate the relations among this inconceivable divine Good, the mystical dispossession through which alone it is known as unknown, and the death that so indiscretely resembles such dispossession.

SIX

The Naming of God and the
Possibility of Impossibility:
Marion and Derrida between
the Theology and Phenomenology
of the Gift

*T*hrough the preceding analyses both of finitude in Heidegger and of mystical unknowing in Dionysius, two key themes arose which come to dominate contemporary discussion of the apophatic traditions: that of the "gift" and that of the "impossible." In the post-Heideggerian context especially, recent attempts to interpret giving or givenness as absolute or unconditional almost invariably end up characterizing "the gift" in terms of "the impossible"—but one can distinguish here at least three figures of "the impossible."

First, the absolute gift is associated in theology with an ineffable and inconceivable Good "beyond Being"[1]—a love or charity that opens the "indisputable and definitive impossibility" of thinking God as such (GWB 45). Reaching back in the Christian traditions most notably to Pseudo-Dionysius, the Good beyond Being would constitute the divine cause (αἰτία) of all things which is itself no-thing, the source of all beings which itself is not or "is" "beyond" Being (ὑπερούσιος). To the extent that the Good remains beyond Being, it marks the limit of all possible thought or language on the part of created beings. Mystical union with the divine would thus occur only in an ineffable unknowing (ἀγνωσία) that knows nothing, an unknowing where, "being neither oneself nor someone else" (MT 10001A), one is undone as a speaking or knowing subject.

Second, the absolute gift is approached phenomenologically in terms of an unconditional givenness (*Gegebenheit, donation*) that appears in a call whose source and identity remain by necessity indeterminate. When the phenomenon is understood unconditionally, without any a priori and according to its pure givenness alone, any theological identi-fication of the gift or its giver would become impossible. Indeed, any identification of the gift at all becomes impossible insofar as its most radical givenness, its purest presence in the "saturated phenomenon,"

---

1. First appearing in the famous passage from Plato's *Republic*, 509b, the ἐπέκεινα τῆς οὐσίας has a rich history through Plotinus (e.g., Ennead., V, I, 8, 6–8: τοῦ δὲ αἰτίου νοῦ ὄντος πατέρα φησὶ τἀγαθὸν καὶ τὸ ἐπέκεινα νοῦ καὶ ἐπέκεινα οὐσίας), Iamblichus (e.g., *De Mysteriis*, sec. 1, chap. 5, p. 8, 2–4: ἔστι δὴ οὖν τἀγαθὸν τό τε ἐπέκεινα τῆς οὐσίας, καὶ τὸ κατ᾽ οὐσίαν ὑπάρχον), and Proclus (e.g., *Commentary on the Republic*: ἐπέκεινα ὂν οὐσίας αὐτὸ [τὸ ἀγαθόν]). For these and further references, see René Roques, *L'Univers dionysien* (Paris: Editions du Cerf, 1983), pp. 72–73, 316–17.

amounts to invisibility or unavailability. Characterized by its remaining unforeseeable, nonpresentable, and nonrepeatable for the intentional subject of consciousness, such a givenness would indicate the radical possibility "of the impossible itself" (MP 590).

Finally, the absolute gift can be associated with death—understood as the "possibility of impossibility"—insofar as death marks the limit at which subjective consciousness cannot return to itself or reappropriate itself in its self-identity. By disrupting the return of the subject to itself, death would interrupt the subject's economy of Being. Like the "unavailable" givenness of a saturated phenomenon, death would remain unforeseeable, nonpresentable, and nonrepeatable. It would signal the ultimate horizon of Dasein's Being which gives to Dasein nothing that Dasein might actually be or experience. The most radical possibility of Dasein's impossibility, death gives to Dasein all that it might have or be even as it signals the final and insurmountable dispossession of Dasein.

How are these three figures of the impossible—and the discourses in which they appear—to be understood in relation to one another? If the first remains primarily theological, while bearing the imprint of Neoplatonic philosophy; and if the second would be primarily phenomenological, while pertaining nevertheless to a thought of God or revelation; the third might offer a terrain where the ambiguity and instability of borders between the theological and phenomenological thought of givenness might be—rather than clarified and overcome—drawn out and exploited. By means of such an approach, I will argue through what follows that mystical union with a God beyond Being can be described (and indeed has been described within the textual history of Christian mysticisms)[2] in terms that recall the phenomenological account of death strongly enough to establish an analogy between the two. When "gift" is thought in terms of "the impossible," it would resist any experience implying the presence or self-presence of a thinking, speaking subject. Thus resisting "experience," death itself appears in remarkable proximity to the mystical dispossession of the subject—both of which would pertain to the paradoxes operative in any thought of radical given-

2. For a fine overview of death in the textual history of mysticism (esp. German), see Alois M. Haas, "*Mors Mystica:* Thanatologie der Mystik, inbesondere der Deutschen," *Freiburger Zeitschrift für Philosophie und Theologie*, vol. 23, no. 3 (1976): 304–92; reprinted as "*Mors Mystica—*Ein mystologische Motiv," in *Sermo Mysticus: Studien zu Theologie und Sprache der Mystik* (Swiss Freiburg: Universitätsverlag, 1979).

ness.[3] Crucial, then, to articulating these theological and thanatological spheres will be the phenomenological account of givenness as a "saturation" or "revelation" which allows for—or requires—a blinding indeterminacy of the given or revealed, an indeterminacy where, precisely, the negativity of theological and thanatological excesses might prove indistinguishable but not necessarily identical.

The present chapter seeks, then, to elicit such indeterminacy by explicating the positions of—and the tensions between—two of the strongest contemporary interpreters both of apophatic theology and of the gift: Jean-Luc Marion and Jacques Derrida.

Marion's Theology

In a theology that has generated significant discussion among philosophers, theorists, and students of religion alike, Jean-Luc Marion formulates a twofold critique that targets two distinct "idolatries." On the one hand, the critique aims at conceptions of God from the metaphysical, or onto-theological, traditions of Western philosophy and theology,[4] while on the other hand, the critique turns against onto-theology's primary critic, Martin Heidegger. While Marion remains indebted to Heidegger (in the critique of onto-theology), as well as to post-Heideggerian thinkers such as Emmanuel Levinas (in the critique of Heidegger himself), an indispensable foundation for his theology must be seen in the writings of the Pseudo-Dionysius, who precedes the post-Heideggerian context by nearly fifteen centuries. In his turn to the Dionysian notion of a Good

3. Though I will not treat him here, I should note a major resource on the question of "impossible" experience and its relation to both death and mysticism: Georges Bataille—whom Derrida treats at length but Marion ignores.

4. The question of the relation between metaphysics and revealed theology is a difficult one. Marion currently argues for a clear distinction between the two (see MP), and yet he has also recognized their historical imbrication: "It would be a little too clearly facile to oppose a 'true' God to the 'God' of onto-theology, since, in fact, for us the one and the other are historically imbricated" (IED 35–36). Aquinas marks a particularly difficult figure here, for Marion suggests both that Aquinas, as a Christian speculative theologian, does not belong to metaphysics insofar as he responds to "the peculiar conceptual demands" that prompt his (nonmetaphysical) theology (MP 573), *and that—* to the contrary—Aquinas is directly responsible for initially imposing a metaphysical stamp on the Christian God of charity. Indeed, according to *God without Being*, it is precisely this stamp that will allow for the construction of the metaphysical idol that constitutes the sole "God" who dies in the death of God (see GWB 82).

beyond Being, Marion discerns a thought of givenness that defies historical boundaries "according to an essential anachronism: charity belongs
neither to pre-, nor to post-, nor to modernity, but rather, at once abandoned to and removed from historical destiny, it dominates any situation
of thought" (GWB xxii). Through this anachronism, Marion brings both
onto-theology and its Heideggerian destruction into the light of the Dionysian Good.

Marion organizes his theology according to the poles of "idol" and
"icon," which he seeks to define in and as phenomenological terms. Idol
and icon signify two distinct modes of visibility for the divine, or two
distinct ways of apprehending the divine: the idol is defined by the primacy of the human subject's intentional consciousness, while the icon
would radically disrupt or reverse that primacy. In the idol, I finally see
only the invisible mirror of my own thought, whereas in the icon I see
the fact that, prior to such thought, I am envisaged by the gaze of an
irreducible other.[5] Marion's critique of onto-theology is based on the assertion that its "God" amounts to an idol of human thought, and he
relies for that assertion on Heidegger's definition of onto-theology.

Within the metaphysical forgetting of Being, according to Heidegger, even the highest questions concern only the representation of beings, and thus the ultimate question of metaphysics leads to a representation of the *ens supremum* taken as first cause of all beings (see ID 70–71).
The theo-logical aspect of metaphysical thought reduces the question of
Being to the question of a supreme being on which all other beings
would depend as on their cause or ground—and it is in these terms that
Heidegger provides Marion his understanding of the metaphysical idol
that needs to be critiqued: "The Being of beings is represented fundamentally, in the sense of the ground, only as *causa sui*. This is the metaphysical concept of God. . . . The cause (*Ur-Sache*) as *causa sui*" (Heidegger quoted in GWB 35). For Marion, this metaphysical conception of
God as a supreme, causal being amounts to a conceptual idol because it
is defined according to what the limits of thought can contain. Within
those limits, a *concept* of the supreme being as *causa sui* is posited as equivalent with *God*, thus creating a well-defined, but thereby limited, "God."[6]

5. Here we can see the "reversal of intentionality" that Marion will borrow from
Levinas's ethics and eventually generalize to all phenomena. On the idol and icon in
theology and metaphysics, see esp. chaps. 1–2 in GWB.
6. Marion will argue insistently that the "death of God" is always the death or
twilight not of God himself but of a concept or idol, "God." Any argument for the death

As Marion indicates, Heidegger himself saw the insufficiency of any such conception of "God": "Man can neither pray nor sacrifice to this God. [. . .] The god-less thinking which must abandon the God of philosophy, God as *causa sui*, is thus perhaps closer to the divine God" (in GWB 35).

In his critique of the idolatry of onto-theology, Marion thus takes up a challenge posed by Heidegger that derives from Saint Paul's insistence on the clash between Greek wisdom and Christian Revelation. "Will Christian theology make up its mind," Heidegger asks, "to take seriously the word of the Apostle and thus also the conception of philosophy as foolishness?" (in GWB 62 and IED 36). And Marion gives his response:

> To take seriously that philosophy is foolishness [. . .] means first (although not exclusively) taking seriously that the "God" of onto-theology is strictly equivalent to an idol, one that presents the Being of beings as the latter are thought metaphysically; and thus it means that the seriousness of God can begin to appear and to grab hold of us only if, through a radical inversion, we claim to advance outside of onto-theology. (IED 36–37)

Marion here clearly indicates the direction he will take in his theology (and later in his phenomenology). To advance beyond onto-theology proves necessary for any escape from the first form of idolatry.

However, Marion's appropriation of Heidegger reaches a limit, for while Heidegger's ontology may offer a path for destroying onto-theology's reduction of Being to the supreme being of the causa sui, that ontology itself harbors a second idolatry. Having freed God from the idolatrous formulation of onto-theology's *causa sui*, Marion argues, Heidegger goes on to submit God to a new set of conditions—those marked by the horizon of Being itself.[7] While Heidegger explicitly maintains that God and Being are not identical, he nevertheless does submit the experience of God to the prior condition of Being: "I believe that Being

---

of God, then, can be only as forceful as its concept of God is limited. On this, see GWB 29–33, 37–39, 58–59, as well as the article "De la 'mort de dieu' aux noms divins: L'Itinéraire théologique de la métaphysique," in *Laval théologique et philosophique*, vol. 41, no. 1 (February 1985): 25–41.

7. In fact, the idolatry of Heideggerian ontology would display two aspects: the priority of the question of Being over the question of God in Heidegger's later writings grows out of the phenomenological priority of Dasein already operative in Heidegger's earlier writings. See GWB 68.

can never be thought as the ground and essence of God, but that nevertheless the experience of God and of his manifestedness, to the extent
that the latter can indeed meet man, flashes in the dimension of Being"
(in GWB 61–62; see also GWB 39–40; 207–8).[8] Because the appearance
of God would occur only within the dimension of Being, human being's
experience of God can be thought only on the prior basis of that Being.
In this submission of the human experience of God's appearance to the
prior conditions of Being, Marion discerns a second form of idolatry,
"proper to the thought of Being as such" (GWB 41), which appears once
the idolatry of onto-theology has been overcome.

The appearance of this second, Heideggerian idolatry leads Marion
to pose the question that constitutes the very heart of his theological
thinking (and, if one substitutes "phenomenon" for "God," the very
heart of his phenomenology): might not a search for the "more divine
god" (or the most phenomenal phenomenon) lead one "to think God [or
the phenomenon] without any conditions, not even that of Being, hence
to think God without pretending to inscribe him or to describe him as a
being"[9] (GWB 45)? In formulating this question, Marion turns from the
two critical moments of his theology to a constructive attempt "to give
pure giving to be thought" (GWB xxv). Such a thought of pure giving
would elude both the unthought ontological difference that grounds
metaphysics (and its reduction of the divine) and the thought of Being
and of ontological difference that defines the work of Heidegger. Now,
according both to metaphysics (implicitly) and to Heidegger (explicitly),
to think outside of ontological difference or outside of Being is finally
no longer to think at all. For Marion, however, this "no longer to think"
does not indicate a simple dead end but rather serves as a "negative propaedeutic" to a properly theological form of thought: "One therefore
must recognize that the impossibility, or at least the extreme difficulty,
of thinking outside of ontological difference could, in some way, directly

8. For a differing view, see John Macquarrie, *In Search of Deity* (New York: Crossroad, 1984), pp. 153–67, esp. pp. 163–64, where, in order to construct a concept of God
from the perspective of the Heideggerian horizon of Being, Macquarrie cites the same
passage from the *Letter on Humanism* that Marion attacks as an idolatrous reduction
of God.

9. The attempt to remove the thought of charity (as later that of the phenomenon)
from all conditions marks a tendency that Marion shares with Emmanuel Levinas, who
seeks to understand the significance of responsibility as fundamentally unconditional,
or "without context." Of the numerous pertinent passages in Levinas, *Otherwise than
Being or Beyond Essence*, trans. Alphonso Lingis (Boston: Martinus Nijhoff, 1981), see
esp. pp. 86, 105, 116, 144, 182, 192, 195.

suit the impossibility—indisputable and definitive—of thinking God as such" (GWB 45).[10]

Moving toward a thought concerning the "impossibility" of thinking God "as such," Marion faces the necessity and the difficulty of articulating such an impossibility—and thus he inevitably faces the question of theological language. In seeking a language suitable to the thought of a God who exceeds the conditions of Being/beings—and so the very conditions of thought and language—Marion appeals to the biblical and theological traditions in which God is articulated first not as Being but as love. Noting the failure of both metaphysical and Heideggerian thought to develop the "speculative power" of love, Marion takes love—or the gift, or giving, or charity, which in *God without Being* appear interchangeable—as the means for passing beyond all idolatry into the impossible possibility of thinking God "without idolatry": "God can give himself to be thought without idolatry only starting from himself alone: to give himself to be thought as love, hence as gift; to give himself to be thought as a thought of the gift. Or better, as a gift for thought, as a gift that gives itself to be thought. But a gift, which gives itself forever, can be thought only by a thought that gives itself to the gift to be thought" (GWB 49). The fundamental question of theology (as later of phenomenology), then, is the question of the gift, which has two modes: that in which it is given and that in which it is received. To receive the gift, one must give oneself (or be given) to it. Reception is itself a repetition or imitation of the initial giving—and thus an indispensable aspect of its appearance. To receive the gift, thought must give itself to the gift—and to give oneself to the gift is nothing "if not to love" (GWB 49). For Marion, as theologian, this thought of the pure gift, or love, assumes its rigor in the theology of Dionysius.

In developing the theological question of divine names, as seen in the preceding chapter, Dionysius is concerned to think and express that which by definition remains inconceivable and ineffable. From within this concern, Dionysius insists on the coimplication of God's self-revelation and self-concealment—and for Marion this coimplication is crucial to any adequate theological language.

Drawing on Pseudo-Dionysius, Marion articulates such a coimplication christologically according to the figure of "the Name": "The

---

10. For an elaboration of the positive significance of this limit to thought, see Marion's essay on the *aliquid quo majus cogitari nequit:* "L'Argument, relève-t-il de l'ontologie?" in *Questions Cartésiennes* (Paris: Presses Universitaires de France, 1991), p. 221 ff.

Name," writes Marion, "comes to us as the unthinkable within the thinkable, because the unthinkable *in person* delivers it to us" (IED 187). This christological articulation of the unthinkable within the thinkable assumes its significance within an interpretation of language that is determined by the function of "distance": "The unthinkable speaks even before we think that we hear it; the anteriority of distance holds out to us a language that both precedes and inverts our predication. More essential than the predication that we can (not) employ concerning the unthinkable, there appears the giving of the Name" (IED 187). The absolute priority of this "giving of the Name" in and through the Christ amounts to the absolute priority of the Good given in distance. Recalling the radical an-archy of the call in Levinas, according to which I am called to responsibility even before I could have been present to receive that call, this "distance" marks the profound passivity of the linguistic subject—situated as one who fundamentally receives before intending or conceiving and who, therefore, cannot master or comprehend the given through a language of knowing and predication.

Throughout Western thought, of course, the language of knowing and predication has been the language of Being. A classic Christian formulation of this interdependence of Being, knowing and predication can be found in Thomas Aquinas, who maintains that "everything is named by us according to our knowledge of it" (*Summa Theologica*, I, q. 13) and that "the first thing conceived by the intellect is being, because everything is knowable only inasmuch as it is" (*Summa Theologica*, I, q. 5, resp.). In privileging a language of praise over the language of predication, Marion will suggest the priority of the Good over Being, and to that degree he sides with Dionysius against Aquinas.[11] In this sense praise would constitute the primal form of theological language: the anteriority of an unthinkable distance that speaks before I can hear—a distance with respect to which my thought and language are always in delay—marks the precedence of the Good over Being and demands the priority of praise over predication.

This fundamental passivity out of which I receive language—resonating with so many post-Heideggerian thinkers from twentieth-century France—constitutes what Marion names the "Christic mode" of

11. Marion's position has now shifted, even to the point that a God without Being can be found in Aquinas himself. The shift begins already in the preface to the English edition of GWB (see, e.g., pp. xx–xxiv), and it is developed at length in his "Saint Thomas d'Aquin et l'onto-théologie," *Revue Thomiste* (January–March 1995).

humanity (IED 188) and leads to a "linguistic model of the dispossession of meaning" (IED 189). Just as the Word receives his Name from the Father and submits his will to the will of the Father even unto death, so do we receive our language in such a way that our possession of meaning through predication is lost, and our discourse "dies" through negation and silence. But just as Christic death gives way to Resurrection, so our silence can give way to proclamations of praise (IED 188–89).

Within this linguistic model of dispossession, the privilege of praise over predication derives largely from Dionysius's thinking on divine names. Marion rightly argues that Dionysian theology exceeds the distinction between negative and affirmative theology—both of which, if based in categorical statements on the essence of God, would amount to idolatry. The real contribution of the negative moment in theology is to open "a beyond of the two truth-values of categorical predication" (IED 192), and that beyond, transcending affirmation and negation, is articulated through the "hyper-" terms that characterize the mystical moment.

This third moment alone (in)adequately expresses at once the immanence and the transcendence of the divine: through a logic and language of the "neither . . . nor . . ." it expresses the christological truth that God advances by way of withdrawal and withdraws in and through his advance.[12] Marion articulates this dynamic through his central notion of distance: "The distance of God is experienced first in the figure of Christ: therein it finds its insurpassable foundation and its definitive authority" (IED 203). The same point is expressed also in terms of the icon, itself already determined christologically: "The icon has a theological status, the reference of the visible face to the intention that envisages, culminating in the reference of the Christ to the Father: for the formula *eikon tou theou aoratou* concerns first the Christ. It would remain to specify in what measure this attribution has a normative value, far from constituting just one application of the icon among others" (GWB 23–24).

In and through Christ or the icon (the distance of God made flesh, the reference of the visible Christ to the invisible Father), the conscious I is overwhelmed or undone by that which irreducibly precedes it. The only form of language suitable to that distance would be praise or prayer (which Marion does not clearly distinguish), since the capacity for prayer would be the capacity (or incapacity) of the I to receive more than its

---

12. In his insistence on the christological aspect of Dionysius, Marion differs from several important Dionysian scholars, such as René Roques, Jan Vanneste, and Paul Rorem.

thought or language might ever grasp or contain: "Praying, man acknowledges the unthinkable. [. . .] That distance cannot be comprehended but must be received implies that one's overall bearing . . . should welcome and pass through it" (IED 205). Prayer marks a response to the absolute anteriority of distance and thus actually "performs distance" (IED 207). To the giving of the Name by the Father would correspond our recognition of distance through prayer.

This nonpredicative discourse of praise/prayer in Marion—the sole discourse that would not abolish distance through idolatry—derives from the central function in Dionysius of the *hymnic* form of language. Following Hans Urs von Balthasar, as well as Maximus Confessor, Marion emphasizes that "Denys tends to substitute for the *saying* of predicative language another verb, *humnein*, to praise" (IED 232), and to illuminate the significance of this, he quotes the *Divine Names*:

> We must simply recall that this discourse does not aim to bring to light (*ekphainein*) the super-essential essence inasmuch as superessential (for it remains unspeakable, unknowable, and therefore totally impossible to bring to light, withdrawing itself from all union), but much rather *to praise* the procession that makes the essences and that comes to all beings from the [Trinitarian] Thearchy, the principle of essence. (DN 816B)

Marion interprets this substitution of the verb *humnein*, to praise, for verbs of predication and manifestation as a move from predicative discourse to prayer, for, as he cites Aristotle, "prayer is a *logos* but neither true nor false" (IED 232). In other words, when language assumes the form of praise or prayer, it becomes possible to surpass the "categorical alternative" between affirmation and negation: praise would state nothing positively or negatively about the nature or essence of the divine but rather would direct itself endlessly toward the divine. This model of praise is organized around the literal anonymity of the transcendent Cause (αἰτία), for as Dionysius notes, "the theologians praise the Cause [αἰτία] as anonymous, outside of all names" (DN 596A).[13]

---

13. One should call to mind here Augustine's famous remarks on the aporia of God's ineffability, which finally demands our praise (*De Doctrina Christiana*, 1.6): "And a contradiction in terms is created, since if that is ineffable which cannot be spoken, then that is not ineffable which can be called ineffable. This contradiction is to be passed over in silence rather than resolved verbally. For God, although nothing worthy may be spoken of Him, has accepted the tribute of the human voice and wished us to take joy in praising Him with our words."

According to Marion, this anonymity of the transcendent marks "less an inverted category [i.e., negation], than an inversion of the category. The absence of names turns into the name of absence, even the name of the Absent" (IED 232).[14] Marion bases this interpretation in the Neoplatonic distinction between negation according to lack and negation according to excess. The name of "the Absent" would not indicate a lack of the divine but rather the inadequacy of human language with respect to the divine excess. Within the language of praise, God is always praised "*as* . . ." (Goodness, Trinity, etc.), where the "as" (ὡς) constitutes an "index of inadequation."[15] Marking the inadequation between our language and the transcendence of God, the radical openness of praise—polyonymy—simply marks the reverse side of a radical anonymity. In other terms, one might say that the difference between praise and predication in Marion marks a distinction—much like Levinas's between the saying and the said—between a pure signifying or endless reference, on the one hand, and a determinate meaning or referent, on the other. The naming of God in praise would signify endlessly toward God without securing (predicatively) any final meaning for God, and in this sense anonymity and polyonymy would remain "two sides of the same distance" (IED 234).

Now, while Marion insists that the language of praise would refer infinitely to the divine Cause or Requisite (αἰτία) and to that degree fall ever short of it, the Requisite nevertheless proves to be, as theological referent, required. To this extent, Marion's position here would have to be contrasted with that of Derrida, who from the same apparent operation of language is able to draw radically different conclusions: "There is only the edge in language. . . . That is, reference. From the supposed fact that there is never anything but reference, an irreducible reference, one *can equally well* conclude that the referent is or is not indispensable. All history of negative theology, I bet, plays itself out in this brief and slight axiom" (PS 303). Marion will not, and perhaps cannot (as theologian), draw such a conclusion from the premise that praise refers infinitely to the Requisite. However anonymous or even Absent he may claim the Requisite to be, it nevertheless remains, as referent, required.

14. For a very different take on the relation between an absence of naming and the naming of absence, see Thomas J. J. Altizer, *Total Presence* (New York: Seabury Press, 1980), p. 26.

15. Though Marion insists, like Dionysius, on the inadequacy of human language with respect to the divine, he no doubt also holds, again like Dionysius, that some language remains more inadequate than other language.

This requirement, however, seems to hold only for reasons of theological commitment, and not for reasons pertaining to a philosophy of language.

The difference here between Derrida and Marion points to a significant ambiguity in Marion between theological and philosophical reflection—for in his discussion of divine names, Marion wants not only to speak about and within a particular theological discourse but indeed to make claims about the "very essence of language." The radical plurality of theological praise indicates for Marion nothing less than that "the very essence of language, comprehending and anticipating us by its overflow, comes to us, in distance, as a fact—that is to say, a given, a gift" (IED 242). An almost identical understanding of language will be central to Marion's later phenomenological position, which maintains that language and *logos* are not properties of a subject but rather "gifts" that can only be received (by a radically passive self) through the "response" that makes them manifest (see ED 397). Marion thus seems in his theology to be making an already phenomenological point. But while Marion wants to indicate—within a theological horizon—that "the very essence of language" would come to us as "a given, a gift," it remains the case also that such a gift comes to appearance here only within the determinate limits of that horizon; it is given not through an indeterminate givenness of language "as such" but in fact through very determinate forms of Christian language—whose referent can remain for the theologian neither indeterminate nor dispensable. The first form of such language would be the biblical *logia* which become iconic in and through their investment by the *Logos*, who is taken as the source, norm, and definitive authority of iconic distance—which would mean the source, norm, and definitive authority of the gift itself. The second form would be the words of prayer: the *Pater Noster*, handed over to believers by the Son, and the *Credo*, wherein the Trinity is praised by believers on the basis of Christic Revelation (IED 243). While one might claim that such language forms refer ever inadequately to their referent, that reference would nonetheless imply more than a pure signifying, for it would be tied necessarily to a referent of some determinate content.

The relation between theology and philosophy becomes a question here precisely because, on the one hand, Marion wants to make claims about the gift as such, or the "very essence of language" as gift, while, on the other hand, he makes those claims by speaking more specifically about the gift of God in Christ and by using the language of a determinate theological tradition issuing from that gift. Perhaps recognizing the difficulties of thinking givenness as such, in its unconditional character, in and through a determinate tradition with determinate content, Marion will later seek to advance his thought on givenness by means of a phenomenology that would be free of all such determination. This second approach, however, is not without its own ambiguities, for just as Marion's theology seeks already to be phenomenological, so his later phenomenology, to which I now turn, continues to bear traces of his theology.

Revelation and Phenomenology

In his recent phenomenological writings, Marion pursues a question that he argues to have been presupposed but never fully developed by all previous phenomenology: "What does giving mean, what is at play in the fact that all is given, how are we to think that all that is is only inasmuch as it is given?" (RG 38–39; quoted in GT 51). Straightaway, I would emphasize that from Marion's own perspective, this question had also been at the heart of his theological work: "To give pure giving to be thought—that, in retrospect it seems to me, is what is at stake in *God without Being*. It is also the task of my future work" (GWB xxv). While Marion's theological thought of the gift would have been shaped and limited by the presuppositions of a particular Christian faith, his phenomenology would in principle be capable of thinking givenness as such—beyond the determination of any such presuppositions.[16] Thus, seeking to advance phenomenologically the question that is first given in his theology—the question of givenness itself—Marion will attempt to move beyond 1) Husserl's transcendental reduction to the constituting I, and beyond 2) Heidegger's "existential reduction" to Dasein, in order to establish 3) an indispensable third reduction to pure givenness itself.

Following within a rich tradition of reflection on "the call," Marion's third phenomenological reduction, a "donative" reduction, is also fundamentally vocative: reduction to unconditional givenness is a reduction to the unconditional givenness of the call or the claim exercised over me by the phenomenon as such. Within this third reduction, there appears, prior to the constituting I and prior to Dasein, what Marion names the *interloqué:* one who is called before being (in the mode of consciousness, intention, or decision) and who, therefore, is radically surprised in its

16. On the distinction between theology, which would be burdened (or blessed) with faith's presuppositions, and phenomenology, which would be free of any such burden or blessing (and so emptier, less determinate), see RMM 67–68.

very birth. Called before being, the one called is always already given over as witness to the pure givenness of the call, which alone first gives the recipient to himself—and in this sense the *interloqué* who bears witness to the call is ultimately the *adonné*, the devotee or addict who is given to himself in being given to the call, a "subjecti(vi)ty entirely in keeping with givenness—one that receives itself entirely from what it receives, given by the given, given to the given" (ED 373).

In its birth by surprise, where it is given over in response to the call of the phenomenon's unconditional givenness, the *interloqué* or *adonné* receives a subjectivity that is always already wounded or divided, a subjectivity that is radically in delay with respect to itself: "I have therefore been said and spoken before Being, I am born from a call that I have not issued, nor willed, nor even heard. Birth consists solely in this excess of the call and in the delay of my response (*répons*)" (ED 400).[17] Within this phenomenological model of that which "comes after the subject" that has dominated modern philosophy, the dative *me* (the "to whom" of the call) radically precedes the nominative *I*, whose intentional consciousness can therefore never account for its own origin. In other words, through a radical reversal of intentionality (and here Marion is deeply indebted to Levinas), the *I* is given over to itself by the call that gives rise first to the *me*, which is prior to any conscious, intentional, or resolute *I* who might have been present to think, constitute, or decide on the call. The excessive priority (and thus radical anonymity) of the call, which goes hand in hand with the irreducible delay between the call and my response to it, would mark the originary *inauthenticity*, or dispossession, of the *adonné*; the I is undone by the primal gift of the *me*, which is given in and through the anonymous call to which the *me* answers.

In terms similar to those Derrida will employ in his discussion of language and passivity, and in a structure almost identical to Marion's own theological model of linguistic dispossession, Marion's phenome-

17. Marion coins the term *répons* to indicate his phenomenological understanding of the relation between call and response in the constitution of the *adonné*: "If the call resonates only in the response, then it follows that the response becomes phenomenologically primary—the first manifestation of the call. The response comes after (echoes, returns, corresponds), but nevertheless, for the *I* become an *adonné*, it allows the first sound of the call to be heard, it frees the call from the original silence and delivers it into patent phenomenality. Such a response (*réponse*), which opens visibility and gives voice to the call, which makes it into a phenomenon instead of refuting and degrading it, I will name the *répons*" (ED 397).

nology develops this originary dispossession or inauthenticity of the *adonné* within a theory of language where the ex-propriating "proper name" is central. "The *adonné* has neither language nor *logos* as its properties, but rather it finds itself endowed with them—as gifts, which show themselves only if the *adonné* gives them back (*redonne*) to their unknown origin. —Thus, only the response performs the call, and the *adonné* renders visible and audible what is given to it only by corresponding to it in the act of responding 'here I am!' (*me voici!*)" (ED 397). Just as, theologically, language would appear as a given or gift that is received only to the extent that it is regiven (through the prayer that responds to the incomprehensible distance of God), so here the gift of language appears phenomenologically only to the degree that a response receives it by giving it back (to a now wholly indeterminate origin).

Likewise, just as the theological model of linguistic dispossession centers around the gift of the Name, so here the phenomenological model of "inauthenticity" focuses on the "proper name" that undoes me even as it gives me to myself: "The 'proper' name results above all else from a call: it was given to *me* before I choose it, know it and even hear it: it was given to *me* because in fact *I* have been given (*interloqué*) as and to *me* (literally: *I* has been given as and to *me*) by the fact of this name" (RMM 93; see also ED 401–4). The fact of the "proper" name, which signals the paradigmatic facticity of speech itself (ED 372), imposes an originary impropriety, dispossession, or inauthenticity: "What is proper to me results from an improper appropriation, and therefore identifies *me* only by an originary inauthenticity—the difference of the claim" (RMM 94). More originary than the difference of consciousness (Hegel), the difference between intention and intuition (Husserl), the ontological difference (Heidegger), or *différance* (Derrida) would be this difference of the claim, which eludes or undoes consciousness, the I, and the circle of Being by marking the radical precedence of an absolute givenness:

> The call thus produces the original difference: at the origin, in what concerns the origin, there is no coincidence, no identity, no authenticity, but rather the gap between the call and the *me/I* that it overtakes with surprise—the delay of the surprised *me* with respect to the call that has always already been issued marks the unique origin of difference, or rather the origin as difference. What differs has to do with the claim: before the fold between Being and beings, older

also than the delay of intuition with respect to intention (or of the sign with respect to presence), the claim differs and defers [*diffère*]. (RMM 92; see also ED 405–8)

In sum, the origin as difference signals the disaster of the I by the call as gift.

Now, a question commonly posed at this point concerns the identity of the caller or the source of the call. Derrida in particular will challenge the thought of pure givenness in Marion precisely by questioning—on the basis of a suspected paternal identity—the purity of the call "as such." Derrida suggests that this *pure* call, the call *as such* in Marion, is finally not simply a call in general, an indeterminate call, but rather the very specific and determinate call of the father: "Marion . . . seems to me also to make '*the* call as such,' 'the pure form of the call,' conform to the call of the father, to the call that returns to the father and that, in truth, would speak the truth of the father, even the name of the father, and finally the father inasmuch as he gives the name" (GT 52). By suspecting a determination of the call that would identify the call as *returning* to the father, to the *name* of the father, and to the *truth* of the father—all of which would signal a circle or economy that would threaten or annul the gift— Derrida calls into question the success of Marion's overall attempt to think an unconditional givenness in terms of the *interloqué* or *adonné*.

Explicitly, Derrida bases his challenge on a note within Marion's discussion of "*the* call as such" where Marion indicates—referring to Heidegger's admission of the possibility of a call other than that of Being— that "indeed, the claim here no longer exerts itself in the name of Being (but of the Father), nor with the destination or starting point of a being. Thus arises the pure form of the call" (RG 248 n. 82; quoted in GT 52). I suspect, however, that Derrida's explicit challenge relates implicitly, and more forcefully, to the questions that Derrida poses to Marion's theological reading of Dionysius—where it is more clearly the case that the gift, call, and name are indeed the gift, call, and name of the Father given through the Son within the Trinitarian play of distance. Derrida's challenge concerning the identity of the call, it therefore seems to me, might hold with respect to Marion's theological position, but not necessarily with respect to his phenomenological position[18]—but in both cases a

18. Indeed, the note on which Derrida bases his challenge is, at the very least, ambiguous. That ambiguity is covered over to the extent that Derrida's quotation of the note takes it out of its context: in fact, the note follows a quotation from Heidegger, such that the "here" ("in fact the claim is no longer exerted, *here*, in the name of

THE POSSIBILITY OF IMPOSSIBILITY

deep ambiguity does remain insofar as Marion's theology would already point toward a general thought of givenness, and insofar as his phenomenology might bear a debt to his initially theological understanding of revelation. Derrida's challenge can thus both miss and hit the mark.

It misses the mark to the degree that, within Marion's phenomenology of the *interloqué* or *adonné*, the "source" of the call, or the instance of absolute, unconditional givenness, must—contra Derrida—necessarily remain indeterminate, unknown, and anonymous. The necessity of such indeterminacy—on this point Marion is clear and insistent—stems from the basic definition and structure of the *interloqué*. Countering objections that within a thought of the call the claiming agency would have, necessarily, some determinate identity—for example, "God, the other, moral conscience, auto-affection, figures of difference, Being itself, etc.," (INT 244)—Marion insists on the essential anonymity of the call:

> This objection rests . . . on the illusory presupposition that it is necessary to name the instance that claims in order to suffer its convocation. Now, following the order of a strict phenomenological description, the reverse happens: I recognize myself as *interloqué* well *before* having consciousness or knowledge not only of my eventual subjectivity, but especially of what leaves me *interloqué*. (RG 202; see the almost identical passage in INT 244; and further argument in ED 408 ff.)

The anonymity of the call, or the unknowability of the donor agency, follows from a phenomenological necessity, and at this strictly phenomenological level, the source of the call is unidentified not only provision-

---

Being . . .") can be taken to refer to a particular passage in *Heidegger* and thus not to indicate *Marion's* phenomenological position. Against Derrida, one could argue that Marion is simply establishing the fact that, even in Heidegger, there is an alternative (not necessarily *the* alternative) to the *Anspruch des Seins*—namely, the *Anspruch des Vaters*. On this reading, Marion would not be suggesting that the pure form of the call comes down to the claim of the father, but rather he would be suggesting that, since Heidegger himself acknowledges at least one claim other than that of Being, Heidegger implicitly recognizes that prior to any determined claim—either of Being *or* of the Father, to name two—there operates the pure form of the claim or call as such. Marion seems to state this explicitly, furthermore, in passages that Derrida does not quote: "It is obviously not a question here of invoking revealed authority in order to broaden the field of phenomenology, but of confirming that another call—no doubt the call of the other—might dismiss or submerge the first call issued by the claim of Being. [. . .] Before Being has claimed, the call as pure call claims" (RG 197).

ally or accidentally but permanently and essentially:[19] "Anonymity therefore plainly belongs to the conditions of possibility of the call, because
it defines the call's unconditional poverty: in conformity with the principle of insufficient reason, the call does not have to make itself known
in order to make itself recognized, nor to identify itself in order to exert
itself. This poverty alone manages to wound 'the subject' and to cast it
into exile, beyond any authenticity, as an *adonné*" (ED 413). Lacking
the presupposed determinations of faith or history (as are operative in
Marion's theological and historical works), the phenomenological analysis of the call must leave the call in the poverty of utter indeterminacy.
Indeed, only such a poverty would deliver the wound that characterizes
the *adonné* in its definitive dispossession. At this phenomenological level,
then, Derrida's challenge to Marion may indeed miss the mark.

At the same time, however, in support of Derrida's challenge, one
can argue that the separation between phenomenology and theology
in Marion is not absolute and the distinction not entirely stable: while
seeking to think givenness—and even revelation—in purely phenomenological terms, Marion will still seem to draw on the thought of givenness and revelation that are given first in his theology. Likewise, conversely, his theology of the gift can often seem already to be drawing
on a phenomenology that extends beyond the limits of theology. How
so?

To begin, already in *God without Being* and *L'Idole et la distance*, the
relation between phenomenological and theological thinking is subtle
and shifting. On the one hand, Marion argues that idol and icon constitute purely phenomenological descriptions concerning two modes of the
apprehension of the divine in visibility. On the other hand, he suggests
that Christ would constitute the very source and norm of the icon—the
fundamental embodiment of distance, the paradigmatic visibility of the
invisible, the givenness of the gift itself. A theological determination—
that of Jesus as Christ—would thus become the source and norm for a
phenomenological definition—that of icon as the gift or revelation of
distance and the reversal of human intentionality. In his move toward
a pure phenomenology, I believe, one can see an attempt to shed this

---

19. As Marion elaborates, under each of the four headings that characterize the
interloqué/adonné—convocation, surprise, interlocution, and facticity—the necessary
unknowability and anonymity of the call impose themselves. On this see RG 200–202;
RMM 87–91; ED 369–73.

theological determination of the phenomenological. But does (or can) that move fully succeed?[20]

In attempting to make such a move, Marion takes up the question of revelation—outside of an explicitly theological context—within what he claims to be a strictly phenomenological philosophy, where he distinguishes between revelation as pure possibility ("revelation") and revelation as actuality, historicity, and real experience ("Revelation") (ED 329; MP 590). The former, on his account, would fall rightly within the domain of phenomenology, while the latter would pertain solely to the domain of revealed theology. Now, insofar as Marion defines revelation phenomenologically in terms of the "saturated phenomenon" whose presence is so overwhelming that it can seem to be absent or unavailable, his distinction between revelation and Revelation leads to a strange bind: either the phenomenology of revelation sheds no light on Revelation[21]—which leaves one to wonder what meaning or purpose such a phenomenology might have—or else Revelation can indeed be described according to the phenomenology of the saturated phenomenon[22]—in which case one is left to wonder how the saturated phenomenon's "unavailability" relates to the real, historical experience that would define Revelation. In order to pursue the implications of this bind, I should outline the traits of the saturated phenomenon and indicate how for Marion it would amount to a "revelation."

Marion seeks in his phenomenology to think the phenomenon in terms of a "saturation" of intuition that would render the phenomenon paradoxical to the point of nonappearance. Developed according to the saturation and thus inversion of the four Kantian categories of the understanding, the "saturated phenomenon" gives an intuition that always precedes and exceeds any concept (rather than coming after the concept simply in order to fill it).[23] Phenomenologically, this means that the satu-

---

20. One can articulate this suspicion very simply as follows: would Marion's phenomenology of revelation look like it does if his theology were more in line with Rahner (or Tillich) than with von Balthasar (and Barth)?

21. Marion suggests this may be the case on p. 329 of ED.

22. This seems to be the implication on p. 327 of ED.

23. For the development of the saturated phenomenon vis-à-vis the categories, see §§ 21–23 of ED. Marion argues that the saturation of the category of quantity is given in the "event" (which would find its exemplary phenomenological analysis in Ricoeur); the saturation of the category of quality is given in the "idol" (which finds an exemplary, though inverted, analysis in Derrida); the saturation of the category of relation is given in the "flesh" (which finds its definitive analysis in Michel Henry); and the saturation of

rated phenomenon would constitute an unconditional and irreducible givenness that overturns the two a priori that Husserl establishes for the appearance of any phenomenon: the horizon of appearance and the reduction to a constituting *ego*.[24] "Can we not envisage a type of phenomenon," Marion asks, "that would reverse the condition of a horizon (by surpassing it, instead of being inscribed within it) and that would reverse the reduction (by leading the 'I' back to itself, instead of being reduced to the 'I')?" (SP 107). Beyond 1) the "poor" phenomenon found in mathematics and logic, which gives a very high level of certainty but almost no intuitive content; and beyond 2) the "common law" (or garden variety) phenomenon which would seek an adequation between concept or intention and its fulfilling intuition; Marion's 3) "saturated phenomenon" would be defined by the unconditional givenness that gives *more* intuition than the intention might ever foresee or conceive rather than a relative poverty or adequacy of intuition. Through this excessive givenness of intuition the saturated phenomenon erases every horizon by inundating all horizons, and it overwhelms the I in remaining irreducible to the I. Givenness becomes *originary* in every sense.

In a crucial and provocative move, Marion equates this saturated phenomenon, which as unconditional appearance would constitute the true fulfillment of the phenomenon as such, with "revelation"—here intended in a strictly phenomenological sense:

> It indicates . . . the coherent and conceptual completion of the most operative definition of the phenomenon: it alone truly appears as itself, of itself and starting from itself, since it alone appears without the limits of a horizon and without the reduction to an I. We will therefore call this appearance that is purely of itself and starting from itself, this phenomenon that does not subject its possibility to

the category of modality is given in the face as "icon" (which finds its definitive analysis in Levinas).

24. The "horizon" is overturned in and through the saturation of the categories of quantity, quality, and relation (ED § 21) and the "I" is overturned in and through the saturation of modality (§ 22). I should note that Marion discerns the givenness that would undo such a priori in Husserl's own *Ideen* § 24, on the famous "principle of all principles," which states that "every originarily giving intuition (*Anschauung*) is a source of right (*Rechtsquelle*) for cognition, that everything that offers itself to us in 'intuition' (*Intuition*) is to be taken quite simply as it gives itself out to be, but also only within the limits in which it is given there." See the English translation by F. Kersten, *Ideas Pertaining to a Pure Phenomenology and to a Phenomenological Philosophy* (The Hague: Martinus Nijhof, 1982).

any preliminary determination, a revelation. And—we insist on this—here it is purely and simply a matter of the phenomenon taken in its fullest meaning. (SP 120)[25]

On this view, the very fulfillment of the phenomenon—defined in terms of Heidegger's "*Sich-an-ihm-selbst-zeigende*," but nearly identical also to the definition of God in *God without Being*[26]—would consist in an unconditional and irreducible appearance best described as "revelation." Indeed, as an unconditional and irreducible appearance, "revelation" would become the norm against which all other (poor, common) phenomena would be measured (as deficient modes). Resting neither on the authority of scripture nor on that of tradition, "revelation" here would be purely self-authorizing because unconditionally self-manifesting.

Having thus defined the unconditional givenness of the phenomenon itself as a revelation, and insisting that revelation can be thought in a purely phenomenological manner, Marion attempts to outline the traits of a God in phenomenological terms—in terms of the "being-given" par excellence.[27] This God of phenomenology has at least three

25. In ED, the almost identical passage changes "revelation" to "self-manifestation" (ED 305). This change results from a refinement of the phenomenological definition of "revelation," which would become the "saturation of saturation" or the "paradox of paradoxes," which includes all *four* modes of the saturated phenomenon in one. The exemplary instance of this saturation of saturation would be given for Marion in the Christ (see ED 331–35).

Without resolving the question here, I would note that this refinement of the phenomenological understanding of revelation involves a significant shift in the definition of the "idol." Whereas the idol in Marion's theological works would in fact block the true revelation of the icon (since the former is defined by the primacy of the human gaze while the latter would overturn such a primacy), the phenomenological treatment of revelation in ED seeks to bring idol and icon together within one phenomenon of revelation. This redefinition of the idol would seem to compromise the very significant antagonism of idol and icon in Marion's earlier works (see esp. GWB 10, 16, etc.).

26. On the phenomenon as "the showing-itself-in-itself (*das Sich-an-ihm-selbst-zeigende*)," see SZ 54; H 31, and Heidegger's *History of the Concept of Time* (trans. Theodore Kisiel [Bloomington: Indiana University Press, 1985], p. 85), which speaks of "*letting the manifest in itself be seen from itself (das an ihm selbst Offenbare von ihm selbst her sehen lassen)*." On the very similar definition of God, see GWB 49: "God can give himself to be thought without idolatry only starting from himself alone." The terms here defining the phenomenon and God appear similar enough to suggest that idolatry would constitute, at bottom, an insufficient understanding of "the most operative definition of the phenomenon."

27. The interpretation of God as the most excellent "being-given" occurs in conjunction with Marion's phenomenological redefinition—or relief—of the three domains

characteristics: 1) "That he is the given par excellence implies that 'God' is given without restriction, without reserve, without restraint" (MP 588). Like the iconic God of *God without Being*, the God of phenomenology displays himself, on the basis of himself alone, in the mode of bedazzlement. He is the Good that is diffusive of itself, standing ecstatically outside of himself while remaining wholly within himself. 2) This givenness par excellence gives "an absolute mode of presence," which, because unlimited or without horizons, "cannot present itself as an object, which is necessarily limited. Consequently, it occupies no space, fixes no attention, draws no look." In other words, it is *present precisely by its absence:* "The absence or unknowability of 'God' does not contradict his donation, but on the contrary attests to the excellence of that donation. 'God' becomes invisible not in spite of his donation, but by virtue of that donation. [. . .] If we saw it, then it would not be 'God'" (MP 589). The absent presence of God here points to the third aspect of the God of phenomenology: 3) Abandon:

> Donation par excellence can thus turn immediately into donation by abandon. The being-given that is absolutely without restraint exerts a phenomenality of such a sort that, according to its intrinsic invisibility, its status as phenomenon might never be acknowledged. The phenomenon par excellence exposes itself, for that very excellence, to not appearing—to remaining in a state of abandon. [. . .] Here . . . a radical unavailability follows from radical donation. Donation can thus pass for abandon. (MP 589)

In sum, the God of phenomenology gives without reserve, in an excess so extreme that that God is present only as absent, to the point of remaining unavailable.[28] But at precisely this point, the question becomes unavoidable: how should we understand the relation between, on the one hand, a God who appears historically, is really experienced and supports (or is supported by) a community and a tradition, and, on the other hand, a God who, in the unconditional givenness that Marion so rigorously defines, does not appear and remains radically unavailable? Are real experience, historicity, community, and tradition actually compatible with such

---

of the traditional *metaphysica specialis* (*theologia rationalis, psychologia rationalis, cosmologia rationalis*). While God is reinterpreted as the being-given par excellence, finite mind becomes "the closest being-given" and world becomes "the first being-given that comes to me" (MP 586).

28. Here, somewhat unexpectedly, Marion's position can begin to resemble that of Altizer.

an unconditional givenness? Or, on the contrary, might experience, history, community, or tradition contradict the very definition of the unconditional as unforeseeable, nonpresentable, and nonrepeatable?

More important: is the indeterminacy of the call that would be given in the saturated phenomenon really enough to distinguish the God of Marion's phenomenology from the God of his theology? Derrida, among others, suspects that, in fact, the "pure call" in Marion might well remain the call of the Father. And while Marion's insistence on the indeterminacy of the call in strict phenomenology is clear, given the deep parallels between the phenomenological thought of givenness and the theological thought of the Paternal gift, one can understand a suspicion like Derrida's that the theological privilege of the Father might haunt the phenomenological thought of "the call as such."

To highlight the persistence of an ambiguity in Marion between his theology and phenomenology, one can sum up those parallels as follows: 1) While Marion's theology seeks to think God without conditions (of Being or thought) in terms of an inconceivable charity given in the call of the Father, his phenomenology seeks to think the phenomenon without conditions (of Being or thought) in terms of a pure givenness given in the call as such. 2) Just as the theological thought of charity, the call, and the giving of the Name necessitates a model of the linguistic dispossession of the Son, so likewise the phenomenological thought of givenness, the call, and the gift of the name requires the model of an originary dispossession or inauthenticity of the I as *interloqué* and *adonné*. 3) Finally, in both the theological and the phenomenological thought of the gift, reception coincides inextricably with a regiving or repetition of the gift. Within the phenomenological reduction to the call, "that which gives itself gives itself only to the one who gives himself over to (*s'adonne à*) the call and only in the pure form of a confirmation of the call, which is repeated because received" (RG 197–98). One can indeed discern here, in the phenomenological thought of the givenness of the call, an echo or recasting of the theological thought of the gift in terms of its necessary regiving, repetition, or redundancy (*redondance*) (see IED 212). As *God without Being* indicates, a gift "can be thought only by a thought that gives itself to the gift to be thought" (GWB 49). Now, the redundancy of the theological gift finds its primal expression in the Christic mode of hierarchy, where each figure in the hierarchy receives the paternal gift only in the measure that the gift is given again in imitation of the paternal generosity. How would it be that the call of charity, the dispossessing name, and the coincidence of reception and repetition would no longer find their source, norm, and authority in the reference of the Christ to the Father? Or, conversely, how could they do so and still maintain the indeterminacy that a radical apophaticism seems to demand? The bind here is at least double for Marion. On the one hand, if Marion's theology pushes the absence and unknowability of God to an extreme, then the theology loses its distinctively Christian content. On the other hand, his phenomenology, which seems able to articulate the absence and unknowability of God even more effectively than can his theology, at the same time seems to bear traces of that theology's distinctive shape and content. What might be the significance of the parallels just noted between the theological and the phenomenological in Marion, and what would be at stake in maintaining the distinction between an identifiably Christian God the Father and a completely indeterminate God of phenomenology?

To address these issues, I turn to questions that Derrida poses in his interpretations of Dionysius, specifically, of "negative theology," generally, and finally of the gift itself. On the basis of Derrida's analyses, I will be able to clarify and intensify the ambiguities that characterize the relation of phenomenology and theology in Marion, and I will argue that the same type of ambiguity is in fact internal to the project of any negative theology. As Derrida will say of the relation between a would-be pure ontology and the historical Christian traditions in Heidegger, so I would say of the relation between phenomenology and theology in Marion, or between the apophatic and the kataphatic within theology: it is a relation of "irreducibly double inclusion: the including and the included regularly exchange places in this strange topography of edges" (AP 80).

Derrida on Dionysius

One can distinguish at least three key points in Derrida's response to Marion concerning the interpretation of Dionysius and "negative theology": 1) the status of "hyperessentiality," 2) the character of nonpredicative discourse (prayer and/or praise), and 3) the role of iterability or citationality in discourse. A consideration of these three points leads to a fourth and essentially related issue: the antagonism of economy and the gift. All of these issues can be tied, in turn, both to the question of community and tradition and to the question of experience. That is, they all concern the identity or identifiability of the inconceivable and ineffable within a determinate community and tradition, the consistency of any language that would there give expression to the inconceivable and inef-

fable, and the limits of "experience" as a term for articulating any relation to the inconceivable and ineffable. The inconceivable and ineffable
would, on the one hand, threaten all determinacy, and thus all tradition
or community, and yet, on the other hand, they would seem never to be
given apart from such determinacy.

To begin, Derrida argues that the apophatic movement articulated
by Dionysius through the use of "hyper-" terms may in fact not avoid
speaking (of) Being insofar as it seeks to designate, precisely, the way in
which God *is*—namely, beyond or above Being, in a hyperessential
mode. On this reading, "hyper-" terms do not avoid but rather aim at
speaking of the divine "properly," such as the divine really "is" beyond
Being. Derrida's emphasis on the persistence of some hyperessence in
negative theology is long-standing. In distinguishing his own notion of
différance from any possible "negative theology," Derrida indicates that
the two differ "in the measure to which 'negative theology' seems to
reserve, beyond all positive predication, beyond all negation, even beyond Being, some hyperessentiality, a being beyond Being" (HAS 77).
Referring explicitly to Dionysius and implicitly to Marion, Derrida here
argues that the terms passing beyond both negation and affirmation in
Dionysius's theology, the "hyper-" terms, do not indicate a liberation of
God from Being but rather the excellence of God's mode of Being. Derrida insists that the forms of negation in negative or apophatic theology
(at least in Dionysius) do not indicate an absence or lack of the negated
terms but rather an excess or overabundance, for "God is refused the
predicate of existence, only in order to acknowledge his superior, inconceivable, and ineffable mode of being."[29]

On Derrida's reading, then, the language of apophatic or mystical
theology still speaks (of) Being, if in an excessive, hyperbolic mode, and
therefore remains faithful to what he identifies as the fundamentally
onto-theological imperative to speak the being of God truly (PS 309).
The infinite play of negations in apophatic or mystical theology, the end-

---

29. Jacques Derrida, "Différance," in *Margins of Philosophy*, trans. Alan Bass (Chicago: University of Chicago Press, 1982), p. 6. This passage is quoted (at greater length)
and commented on by Marion in *L'Idole et la distance* (Paris: Grasset, 1977), p. 318, to
which Derrida then responds in "How to Avoid Speaking" (HAS 132). I will not elaborate these aspects of the Marion-Derrida debate. The three central issues are 1) the
status of Derrida's initial remarks with respect to Dionysius specifically, 2) the presence
or absence of the distinction between essence and existence in a given stage of the Greek
language (here, Dionysius's stage), and 3) what negative theology "in its depths" intends,
and what is at stake in the qualifier "in its depths" when applied to negative theology.

less renewal (or exhaustion) of its referential movement, its insistence on the irreducible inadequation between its language and the referent of that language—all of this would operate with a view toward speaking the truth of God:

> to say God such as he is, beyond his images, beyond this idol that being can still be, beyond what is said, seen, or known of him; to respond to the true name of God, to the name to which God responds and corresponds beyond the name that we know him by or hear. It is to this end that the negative procedure refuses, denies, rejects all the inadequate attributions. It does so in the name of a way of truth and in order to hear the name of a just voice. (PS 310)

Thus, for Derrida, the God of apophatic theology does not stand free of the truth that is sought, within onto-theology, under the name of Being.

This being so, however, Derrida also stresses the complexity of the relation between apophatic theologies and the function of tradition: if indeed faithful to the originary injunction of onto-theology to speak of God truly, apophatic theologies would at the same time always pose the threat—through a suspension or destruction of all ontological and theological theses—of a certain "internal rebellion" (PS 309): "Placing the thesis in parenthesis or in quotation marks ruins each ontological or theological proposition, in truth each philosopheme as such. In this sense, the principle of negative theology, in a movement of internal rebellion, radically contests the tradition from which it seems to come" (PS 308–9). Negative theology would thus oscillate between, on the one hand, an affirmation of the onto-theological injunction to speak the name of God in its truth, according to the true (hyper-) being of God and, on the other hand, the refusal of this injunction through a suspension or destruction of all positive (or negative) theses—in a movement that might invite one to see a parallel between negative theology and the phenomenological *epoché*.[30]

Derrida nicely articulates this oscillation when he states that "nega-

---

30. On this, see Derrida: "On the one hand, in effect, this theology launches or carries negativity as the principle of auto-destruction in the heart of each thesis; in any case the theology suspends every thesis, all belief, all *doxa*. . . . —In which its *epoché* has some affinity with the *skepsis* of skepticism as well as with the phenomenological reduction. And contrary to what we said a few minutes ago, transcendental phenomenology, as it passes through the suspension of all *doxa*, of every positing of existence, of every thesis, inhabits the same element as negative theology. One would be a good propaedeutic for the other" (PS 308).

tive theology is everywhere, but it is never by itself. In that way it belongs, without fulfilling, to the space of the philosophical or onto-theological promise that it seems to break (*renier*)" (PS 310). This oscillation between an affirmation and a suspension of its "own" tradition is, indeed, inherent to the question of negative theology. At once dependent on and destructive of the self-identity of its tradition, negative theology would be "one of the most remarkable manifestations" of the "self-difference" of all tradition (PS 311). This tension, I would note, repeats the tension in Marion between the determinacy of his theology and the indeterminacy of his phenomenology, thus reinforcing the parallel Derrida suggests between apophaticism and the *epoché*.

Now, the question of hyperessentiality and of its relation to the onto-theological injunction to speak the name of God truly is intimately bound with the question of predicative and nonpredicative discourse in Dionysius's theology. If the God named in that theology does not exceed Being, but rather "is" exceedingly—in an overabundant mode—then the language of negative theology will bear that fact. That is, if the God named by Dionysius's theology is named such as he "is" (beyond Being), then even the most deeply apophatic or mystical naming of God remains, however minimally (or excessively), predicative.

Through his analyses of prayer (εὐχή) and praise (ὑμνεῖν) in Dionysius, Marion formulates a theory of "nonpredicative" discourse, which he argues to constitute the sole discourse suitable within a theology that would speak and think of the God who is without Being and therefore definitively beyond speech and thought. Derrida responds that Marion wrongly supposes there to be an immediate, even analytic relation, between praise, on the one hand, and prayer, on the other. Marion passes too quickly to prayer, which as a pure appeal or absolute address might well constitute a nonpredicative discourse (HAS 110), from praise, which in fact "preserves the style and the structure of a predicative affirmation. It says something about someone" (HAS 137). By contrast to the nonpredicative, nonconstative, nontheo*logical* form of discourse, which "implies nothing other than the supplicating address to the other [. . .] to give the promise of His presence as other, and finally the transcendence of His otherness itself, even without any other determination" (HAS 111), *praise* would in fact convey a content that renders prayer other and more than nonpredicative. Maintaining a measure of predication, praise would add to prayer some *other determination* and thus call into question both the purity of its address and the indeterminacy of its destination.

With this determination through praise of the addressee of prayer, the question of tradition and of community necessarily arises, for the identification of the ineffable and inconceivable does after all occur in and through the tradition and community that praises it as such:

> [H]ow can one deny that the encomium qualifies God and *deter-mines* prayer, *determines* the other, Him to whom it addresses itself, refers, invoking Him even as the source of prayer? How can one deny that, in this movement of determination (which is no longer the pure address of the prayer to the other), the nomination of the *trinitary* and superessential God distinguishes Dionysius' *Christian* prayer from all other prayer? (HAS 111)

To determine prayer in this way, which constitutes one of the key functions of praise, is to compromise the purity or absolute character of the address that would define prayer. Prayer, which taken absolutely would speak only *to*, is determined through praise to speak also *of*. According to the framework established by this distinction, a third alternative— praise "*as*" [ὡς], wherein Marion locates the "index of inadequation"— would not suffice to counter Derrida's argument that praise determines the addressee of prayer: praise *of* God "as" Good beyond Goodness, and so on, may well signify the ultimate inadequacy of our language and its determinations, but it remains nonetheless a determination—with grounds in a tradition and community—that is not simply a pure address. Only insofar as prayer speaks "*of. . .*" can it assume an identity and thus sustain, or be sustained by, a community and tradition—for example, Dionysius's community and tradition, which do after all bear a Christian (and Neoplatonic) identity.

The identity of Dionysius's prayer as Christian prayer, as a prayer belonging to an identifiable tradition or community, is determined as such by the distinctive character of its attributive language—its praise. That identity, from Derrida's perspective, would annul the purity of address that might have characterized prayer. Indeed, the condition of possibility for such a determinate, tradition-bound prayer—namely, its iterability or citationality—might well call the possibility of pure address as such into question. The ability to cite a prayer, to repeat it through quotation, to address it not only to God but also to a disciple or reader, belongs among the conditions of possibility for teaching and initiation, for the establishment and maintenance of a discrete community, for the transmission of doctrines and texts (tradition as παράδοσις). Insofar as

Dionysius's theology refers to and sustains a tradition of teaching and initiation, the form of its language and whatever content that form might convey necessarily require both the possibility and the actuality of this repetition and determination.

Now, as Derrida will argue, repetition is both a chance and a danger for prayer and theology—a condition of possibility and a condition of impossibility at once (HAS 119). First, the possibility: Dionysius's work begins with prayer to God; the prayer as received by the reader of Dionysius, however, marks a quotation of the "initial" prayer, an inscription of the prayer within Dionysius's written corpus; further, that corpus is itself also addressed to a disciple (Timothy) whose initiation depends precisely on the possibility of this quotation and inscription. After laying out this complex structure, which can be generalized to all texts, Derrida notes:

> None of this would be possible without the possibility of quotations (more generally, of repetition), and of an apostrophe that allows one to speak to several people at once. To more than one other. The prayer, the quotation of the prayer, and the apostrophe, from one you to the other, thus weave the same text, however heterogeneous they appear. There is a text because of this repetition. (HAS 117)

This possibility of quotation or repetition, however, signals at the same time an impossibility which arises in the contradiction or incompatibility between the repetition that permits a text, on the one hand, and, on the other hand, the singularity of an appeal, the purity of an address that would not be reducible to a code or language: "Repetition appears at once proscribed, impossible and necessary, as if it were necessary to avoid the unavoidable" (HAS 138). If prayer were absolutely pure appeal, it could "occur" only once; it would prove singular, unique—to the point of resisting all repetition, which would reduce the singularity of the appeal to the iterability of a name, a common name, or even a concept, transmissible by tradition.

Repetition alone allows for a tradition of prayer, even as the singularity of prayer might resist all repetition. As throughout his work, Derrida here highlights well this tension or ambiguity, this oscillation between the possible and the impossible:

> Does one have the right to think that, as a pure address, on the edge of silence, alien to every code and to every rite, hence to every repetition, prayer should never be turned away from its part by a nota-

tion or by the movement of an apostrophe, by a multiplication of
addresses? That each time it takes place only once and should never
be recorded? But perhaps the contrary is the case. Perhaps there
would be no prayer, no pure possibility of prayer, without what we
glimpse as a menace or as a contamination: writing, the code, repetition, analogy or the—at least apparent—multiplicity of addresses,
initiation. If there were a purely pure experience of prayer, would
one need religion and affirmative or negative theologies? (HAS 131)

Religion as such, negative and affirmative theologies, would move within
this space of oscillation between the unicity of pure appeal, on the one
hand, and the repetition of code, language, or rite, on the other. The
pure appeal to which a nonpredicative discourse (such as Marion's) might
aspire could render a determinate theology unnecessary or even impossible. Conversely, the very notion or possibility of pure appeal or nonpredicative discourse would not arise without such a theology.

This tension, I stress again, repeats the ambiguity in Marion between a determinate thought of paternal givenness in theology and a
purely indeterminate thought of givenness as such in phenomenology.
To elucidate further the implications of such a tension, I turn finally to
Derrida's consideration of the gift.

Gift, Economy, and Identity of the Giver

From the Derridean perspective, perhaps the strongest challenge to
Marion's thinking on charity concerns the structural paradox of the gift.
The basic schema of the gift would be that wherein someone gives something to someone. Derrida argues that if any of these conditions were
actually met, the gift as such would be annulled by its reduction to, or
reinscription in, a cycle of economic exchange.[31] From receipt or recognition of the gift would follow the annulment of its unconditionality
through the circularity of economy, the unavoidable cycle of gift and
countergift, donation and debt, receipt and the obligation of repayment.
This annulment relates fundamentally to the questions of hyperessentiality, predication or attribution, repetition, tradition, and the identity
of God in nonpredicative discourse—that is, the identity of the giving
instance. Just as the identification of the hyperessential God by an attrib-

31. In explicating the destruction of the gift by the circle, Derrida is playing on
the notions of annulment (annul deriving from the Latin *annulare*, to bring to nothing,
ad-nullum) and the annular (from *annularis*, pertaining to a ring, *annulus*).

utive language of praise would both sustain a tradition and threaten the unconditionality and singularity of prayer and its addressee, so recognition of the gift threatens to annul the unconditionality of its givenness. This tension—and the oscillation it engenders—might be used to interpret the relation between theology and phenomenology in Marion, the tension between "the impossible" as in fact identified (the distance of the Father) and "the impossible" as utterly indeterminate (the saturated phenomenon).

The question of the gift is posed by Derrida in relation to the question of the circle and economy. Economy is essentially *odyssean* in the sense that it always seeks a homecoming, a return to self and to self-possession (GT 7). The insistence of the economic circle is such that Derrida always mentions the gift hypothetically, with the condition *"if there is gift."* The conditional indicates that the gift constantly risks falling into a structure and dynamic of exchange, circulation, reciprocity, symmetry, recognition, calculation, and so on—all of which annul the gift in its definitive unconditionality. Derrida very clearly sets out the terms and stakes of the issue:

> Now the gift, *if there is any,* would no doubt be related to economy. One cannot treat the gift, this goes without saying, without treating this relation to economy, even to the money economy. But is not the gift, if there is any, also that which interrupts economy? That which, in suspending economic calculation, no longer gives rise to exchange? That which opens the circle so as to defy reciprocity or symmetry, the common measure, and so as to turn aside the return in view of the no-return? If there is gift, the *given* of the gift (*that which* one gives, *that which* is given, the gift as given thing or act of donation) must not come back to the giving (let us not already say to the subject, to the donor). It must not circulate, it must not be exchanged, it must not in any case be exhausted, as a gift, by the process of exchange, by the movement of circulation of the circle in the form of return to the point of departure. If the figure of the circle is essential to economics, the gift must remain *aneconomic.* Not that it remains foreign to the circle, but it must *keep* a relation of foreignness to the circle, a relation without relation of familiar foreignness. It is perhaps in this sense that the gift is the impossible.
>
> Not impossible but *the* impossible. The very figure of the impossible. It announces itself, gives itself to be thought as the impossible. It is proposed that we begin by this. (GT 7)

Beginning with the hypothesis of such a paradox, a paradox of *the* impossible that nevertheless announces and gives itself, Derrida draws out several consequences.

Because any recognition of the gift threatens to annul it (by inscribing it in the circle of debt, gratitude, obligation, self-satisfaction, etc.), the gift must not be recognized either by the donor or the donee, and yet it must indeed give itself. Because nonrecognition cannot mean "a simple non-experience," or "non-appearance" (GT 17), the gift must somehow efface itself in its very occurrence. Such a self-effacing occurrence is articulated according to the "time without time" of the *event* or the *instant:* "There would be a gift," writes Derrida, "only at the instant when the *paradoxical* instant (in the sense in which Kierkegaard says of the paradoxical instant of decision that it is madness) tears time apart" (GT 9).[32]

The event "tears time apart" precisely to the degree that it remains nonforeseeable, nonrepeatable, and, thus, never actually or fully present. The instantaneous irruption of the gift would thus obey a mad "logic" of pure chance:

> The gift, like the event, as event, must *remain* unforeseeable, but remain so without keeping itself. It must let itself be structured by the aleatory; it must *appear* chancy or in any case lived as such, apprehended as the intentional correlate of a perception that is absolutely surprised by the encounter with what it perceives, beyond its horizon of anticipation—which already appears phenomenologically impossible. (GT 122)

Defined by a phenomenological impossibility which is for Marion likewise the defining characteristic of givenness, the unconditionality of the gift or of the event, of the gift-event, runs counter to any anticipation that would inscribe the gift-event within a horizon established before the irruption of the gift-event itself. The surprise of the gift would resist all mastery or appropriation on the part of a subject who might anticipate it,

32. For more on Derrida's reading of Kierkegaard, within a context addressing especially the ethical implications of the madness of decision, see Derrida, *Donner la mort* (Paris: Métailié-Transition, 1992), esp. § 3. See also John Caputo, "Instants, Secrets, and Singularities: Dealing Death in Kierkegaard and Derrida," in Martin Matuštík and Merold Westphal, eds., *Kierkegaard and Postmodernity* (Bloomington: Indiana University Press, 1995). One of the first to recognize the profound connections between Derrida and Kierkegaard, of course, was Mark C. Taylor. See esp. his *Altarity* (Chicago: University of Chicago Press, 1987).

since "a gift or event that would be foreseeable, necessary, conditioned, programmed, expected, counted on would not be lived either as a gift or as an event" (GT 122–23). Similarly, that which surprises absolutely remains absolutely nonrepeatable, for the "sudden coming of the new" signals "that which cannot be anticipated *or repeated*" (GT 146; my emphasis).

Unforeseeable and also nonrepeatable, the gift would fall instantaneously and decisively between absolute surprise and radical forgetting—thus never becoming present as such:

> For there to be gift event (we say event and not act), something must come about or happen, in an instant, in an instant that no doubt does not belong to the economy of time, in a time without time, in such a way that this forgetting forgets, that it forgets *itself*, but also in such a way that this forgetting, without being something present, presentable, determinable, sensible or meaningful, is not nothing. (GT 17)[33]

In Derrida's thought of the gift, the forgetting of the gift would not be a forgetting of anything that was once or ever present. Rather, in the gift "without present," the forgetting of the gift is primal and originary. As in Heidegger, where the forgetting of ontological difference opens the space in which metaphysical thinking moves according to the circle of beings and Being, a circle which does not contain, but rather depends on, the difference that it leaves unthought, so in Derrida, the forgetting of the gift gives way to the gift-effects that would remain exterior but nonetheless related to the economic circle.

Given the functions of surprise, nonrecognition, and radical forgetting, the gift would be incompatible with the very constitution of subjectivity, since a circle of return "is produced as soon as there is a subject, as soon as donor and donee are constituted as identical, identifiable sub-

33. I should note here the parallel between this radical forgetting that forgets itself and yet remains as trace, on the one hand, and, on the other, the oblivion of the ontological difference which, according to Heidegger, is itself forgotten, veiled, or covered over: "The oblivion here to be thought is the veiling of the difference as such, thought in terms of λήθη (concealment); this veiling has in turn withdrawn itself *from the beginning*" (ID 50). In Heidegger, oblivion does not befall a difference that would have preceded that oblivion; rather, "the oblivion belongs to the difference because the difference belongs to the oblivion. The oblivion does not happen to the difference only afterward, in consequence of the forgetfulness of human thinking" (ID 50–51). Likewise in Derrida's thought of the gift, the forgetting of the gift would not be a forgetting of anything that was once or ever present.

jects, capable of identifying themselves by keeping and naming themselves. It is even a matter, in this circle, of the movement of subjectiva-
tion, of the constitutive retention of the subject that identifies with
itself" (GT 23–24). The self-relation and self-possession of the subject,
the keeping and naming in which the subject as such identifies and sustains itself, would be inconsistent with the surprise, nonrecognition, and
forgetting of the gift—which signal the precedence of the gift over all
intentional consciousness and the resistance of the gift to retention or
memory.[34]

The gift remains incompatible with the very constitution of the subject precisely insofar as the subject in its constitution seeks to master or
exclude that which is given in the gift:[35] "One would even be tempted to
say that a subject as such never gives or receives a gift. It is constituted,
on the contrary, in view of dominating, through calculation and exchange, the mastery of this *hubris* or of this impossibility that is announced in the promise of the gift. There where there is subject and
object, the gift would be excluded" (GT 24). The incompatibility of the
gift and the subject goes hand in hand with the necessary lack or erasure,
at the level of the pure gift, of both an identifiable addressor and an identifiable addressee. Such an erasure of identifiable subjects would be
staged within the "scene of writing," where Derrida articulates the "nonreturn" of the gift in terms of dissemination.

What Derrida identifies—through his interpretation of "writing"—
as the irreducible play or dissemination of meaning becomes crucial for
his interpretation of the gift. Derrida draws out the diversity of meanings
and idioms associated with the very terms of "gift," "giving," "to give,"
and so on, and he understands that diversity in terms of the boundless
play of dissemination. According to the movement of dissemination, the
nonreturn of the gift operates even at the level of the meaning of the term
itself: "This hypothesis of a dissemination without return would prevent
the locution from circling back to its meaning. It thus also concerns—
whence this paradoxical fold—the without-return of the gift" (GT 48).

34. Such, argues Derrida, is the move made by Heidegger: "The question of the
gift should therefore seek its place before any relation to the subject, before any conscious or unconscious relation to self of the subject—and that is indeed what happens
with Heidegger when he goes back before the determinations of Being as substantial
being, subject or object" (GT 24).

35. Marion comes very close to this position when he indicates that "metaphysical
subjectivity could even be defined as the obstinate denial (*dénégation*) of the always already accomplished fact of my birth" (ED 399).

Dissemination prevents any locution, and here that of "the gift" itself, from returning or circling back to its own "proper" meaning; it prohibits any term from constituting a fully or finally stable, discrete, self-identical signification. So operating, dissemination relates to the structure and dynamic of textuality.

According to Derrida's well-known formulations, the signatory of a text delivers the text up "to a dissemination without return" (GT 100). This dissemination without return would operate in spite of the efforts of the calculating subject to produce or reproduce itself, to invent or rediscover itself in its text, in its signature, or in its name, to reappropriate itself in its written production. The signatory of a text abandons it, as an orphan, or is dispossessed of it. Likewise, from the side of reception, the text is delivered "above and beyond any determined addressee, donee, or legatee" (GT 100).

Lacking both an identifiable addressee and a stable addressor, the scene of writing might become the scene of a giving without return, and Derrida will frame such a giving specifically in terms of death. Indeed, it is precisely death that Derrida will name "the fatality that destines a gift *not to return* to the donor agency" (GT 102). The tie that binds the gift, the scene of writing, and death is to be found in the fundamental *passivity* out of which we are related to language. Received out of such passivity, language "carries off the property of our own thoughts even before we have appropriated them" (GT 80). Recalling Marion's Christic model of linguistic dispossession—but lacking the function of Resurrection operative in that model—the gift of language here dispossesses and puts to death *without return*.

Now, as seen above, the irruptive character of the gift—its absolute surprise, instantaneous occurrence, and nonrepeatability—will not be submitted to any horizon or principle that would account for it, motivate it beforehand, or allow its reproduction: "The gift and the event obey nothing, except perhaps principles of disorder, that is, principles without principles. In any case, if the gift or the event, if the event of the gift must remain unexplainable by a system of efficient causes, it is the effect of nothing" (GT 123). As the effect of nothing, the gift is unmotivated, gratuitous, unconditional.

The unconditionality or gratuity of the gift imposes both surprise and forgetting, it gives as both irruption and nonappearance, such that the gift must somehow be without being. The "without being" of the gift allows it, perhaps, to avoid the violence that would surprise or overtake (*sur-prend*) the recipient of the generosity of the gift, for "to overtake the other with surprise, be it by one's generosity and giving too much, is to have a hold on him, as soon as he accepts the gift" (GT 147). Thus:

> So as not to take over the other, the overtaking by surprise of the pure gift should have the generosity to give nothing that surprises and appears *as* gift, *nothing that presents itself as present, nothing that is;* it should therefore be surprising enough and so thoroughly made up of a surprise that it is not even a question of getting over it, thus of a surprise surprising enough to let itself be forgotten without delay. And at stake in this forgetting that carries beyond any present is the gift as remaining [*restance*] without memory, without permanence and consistency, without substance or subsistence; at stake is this rest that is, without being (it), beyond Being, *epekeina tes ousias*. The secret of that about which one cannot speak, but which one can no longer silence. (GT 147)

The character of the gift as irremediably nonforeseeable would correspond to absolute surprise, while the impossibility of repetition would correspond to absolute forgetting. Between surprise and forgetting, the event of the gift occurs instantaneously, without ever being fully present in a presence. The mode of the gift, then, is not being, but "remaining"—without recollection, without presence or subsistence, without return. This mode is not merely impossible, but *the* impossible—a subtle distinction, no doubt, but a crucial one, for only *the* impossible opens (or closes) "the secret of that about which one cannot speak, but which one can no longer silence." In other words, it is with respect to "the" impossible that a thinking, naming, and desiring of the gift would be oriented.

The gift, Derrida suggests, is not simply impossible, but rather *the* impossible. I take this distinction to mark, among other things, the difference between that "about which one [simply] cannot speak" and, by contrast, "that about which one cannot speak, *but which one can no longer silence*." In other words, "the impossible" articulates this double bind: it engenders thought, speech, and desire that remain oriented around what, precisely, thought, speech, and desire can never attain. Indeed, the impossible might well engender thought, speech, and desire to the very extent that it announces itself and yet remains inaccessible: "For finally, if the gift is another name of the impossible, we still think it, we name it, we desire it. We intend it. And this *even if* or *because* or *to the extent that* we *never* encounter it, we never know it, we never experience it in its present existence or in its phenomenon" (GT 29).[36]

If the gift were simply impossible, rather than *the* impossible, it could not maintain the relation that it does with *possible* thought, language, and desire. It remains, after all, possible to think of, speak about, and desire the impossible. But such possible thought, language, and desire occur as such only in relation to the impossible that feeds them; their fulfillment or actualization—their conversion into "philosophy, science and the order of presence"—would be their annulment. It is precisely *the* impossible that *remains* to be thought, spoken, or desired; it remains in what is *not yet* thought, spoken, or desired, in what might still remain possible for thought, language, and desire: "Perhaps there is nomination, language, thought, desire, or intention only there where there is this movement still for thinking, desiring, naming that which gives itself neither to be known, experienced, nor lived—in the sense in which presence, existence, determination regulate the economy of knowing, experiencing, and living" (GT 29). Within this perspective, the impossible is not simply cut off from and opposed to the possible (which might be realized in knowledge or experience). Rather, the possible circles around the impossible. The impossible sets the circle of the possible moving, and thus stands with it in a "relation without relation": "If one wants to recapture the proper element of thinking, naming, desiring, it is perhaps according to the measureless measure of this limit that it is possible, possible as relation *without* relation to the impossible" (GT 29).

Here, a significant point of rapprochement between Derrida and Marion arises. If Marion's *theology* of the gift and *Christic* model of linguistic dispossession remain suspicious to Derrida, Marion's phenomenological analysis of givenness and language could prove compatible with Derrida—first, by recognizing (in a way that the theology does not) a profound tie between the facticity of language and the mortality of the radically passive subject, and then, correlatively, by insisting on the unknowing and radically open character of the mortal's relation to language:

36. Derrida's discussion here of "that about which one cannot speak" (the phrase found in § 7 of Wittgenstein's *Tractatus Logico-Philosophicus:* "That about which one cannot speak one must pass over in silence") seems to me very close to Maurice Blanchot: "Wittgenstein's 'mysticism,' aside from his faith in unity, must come from his believing that one can *show* when one cannot *speak*. But without language, nothing can be shown. And to be silent is still to speak. Silence is impossible. That is why we desire it," in

. . . no mortal has ever lived, even for an instant, without discovering himself preceded by a call already there. The paradigm of this irremediable facticity is found in the fact, always already arrived, of speech [*la parole*] itself: for every mortal, the first word [*parole*] was always already heard before he was able to pronounce it. Speaking always and first comes back to hearing passively a word coming from another, a word that is first and always incomprehensible, that announces no meaning or signification, unless to begin with the very alterity of the initiative, whose pure fact gives (itself to be thought) for the first time. (ED 372)

The gift of language in Marion's phenomenology can and indeed must maintain an anonymity that his theological language (as Derrida argues) may be unable to maintain. Such anonymity would be tied to a radical openness of language that, again, would be consistent with Derrida's approach to language surrounding "the impossible." Indeed, Derrida's argument that "the proper element of thinking, naming, desiring," is possible "as relation *without* relation to the impossible" comes very close to Marion's understanding of the relation between unconditional givenness as anonymous call and the radical incompletion of the *adonné*'s constitutive response. Just as for Derrida "the impossible" ever remains yet to be thought, spoken, and desired, so in Marion, response to the call takes the form of an expectation or desire that knows no end: "The call arouses the response (*le répons*) but never appeases it; every advance remains a beginning, and the response (*le répons*) is never done with beginning (like desire)" (ED 417). Precisely because the response of Marion's *adonné* is ever in delay with respect to the call, it can never come to completion.

Thus, much as in Heidegger, where the past for which I could not have been present (indicated by thrownness) returns in a future that I can never realize (indicated by death), so here for Marion, the originary delay between call and response implies that "the response (*le répons*) always remains to be completed. With this ever to be completed delay, the response is opened to its historicity, which is therefore temporalized radically on the basis of the already given that is not yet shown (*à partir du déjà donné non encore montré*), and therefore on the basis of the past" (ED 418). Ever already past, the call for which I could not have been

Blanchot, *The Writing of the Disaster*, trans. Ann Smock (Lincoln: University of Nebraska Press, 1986), pp. 10–11.

present leaves me straining ever forward toward an open future where I would ceaselessly name and rename that call—which remains, by phenomenological necessity, anonymous. In terms that would recall the hermeneutical openness of mortal existence in Heidegger (see chap. 4), Marion understands this radical openness of response to the call in light of the *adonné*'s relation to death: "The history of the *adonné* consists in nothing other than the uninterrupted but finally suspended series of its responses (*répons*). And the *adonné* dies as soon as it no longer has a respondent and no longer manages to name once again the call without a name" (ED 418). Just as I cannot be present in my death—and thus, as living, remain ever open toward that death, so my language never fully names the anonymous call—and thus remains radically open.

Marion and Derrida on Givenness and the Impossible

Both Derrida and Marion, then, despite their apparent differences, approach gift and givenness in and through figures of "the impossible," which generates thought, language, and desire precisely because it ever eludes them. Such figures of the impossible can tend either in the direction of the theological or in the direction of the thanatological—or, perhaps, in the direction of an indiscretion between the two. To develop the theological figure, one might draw on the Dionysian framework, where that around which thought and language circle in endless desire is the inconceivable and ineffable generosity of the Good beyond Being. The naming of the unnameable in Dionysius, if pushed to its extreme, might thus constitute a relation of the possible to the impossible; the thought and language that are possible, that we live and experience, circle in endless desire around that which remains utterly impossible—to comprehend, speak, and be sated by the Good that ever remains to be thought, named, desired. To develop a thanatological figure of the impossible, one might draw on the Heideggerian framework, where death itself can become a figure of the gift in its "impossibility." Defined as the possibility of impossibility, death becomes a figure of the absolute gift in the sense that death marks a possibility that can never be realized in experience, the horizon of all possibility that itself *remains* at every moment possible and thus marks the impossible. Just as "I," as the speaking, thinking, desiring being that I am, could not be present to experience mystical union with the divine source beyond Being, so as Dasein, I could not be there where my death would "occur." An absolutely measureless limit (since there is no more or less in death), death as the possibility of impossibility dispossesses absolutely even as it gives to Dasein all that it might ever possibly be.

The impossible, then, provides a term through which to compare the naming of the unnameable in the apophaticism of mystical theology and the possibility of impossibility in the Heideggerian conception of death. Rightly, I think, Derrida has indicated such a point of resemblance between the death in which Dasein can no longer be and the mystical moment in which the speaking being can no longer speak: "All the apophatic mysticisms can also be read as powerful discourses on death, on the (impossible) possibility of the proper death of being-there that speaks, and that speaks of what carries it away, interrupts, denies, or annihilates its speaking as well as its own *Dasein*" (PS 290–91). As the possibility of Dasein that renders Dasein impossible, death resembles the mystical union of the speaking self with God, a union in which that self is dispossessed of itself, deprived of its capacity for thought or speech and, to that degree, of its capacity for "experience." The articulation of that union from within thought and speech occurs in a discourse whose referent remains inaccessible, a discourse that enacts a circling of the possible around the impossible. "The impossible," then, might be understood either in terms of mystical union with the Good or in terms of death—or in terms where death and the Good would illuminate one another. Such illumination becomes possible precisely to the degree that "the impossible" allows for an ambiguity between the theological and the thanatological—and that ambiguity can persist thanks to an indeterminacy of the gift which, despite all their apparent differences, may be common to Derrida and Marion. But what are the nature and limits of this commonality?

While Derrida and Marion may have real differences at the theological level, at the phenomenological level they can seem rather close in their approaches to the gift in terms of "the impossible." At the same time, they do have different emphases in their attempts to figure "the impossible." Derrida seems to find a privileged figure of the impossible in "death," though he will also acknowledge the similarity of such a figure to mystical unknowing vis-à-vis revelation. By contrast, Marion finds his most privileged figure of the impossible in revelation—even though his phenomenology also recognizes the significance of mortality vis-à-vis the saturated phenomenon. Now, while Derrida's tendency to think the gift in terms of death can seem to imply a radical lack or absence of the gift, and while Marion's tendency to think the gift in terms of revelation can seem to imply its plenitude and presence, both approaches to the gift suggest to me that the excess of "the impossible" ought rightly to *exceed* any such decision between plenitude and lack, revelation or death. In the end, Derrida may sustain this undecidability in a way that Marion does not, since Derrida recognizes the possible indiscretion between revelation and death, whereas Marion wants finally to avoid it—but Marion's own phenomenology, despite such avoidance, could nevertheless invite a similar undecidability. How so?

We can take a clue here from the interplay of anonymity and polyonymy within *Etant donné*'s analysis of the saturated phenomenon of revelation. According to that analysis, "the call—if it would show itself—would bear no name because it would assume all names; its anonymity would be reinforced by the very excess of the paradox, which would require an infinite denomination; thus, no call would offer *less* of a name than that of a phenomenon of revelation" (ED 410). The unconditionality of the doubly saturated phenomenon of revelation would demand an irreducible polyonymy that constitutes the reverse side of radical anonymity—and this undecidable play of language would correspond to the phenomenological principle that the most radical givenness can be given in and through unavailability or abandon.[37]

But here one should ask again—now on phenomenological and not theological grounds: if an endless de-nomination ensues from the unconditional and thus ultimately unavailable or anonymous saturation of revelation, if in face of that saturation and unavailability the speaking subject would inhabit what amounts to a movement of irreducible linguistic *reference*, why not assert as Derrida does that "one *can equally well* conclude [from the supposition of irreducible reference] that the referent is or is not indispensable" (PS 303)? *This* understanding of irreducible reference before the impossible, an understanding which Marion's "denomination" seems finally to reject or ignore, would be at the basis of Derrida's ability to maintain (where Marion will not) the undecidabilty or indiscretion between Being-toward the impossible death of Heidegger and Being-toward the ineffable God of apophatic traditions. Now, while one can understand why Marion would want, as theologian, to exclude such an undecidability or indiscretion, is such an exclusion justified in phenomenological terms?

37. On this anonymity and unavailability vis-à-vis the Christ, see ED 333–34, where the infinite naming of the paradox of revelation—a naming embodied in history, civilization, spiritualities, literatures, and cultures—would ever "succeed" only by *failing*

Marion's phenomenological thought of givenness in terms of "revelation" can seem to push the excess of givenness to an extreme of blinding indeterminacy between plenitude and lack, or between presence and
absence, and to that degree Marion's position comes close to Derrida's.
At the same time, however, Marion can also seem unfaithful to such indeterminacy—and most notably in his attempt to avoid any indiscretion
between the impossibilities of revelation and of death.

Like Derrida on the gift and death, Marion will indeed approach the
givenness that reaches its height in revelation according to "the possibility of impossibility," but, unlike Derrida, Marion will insist that *this* impossibility is *not* the impossibility signaled in Being-toward-death: "The
phenomenon of revelation," he writes, "would itself also be defined as the
possibility of impossibility—on condition that one no longer understand
here an impossibility confiscating possibility (Being-toward-death), but
a possibility assimilating impossibility to itself (incident, fait accompli)"
(ED 328). In light both of this passage and of my own preceding analyses, one can ask here: is this characterization of death by Marion the
most productive one? And does his attempt to distinguish the impossibilities of death and of revelation contradict a major tendency within his
own thought of saturation?

Marion's characterization of death in this passage is indeed less generous than it could be—if only because he himself recognizes earlier in
the same work that death does *not* simply close up or confiscate all possibility within an utter impossibility but indeed *gives* all possibility precisely by constituting possibility's most radical form—namely, the form
that can never be reduced to actuality for the being whose ultimate possibility it nevertheless is. In attempting to show that "even death" obeys
the logic of givenness, Marion himself indicates, following Heidegger,
that "Death, at least understood as this [originary] possibility, gives itself
to Dasein just as long as Dasein's life—indeed, as that very life, since that
life also gives itself only as a pure possibility. [. . .] Givenness never imposes itself more visibly than in such a possibility" (ED 86). The possibility that defines life itself, then, is given—in Marion's eyes as well as
Heidegger's—by the radical possibility of death—in such a way that
death does not, as Marion implies in this later distinction between death
and revelation, simply "confiscate" possibility.

---

to render manifest, tangible, and effable that which remains unknowable, intangible,
and ineffable.

But if death is in fact *generous* as Marion himself rightly indicates, why does he later imply that death simply "confiscates" possibility? Apparently, in order to distinguish the saturated phenomenon of revelation from that of death. But what motivates such a distinction between two figures of the impossible—two figures of that which should in principle remain "radically unavailable" and thus, it would seem to me, ultimately beyond the possibility of such distinction? Marion's attempt to distinguish the impossibility of death (which he finally associates with a simple lack or deprivation) from the impossibility of revelation (which he clearly associates with a generous plenitude) seems to contradict his own recognition that radical givenness can "manage to give paradoxes (saturated phenomena) without intuition, or without one being able to decide between excess and poverty" (ED 341).[38]

Now, in this gesture toward the undecidability between excess and poverty, Marion is responding to a question regarding how one might reconcile "the description of the phenomenon of revelation according to . . . intuitive saturation" (ED 337–8) with "the apophaticism where God is known only as unknown, in the 'night' of the senses and of concepts, and therefore in a radical intuitive poverty" (ED 338, see n. 1). In that response, Marion argues—very powerfully—that the most excessive givenness (the saturated phenomenon) can render indistinguishable the radical plenitude and the radical poverty of intuition. "The paradox of paradoxes," he insists, "does not have to choose between kataphasis and apophasis any more than between the saturation and the poverty of intuition—it uses them all in order to push to its limit the phenomenality of what shows itself only inasmuch as it gives itself" (ED 340). Alluding here to the endless play in Dionysius between kataphasis and apophasis, Marion would seem to be signaling the radical unknowing that defines Dionysius's third, mystical moment, where the soul could in fact no longer say whether its God gives a plenitude or a poverty, a presence or a lack, a truth or an error, a light or a darkness.[39] From the perspective of mystical unknowing, God would utterly exceed such distinctions.

38. Likewise: "when givenness no longer gives any object or being, but a pure given, it no longer exerts itself through intuition; or rather the alternative between a poverty and a saturation of intuition . . . becomes undecidable" (ED 340).

39. See, e.g., MT 1048A–B: "It falls neither within the predicate of nonbeing nor of being. Existing beings do not know it as it actually is and it does not know them as they are. There is no speaking of it, nor name nor knowledge of it (οὔτε λόγος αὐτῆς ἐστιν οὔτε ὄνομα οὔτε γνῶσις). It is neither darkness nor light, neither error nor truth

But if revelation in phenomenology imposes an undecidability whose theological analogue would be mystical unknowing, how could one securely *decide* (without invoking the Neoplatonic and finally metaphysical distinction between negation according to lack and negation according to excess) that the givenness of the impossible possibility of death is distinct from the impossible possibility of revelation? After all, key Dionysian mystics (well before Derrida) do eventually recognize death as a possible figure of mystical unknowing (or vice versa), and Marion himself acknowledges that "He whom no one can see without dying blinds first with his holiness" (ED 286), that "no one can see [the glory of the Holy] without dying"—in short, that "revelation indeed imposes the worst trial for a gaze—that in which it can and even must perish."[40]

While Marion's phenomenology points powerfully toward the undecidable, he in fact seems nevertheless to have decided. "I will name the phenomena of revelation," Marion writes, "where the excess of the gift can take on the aspect of poverty, with the name of the abandoned" (ED 341). While one might at first see in this concept of "the abandoned" an assertion of some real undecidability between excess and poverty, Marion in fact indicates that he has decided on the meaning of the undecidable: it is excess that takes on the "aspect" of poverty—and not the reverse; if an undecidability arises between lack and plenitude, that undecidability results in fact from plenitude rather than from lack. This (Neoplatonic) distinction, I think, helps to explain Marion's separation between revelation and death, and it confirms that the plenitude of givenness is never in question for Marion but only the capacity of finite beings to *recognize* that plenitude.

As I indicated above, Marion ties his concept of "the abandoned" to the assertion that the given—which would remain without limit—appears only insofar as "received" by the essentially finite *adonné*—the mortal who comes to birth as the devoted or addicted witness to the surprise of the given. On this view, far *more* would always be given than

---

(οὔτε σκότος ἐστὶν οὔτε φῶς, οὔτε πλάνη οὔτε ἀλήθεια). Of it there is neither assertion nor denial (οὔτε . . . θέσις οὔτε ἀφαίρεσις). We make assertions and denials of what is next to it, but never of it, for it is both beyond every assertion (ὑπὲρ πᾶσαν θέσιν), being the perfect and unique cause of all things, and, by virtue of its preeminently simple and absolute nature, free of every limitation; it is also beyond every denial (ὑπὲρ πᾶσαν ἀφαίρεσιν)."

40. *La Croisée du visible* (Paris: Presses Universitaires de France, 1996), pp. 121, 81, respectively.

I could ever actually receive. Givenness would remain without limit, and what gives itself *would* necessarily *show* itself (according to Marion's basic phenomenological principle), but that monstration would not always be "received": "Since its finitude determines the adonné essentially, it cannot by definition receive adequately the given *such as it gives itself*— namely, without limit or reserve" (ED 425; emphasis added). The question, though, becomes unavoidable: from *within* the perspective of essential finitude, how could one distinguish phenomenologically between that which gives itself *such as it gives itself* and that which gives itself only such as I receive it? Doesn't the phenomenological project begin with the *suspension* of such a distinction between what is "in itself" or "as such" and what appears "for me"?

With Marion's introduction of this distinction into his phenomenology of givenness, it is illuminating to note a shift in the theological analogue that one might discern in the background: it would no longer be Dionysius and his mystical unknowing, according to which God might indeed prove radically unknowable, but rather Thomas Aquinas and his doctrine on the illumination of finite intellect. Just as Aquinas insists that God is in himself "infinitely knowable" while the creature can know God only in the finite measure of the glory that the creature manages to receive (*Summa Theologica*, I, q.12, a.7), so Marion finally argues that "the phenomenological principle that what gives itself shows itself remains itself intact, but it is accomplished for us only within the limits where the finite *adonné* manages to put it into operation" (ED 425).

Like Aquinas, who never doubts the knowability of God but only our ability to attain such knowledge, Marion never doubts the unlimited plenitude of the saturated phenomenon—only our ability to see that phenomenon and acknowledge it as gift. In face of what could be a radical undecidability before the excessive impossibility of the gift, Marion has always already decided in favor of the gift's plenitude of appearance. However, according to the very terms of finitude—and mortality—that Marion's phenomenology invokes, one might well move, as Derrida seems to, in the other direction, in the direction where one really could not decide, or where one could really only *decide*—without knowing— whether the impossibility one faces is that of plenitude or poverty, revelation or death.

Exploiting such an indecision or indiscretion, I will lay out in my conclusion the significant ground that might be established for interpreting in light of one another, according to an "apophatic" analogy of relation, the Being of the thinking, speaking being toward the ineffable and inconceivable goodness of God, on the one hand, and, on the other, the Being of that thinking, speaking being toward the possibility of impossibility that is its death. The possibility (or impossibility) of such analogy depends precisely on the radical indeterminacy that might accompany a thought of givenness in terms of "the impossible."

CONCLUSION

The Apophatic Analogy

Less than for any other name, save "God"—and for
good reason, since their association here is probably not
fortuitous—is it possible to attribute to the name "death,"
and above all to the expression "my death," a concept or a
reality that would constitute the object of an indisputably
determining experience.

— JACQUES DERRIDA

*H*ow did I arrive at this question of "experience" and of its limit or undoing in forms of "the impossible" that seem to arise both in a thought of absolute gift or goodness and in the thought of finitude and death? And how are these two distinct figures of "*the* impossible" related to one another? To conclude, I will address these questions by summarizing my path up to this point and by indicating how the language of finitude in post-Heideggerian frameworks and the language of goodness in the mystical traditions might be articulated in relation to one another by means of an analogy that itself proves "apophatic" insofar as it compares terms that remain incomparable because ultimately indeterminate. In evoking unavoidable but not unambiguous ties between a theology and a thanatology, the analogy is able to indicate the presence and significance of a certain negative anthropology within most any negative theology—or perhaps vice versa—and thus to trouble the borders of both these spheres even to the point of indiscretion. Pushed to such a point, negative theology and negative anthropology would alike and in concert force a confrontation with the aporias of "unknowing," a confrontation with the multiple, irreducible, and—I would insist—finally promising uncertainties that befall us when, in our experience, we no longer quite know who we are or what we desire. In this manner, the "apophatic analogy" could provide a powerful trope through which to figure the aporetic not only here, in terms of gift and death, theology and thanatology, but also elsewhere throughout the religious sphere and beyond, wherever "the impossible" weaves its double binds.[1]

Absolute Experience and Absolvent Language in Hegel

As I indicated in the course of the first three chapters, it is precisely through the category of experience—the "experience of conscious-

1. This unsettling force of the apophatic analogy, emerging for us here in the religious sphere, seems to me especially promising also in the aesthetic and ethical spheres. Aesthetically, the operation of apophatic analogy would come very close to Mark C. Taylor's "disfiguring" or, in another sense, Marion's phenomenology of the invisible in painting. Ethically, it would bear strong kinship not only to the aporetic in Derrida and to Levinas's "unsaying," but also to the *ethica negativa* and "generalized apophatics" of John D. Caputo, and to the "saintliness" of Edith Wyschogrod. On these, see Taylor,

ness"—that Hegel will seek to establish the self-presence of the self-conscious subject who realizes itself in its thought and language. As a culminating figure of the modern project of autonomy, Hegel will conceive experience on the basis of absolute, subjective self-presence. That self-presence, I argued, implies the resolution, in and through the temporal experience of consciousness, of the subject's self-difference—which means that the Hegelian conception of experience in terms of absolute subjectivity is tied to a very specific interpretation of temporality.

Insofar as "time" for Hegel is defined as the existence of the concept that has not yet been grasped by and as self-consciousness, that is, the existence of spiritual consciousness in its own self-difference, the resolution through experience of the subject's self-difference amounts essentially to an annulment of time. While realizing itself only in and through this detour of temporality, which amounts to a provisional self-difference of consciousness, the self-presence of absolute subjectivity finally transcends and annuls the difference on which it depends.

This annulment of time, whose ground and character I uncovered in the structure and dynamic of the temporal experience of consciousness (chap. 2), would imply a sublation of finitude corresponding to the "death of death" that Hegel elaborates on the basis of his "death of God" (chap. 1). According to the twofold sense of the Hegelian death of God, God himself negates the unmoving, infinite abyss of his abstract and unknowable eternity in order to become known concretely by finite, human subjectivity within the very movement of historical consciousness. For Hegel, this negation of divine abstraction and unknowability effects at the same time an overcoming of human finitude: through the realized presence of the absolute in this world and its history, the finitude of humanity itself is raised into the infinitude of the absolute. The "death of God" as a self-giving of the divine into the most extreme negativity of finitude and death effects a reversal of that negativity, a death of death according to which finitude itself is overcome. Such a reversal and overcoming occur precisely through the temporal experience of consciousness that would finally annul time.

That annulment implies, then, that death in Hegel is not empty or

Disfiguring: Art, Architecture, Religion (Chicago: University of Chicago Press, 1993); Marion, *La Croisée du visible* (Paris: Presses Universitaires de France, 1996); Caputo, *The Prayers and Tears of Jacques Derrida* (Bloomington: Indiana University Press, 1997), and *Against Ethics* (Bloomington: Indiana University Press, 1993); and Wyschogrod, *Saints and Postmodernism* (Chicago: University of Chicago Press, 1990).

purely negative. Indeed, death itself dies, and time is annulled, only to the extent that death is actually filled with positive, meaningful content. This means that Hegelian consciousness finds and sustains itself even in the most extreme negation marked by death; consciousness realizes its fullness in the self-presence of self-consciousness precisely by maintaining itself in and through the negative.

Philosophically, this positive meaning achieved even by the negativity of death is expressed in terms of "the concept," while religiously it is expressed in terms of "love." The "death of God" that effects the "death of death" is enacted for Hegel through the Christ, the meaning and content of whose death is love. Hegel conceives that love, according to the logic of the concept, in terms of the unity or identity of opposites wherein the infinite becomes finite in order thus to raise the finite into the infinite. Interpreted according to the conceptual logic of reconciliation, love constitutes a movement through which consciousness finds itself or returns to itself in and through the otherness of the beloved. In conjunction with the annulment of time and the death of death in Hegel, then, love is interpreted not as a movement of self-loss or insatiable desire (as, e.g., in Gregory or Dionysius) but rather as one of self-discovery and self-satisfaction.

The movements of love and death that transpire in the religious sphere imply for Hegel a self-negation of the divine according to which the absolute becomes wholly comprehensible—indeed, actually equated with the concept—for a humanity that would thereby surmount its finitude. Love in Hegel constitutes a representation of infinite comprehension or, equally, a comprehension of the infinite, rather than a name for the divine incomprehensibility that created beings might confront in their definitive finitude.

As we saw, these interrelated developments—the annulment of time, the death of death, and the correlative conception of love in terms of infinite self-consciousness—all occur within a framework that subordinates religious to philosophical thought. From the Hegelian perspective, that subordination is necessitated by the inadequacy of the religious, or representational, form of thought with regard to the philosophical, or wholly conceptual, form. The former would remain caught up within the self-difference of consciousness, and for that reason it would remain incomplete and essentially bound to temporality; the latter, by contrast, would resolve and so overcome the difference of consciousness, thus fulfilling rational thought and annulling time itself.

In chapter 3, I examined the manner in which the logic governing this subordination of religious, temporal consciousness to the timeless rationality of philosophical thought determines also Hegel's conception of philosophical language in general and his naming of God in particular. The absolute subjectivity in terms of which Hegel would sublate finitude, annul time, and fill death according to the idea of love, comes to expression ultimately in a philosophical language that would articulate the truth of the experience of consciousness.

Just as the experience of consciousness proves circular in the sense that, through experience, consciousness returns to itself as self-consciousness, so the philosophical language corresponding to that experience proves fundamentally closed in its circularity. Both the Hegelian conception of experience and the Hegelian conception of language interpret the development of the subject (the subject of consciousness or the grammatical subject, which mirror one another) in terms of the subject's self-differing and self-return. Just as the conscious subject of experience ultimately finds and realizes itself in its own self-difference, so the grammatical subject finds and realizes itself in the apparent otherness or difference of its predicates. Predicates that within a nonspeculative understanding of the propositional structure would seem to stand apart from and external to their subject prove here, on the contrary, to be not contingent additions to that subject but rather the essential self-difference of the subject in and through which it realizes itself.

Within the "absolvent" circularity of Hegel's speculative proposition, the name of God in particular takes on a full and fully rational content. Indeed, the naming of God becomes the exemplary instance of the speculative proposition according to whose logic the subject concretizes and realizes itself in and through the (self-) difference of its predicates. Conceptually, God or the absolute is delivered from the one-sidedness that would set the infinite apart from the finite; the infinite realizes itself in and through its finite determination. Likewise at the level of language, the speculative proposition that would express the absolute passes beyond the one-sidedness of the predicative statement where predicates and subject would remain external to one another; the speculative proposition enacts the self-realization of the absolute in and through the determinations of its predicates. In this way, through the speculative form of language, the absolute is fully determined and conceived in its content.

To the full determination and conception of the Hegelian God in thought, then, would correspond the fullness of language articulating that determination and conception. According to such a fullness, language can speak only the rational in its universality. The singular, on this view, or the "mere name" that is not determined conceptually, proves finally irrational and so ineffable; it is necessarily negated by the universal power of language in its all-embracing rationality. According to the absolvent logic embodied in the speculative proposition, the Hegelian absolute is fully conceived and thus named or expressed in such a way as to effect an "exorcism" of the ineffable that goes hand in hand with the erasure of any "mystery" that would remain obscure to rational thought.[2]

Finite Existence in Heidegger and Negative Discourse in Dionysius

Now, if "experience" in Hegel actualizes the self-presence of the self-conscious subject in such a way as to annul finitude and secure the fullness of a conceptual language that names and grasps the absolute, thereby exorcising the μυστήριον, it does so according to a resolution of difference, a negation of negation, that Heidegger and his heirs will identify in its "onto-theological" character.

On the reading I established, with regard to both temporal consciousness (chap. 2) and the language articulating its truth (chap. 3), Hegel's thought of absolute subjectivity proves onto-theological in the degree that it ignores—precisely by attempting to resolve—the "ontological difference" that would underlie the "difference of consciousness." The Hegelian subject's movement between natural consciousness and real knowledge would in fact imply, according to Heidegger, a difference between ontic and ontological consciousness, and thus an ontological difference; but insofar as Hegelian thought attempts to resolve or pass beyond the difference between natural consciousness and real knowledge (the difference of consciousness), it ignores the irreducibility of the ontological difference. Likewise, the speculative proposition that would name God depends on, but does not think, the difference between beings (God is a being) and Being (God, a being, is also Being itself). Now, from Heidegger's perspective, to ignore the ontological difference in its irreducibility is to ignore the radical finitude of that being who inhabits,

---

2. Again, see Cyril O'Regan, *The Heterodox Hegel* (Albany: State University of New York Press, 1994), pp. 31–44, and his article on Hegel and Eckhart in David Kolb, ed., *New Perspectives on Hegel's Philosophy of Religion* (Albany: State University of New York Press, 1992), esp. pp. 121–25.

performs, or makes the difference—human being as Dasein, the mortal who dwells and deals in significance.

Thus, in chapter 4, I explicated the radical finitude of Dasein in terms of the "mortal difference" signaled by its constitutive Being-toward-death. As contrasted with Hegel's difference of consciousness, according to which the temporal experience of consciousness and the language of the speculative proposition will ultimately sublate finitude in such a way that both time and the singular are annulled, Heidegger's "mortal difference" implies a temporality that determines Dasein in its singular existence and insurmountable finitude.

Within this Heideggerian framework, I highlighted the manner in which "significance," and thus meaningful experience (that which might be articulated in thought and language), would be given according to the horizon of a "possibility" that itself remains "beyond" experience: the possibility of death. As the possibility of Dasein's utter impossibility, death opens the horizon of all Dasein's possibility even as it remains be-yond any eventual actualization by Dasein. Thus, at the very "center" or "ground" of significant experience lies that which finally eludes experience.

This understanding of "possibility" and its basic temporality, I argued, differs fundamentally from the Hegelian, and in that difference it opens the ground for numerous contemporary critiques of the modern subject's self-enclosed return to self. According to the Hegelian difference of consciousness, absolute subjectivity is, at least implicitly, ever *already* that which it is *not yet* explicitly—namely, full self-consciousness, or the realized absolute. This means that the "not yet" of the absolute in Hegel is only provisional; the difference it implies is resolved insofar as the absolute does actually realize itself—which for Hegel it cannot fail to do and still remain absolute.

According to the "mortal difference" in Heidegger, by contrast, Dasein is constitutively "not yet" that which, according to its radical possibility, it might at every moment still be. Because Dasein as such is defined by the openness of its "to be," this "not yet" simply cannot be negated or surpassed by Dasein so long as Dasein still *is*. Dasein *is* its own possibility, its "to be," and this necessarily implies the "not yet"; Dasein's possibility depends, precisely, on its essential incompletion—on the finally irreducible gap between that which Dasein actually is and that which it might at every moment yet be. Such a possibility is radical: for as long as Dasein *is*, its possibility can never be reduced entirely to present actuality or actual presence.

The ultimate horizon of that possibility is the death toward which Dasein ever exists but at or in which Dasein can never actually be. Death marks the ultimate possibility of Dasein that undoes Dasein of all possibility. It constitutes a final possibility that can never be made actual. "There" where death is, Dasein is not and cannot be precisely because death would erase or collapse the "there" that defines Dasein. Because Dasein as such cannot *be* in death, cannot find itself in death, it can never give to death the positive content or meaningful experience that is secured (or sought) within the Hegelian sublation of finitude.

Likewise, while the sublation of finitude in Hegel implies the negation of singularity, the irreducible finitude of Dasein indicates the definitive singularity of its existence. In its Being-toward-death, each Dasein confronts the paradoxical possibility of its own impossibility, and that possibility belongs, precisely, to it alone. No one can take my place in dying, and I cannot take the place of another; death thus constitutes an absolute limit to substitution or representation. Leaving me without any support among beings in the world, the possibility of my own nullity individualizes me to the point of singularity; even as it ultimately dispossesses me, that possibility signals my "ownmost" because it dispossesses me alone.

Having contrasted, then, the irreducibly finite temporality of an essentially singular existence in Heidegger, on the one hand, with the temporal experience of an ultimately universal and timeless consciousness in Hegel, on the other, I turned in chapter 5 to a naming of God that would stand in contrast to the absolvent language of Hegel's speculative proposition. If Hegel's speculative language strives through a play of double negation toward a positive fullness that would articulate a wholly conceptual grasp of the absolute, Dionysian language strives through a double play of negation to reach an emptiness, or even a destruction, of language that would signal the utter transcendence of the divine over all representation and all conceptual thought.

While the subject of representational consciousness and language in Hegel would find and realize itself within the speculative form of language, the thinking and speaking being in Dionysius (the created soul) would lose and transcend itself through the hyper-negativity of its language (apophatic and mystical). The use of a hyper-negative language in Dionysian theology, I argued, would serve to carry the soul beyond both itself and all other beings in the world toward an "unknowing" union with the ineffable God. To negate all beings in both thought and language, and in turn to negate those negations themselves, constitutes the doubly negative or hyper-negative path through which the soul might strain toward the ineffable and incomprehensible God who is no being among beings but who calls all beings to be. In this sense, the mystical path in Dionysius aims toward that without which thought and language are not possible but which itself remains beyond any thought or language.

In Heidegger and Dionysius alike, then, we find an articulation of some absolute limit to possible experience (death, the unknowing of God) for the thinking and speaking subject of experience (Dasein, the created soul), and in both thinkers, that limit gives the possibility of all experience (of all language, all thought) even as, or precisely because, it remains in a fundamental sense beyond such experience.

In what sense do death, on the one hand, and the mystical unknowing of God, on the other, remain "beyond" experience? And would the "beyond" in each case differ—insofar as Dionysius could seem to figure the beyond in terms of some super-plenitude while Heidegger might seem to approach it more in terms of lack?[3] This second question finds

3. This question is prompted by the illuminating interpretive framework that Edith Wyschogrod establishes to distinguish between "pleromatic" and "differential" postmodernisms, between the "ecstatics" (such as Deleuze, Guattari, Kristeva) and the "thinkers of difference" (such as Blanchot, Levinas, Derrida). Pleromatic postmodernism, Wyschogrod argues, would fail to conceive desire in terms of true alterity since it reaches a certain satisfaction through a hidden monism, while differential postmodernism, thinking desire as it does in terms of "lack, absence, and negation" would leave open a more radical alterity (on this, see esp. chaps. 7–8 of *Saints and Postmodernism*). Despite the language of ecstasy and union in Dionysius, my reading would place him nonetheless toward the side of Wyschogrod's differential thinking—insofar as "satisfaction" of desire proves wholly elusive in Dionysian unknowing. With more specific reference to the question of negative theology, John Caputo (following Derrida) makes a distinction similar to Wyschogrod's—between "two voices (at least): one of desertification, the other of plenitude; one of the most arid empty intention, the other of the most lush overflowing hyperfulfillment; one a virgin, the other a mother; one of dessicated, desert aridity, the other of an intuitive flood; one of meontic and meontological desolation, the other of hyperousiological saturation" (*The Prayers and Tears of Jacques Derrida*, p. 45). As my argument should indicate, I am seeking in the present work a point of indiscretion where "unknowing" would become radical enough that these distinctions—powerful and productive in so many contexts—would be open to question. The seeming "lack" spelled by Heideggerian death and the seeming "super-plenitude" of Dionysius's God could prove finally indistinguishable insofar as they both defeat the self-presence of any thinking subject who might articulate the distinction. As Caputo indicates of negative theology: We really do not know what we desire—and so, I would argue, we could not really say whether desire's excess is one of lack or plenitude. In its excess, the endless end of desire, precisely, *exceeds* any simple distinction between presence and absence. This seems to have been the insight of the many mystics who themselves were

its response in and through an answer to the first. Death and mystical unknowing remain beyond experience in the precise sense that they mark a limit at which the thinking and speaking being who is capable of experience would be dissolved or undone as such. There where death would have "occurred," Dasein cannot be present to actualize, think, or express it. There where mystical union would be achieved, the soul is carried beyond its own being, thought, and language. In both cases, our thought and language ever remain on "this side" of a boundary or limit beyond which our thought and language cannot pass. In both cases, our thought and language would signal a term that remains beyond the realm of any knowing or speaking, beyond the realm of actual presence for the self-present subject. For this reason, one cannot finally decide whether the negativity of the "beyond" results from an excess of presence or of absence, of plenitude or of lack, for the truly excessive, precisely, exceeds this distinction to the point of indiscretion.[4]

In both Heidegger and Dionysius, then, one can discern an understanding of possibility that differs fundamentally from the Hegelian. While for Hegel the possibility of the absolute is always already determined implicitly by its actuality, which is achieved explicitly in absolute knowing and its absolvent language, for both Heidegger and Dionysius one might say that the possible is given not according to the eventually actual but according to the excess of "the impossible," which stands outside of actual knowledge and its language—outside of "truth" as a present presence in our thinking and speaking. In the case of Heidegger, the horizon of significance, and therefore experience, is the horizon of a death that remains beyond that experience, for it implies the utter collapse of significance. In the case of Dionysius, the "cause" of all thought and language, "that without which" they simply are not, is a God who remains beyond such thought and language, since union with that God would imply a dissolution of the very one who thinks and speaks. In both cases, the being that inhabits thought and language would, according to the existence that defines it, circle around, or strain asymptotically toward, a term that it never attains, and never can attain, "as such."

---

able to hold that desert aridity and oceanic flood, the virgin and the mother, are, indeed, indistinguishable.

4. This "indiscretion" is, to be sure, difficult (perhaps impossible) to maintain. Most all those thinkers who would insist on an excess that exceeds the distinction of presence and absence tend nevertheless to fall toward one side or the other: Marion (or Altizer), for example, tends toward a thought of fullness or presence despite his assertion that a saturation of presence amounts to absence, while Derrida (or Taylor) tends toward

The Contemporary Framework: "The Impossible"

In my discussion of the contemporary debate concerning onto-theology and the apophatic traditions, I found that, despite important disagreements concerning the status of the latter vis-à-vis the former, both Derrida and Marion seem finally to agree that a thought and language of absolute gift or giving would indicate some paradoxical or aporetic thought and language of "the impossible." The significance of "the impossible" in both cases concerns the relation of the thinking subject to the giving or givenness of the gift. Radically preceding or exceeding the subject in its self-identity, an absolute giving or unconditional givenness would remain irreducible to the economy of that subject's Being—irreducible, that is, to the thought and language that would constitute the conditions of its experience.

Marion thinks such a givenness in terms of the "call"—the theological call of the Father and the more indeterminate call of the phenomenon as such—that calls the "I" to be in such a way that the "I" cannot have been present to intend, constitute, master, or even receive the call. Before I am, the call calls me to be, and in this sense the call is given before Being. Radically preceded by a givenness that calls me to be, I am constituted through an originary and irreducible difference or delay between the call and my response to it. That difference prohibits my foreseeing the call so as to calculate it; it disallows my rendering it present in a presence so as to master or manipulate it; it forbids my inscribing it within conditions that would permit its repetition. In sum, the conditions of thought or language do not determine the givenness of the call, but rather the givenness of the call first brings about those conditions. The conditions of thought and language, then, are given to me through the provocation of that which ever exceeds them because it radically precedes them. In this sense the givenness of the call remains "unconditional." Irreducible to the conditions of my own thought and language, the unconditional givenness of the call signals "the impossible" precisely insofar as it remains for intentional consciousness nonforeseeable, nonpresentable, and nonrepeatable; indeed, it does so in such a way that it signals a "radical unavailability," or what Derrida signals as a "phenomenological impossibility." Within this perspective stressing unavailability

---

a thought of lack and absence, despite his insistence on undecidability. Could not the thought of excess shared by all these thinkers finally call these tendencies into question?

or impossibility, radical givenness would exceed the category of "experience" for the intentional consciousness of any self-present I.[5]

In his attempt to distinguish between the giving of a gift and the economy of exchange, Derrida comes very close to Marion's thought of givenness as unavailability or abandon. On Derrida's reading, in order to avoid its reduction to a cycle of economic exchange, the gift and its giving cannot or must not be recognized as such. Giving must remain "without return." Thus, the gift and its giving could not be foreseen, made present in a presence, or repeated, for such foresight, presentation, or repetition would imply an identification of the gift that would allow for its calculation, exchange, or repayment—all of which would annul it as gift. If the gift remains "without return," then "relation" to the gift would be characterized, paradoxically, by surprise, forgetting, and non-recognition. In other words, it would constitute a relation "without relation" that occurs within a paradoxical temporality that, like Kierkegaard's instant, "tears time apart" and disrupts the self-identity of the subject. Indeed, in the measure that subjectivity and its temporality imply for Derrida (as for Marion) a circle of self-identity, a circle wherein the subject relates itself to itself, discovers, maintains, and reproduces itself, the gift would remain incompatible with the subject and its constitutive experience, the truth of whose temporal movement and language I explicated in Hegel—and precisely in Hegel Derrida finds the exemplary case of subjectivity in its circular economy.

Now if the necessary "nonreturn" of the gift would disallow the subject's return to itself in the gift, then, as Derrida shows, the gift might bear a strong relation to death, insofar as death names that wherein the subject cannot return to itself, cannot discover itself, cannot be present to itself in its thought or language—in its experience. And if Marion does not think death and the gift together in quite the intimate way that Derrida does, he nevertheless does think the paradox of radical givenness in terms of an incurably wounded subject that remains ever in delay with respect to itself. Constituted in the irreducible difference between the call of unconditional givenness and the inevitably incomplete response that would bear witness to such a call, Marion's *adonné* is never actually present or self-present to experience the call that brings it to birth—and such a birth therefore signals already the *adonné*'s essential finitude and

5. Indeed, it would impose a "counter-experience" that "offers the experience of that which contradicts the conditions of the experience of objects" (ED 300).

mortality. Like a gift that gives absolutely without ever being actually present, then, death might signal, for Derrida and Marion alike, that which gives all possibility even as it indicates the "impossibility" of the being whose ultimate possibility it is.

Now, if an absolute gift or giving, like death, remains associated with "the impossible," it remains the case also that one can still think and speak about it. Above all, one can still desire it. At this level, Derrida proves particularly helpful when he distinguishes between what is simply impossible, on the one hand, and *the* impossible, on the other. I take that distinction—which involves a critical response to Wittgenstein's "What we cannot speak about we must pass over in silence"—to indicate a difference between that "about which one [simply] cannot speak" and "that about which one cannot speak, *but which one can no longer silence.*" The impossible, precisely, would engender thought, speech, and desire that remain oriented around a term that thought, speech, or desire cannot finally attain as such. Indeed, it would be this very inaccessibility that engenders thought, speech, and desire in their radical openness, for they would live and move only so long as something yet remains to be thought, spoken, or desired. But what remains, radically, at every moment, yet to be thought, spoken, or desired is that possibility which cannot be reduced to actuality—the possibility, precisely, of "the impossible." The possibility that ever remains to be thought, spoken, or desired (the possibility of the impossible) indicates what is—irreducibly—*not yet* thought, spoken, or desired, what still and ever remains outstanding for thought and for language, for desire and the experience it would seek but not attain as such.

As I indicated in chapter 6, according to this Derridean perspective—which is echoed in Marion's approach to the radical incompletion of the response to givenness, the polyonomy that issues from a radical anonymity—the impossible is not simply opposed to the possible but remains that around which the possible ever circles, or that toward which it moves without arriving. For both Derrida and Marion, thought and language remain radically open to the degree that "the impossible" ever remains yet to be thought or expressed. This openness indicates the decisive character of the relation between possibility and the impossible: *the* impossible, insofar as it always remains outstanding, indicates the radical possibility of an ever remaining "not yet." The "not yet" on which all possibility feeds (since without it, one is absorbed already in actuality) would itself appear in its most fundamental form as *the* impossible.

In Heidegger, as I have been suggesting, the radical possibility of the impossible, the "not yet" that ever remains while never being reduced to something actual, is indicated in terms of the anxious "Being-toward-death" of the essentially finite being. In Dionysius, an equally radical possibility, an equally irreducible "not yet," is named in and through the endless, restless desire of the created soul for God. This analogy can be pursued and specified further according to my two main categories of temporality and language.

Both Being-toward-death and the mystical path of Dionysius can be characterized by their ecstatic structure and temporality of radical *expectation*. Called to be from nothing, the soul in Dionysius ex-ists, according to an endless desire, between that nothing from which it is called and the incomprehensible, ineffable, ever desired God who, himself nothing, would give the call. The thrown basis of a nullity, Dasein ex-ists temporally, according to the structures and movement of radical possibility, between a past that was never present and a future, in death, that never arrives. As against Hegel, one thus encounters in both Heideggerian and Dionysian thought a "not yet" that remains irreducible. For Dionysius, that "not yet" issues in the openness or endlessness of desire that characterizes the created soul's relation to God, for as I argued in chapter 5, the return to God in Dionysius does not lead to satiety (as does, e.g., the *apokatastasis* in Origen) but remains ever a movement forward, a straining-beyond, an *epektasis* without end (as developed notably in Gregory of Nyssa).[6] For Heidegger, an irreducible "not yet" is fundamental to finite temporality, which remains radically open precisely because it is finite. The irreducible character of futurity in the Heideggerian temporality ensues from the fact that the temporal being, Dasein, moves ever "between" the nullity of its thrownness and the horizon of a death that remains impossible. The radical futurity of this impossible death marks the return of Dasein's irrecuperable, an-archic past.[7]

6. On Gregory's important notion of infinite progress in desire, which grows out of God's fundamental incomprehensibility, see esp. the remarkable passages in *The Life of Moses* at 2:232–33 and 2:239. See also the numerous passages in Gregory's commentary on the Song of Songs (e.g., J.174/M.888; J.246–47/M.941; J.321/M.1000). The crucial difference between a thought of satiety and one of *epektasis* would have to do with whether one understands God to be limited or unlimited. As contrasted with Gregory, Origen holds that, in order to be knowable, God cannot be unlimited. On this, see Origen, *On First Principles*, book 2, chap. 9, § 1.

7. From this perspective, Marion's attempt to separate birth and existence in order to privilege the former would seem problematic. On this separation, see ED 399—which Marion himself seems to contradict when he recognizes (ED 408) that the "immemorial past" of the call that gives rise to my birth can and must be understood also

To the structure and temporality of radical expectation would correspond, again in both cases, an irreducible openness or incompletion of language. In Dionysius, the endless desire of a soul created ex nihilo is embodied or enacted, precisely, through an infinite naming of the nameless. As I indicated, the apophatic movement, which seeks to undo or pass beyond the affirmative names of God, in fact issues within a ceaseless play between affirmation and negation, a de-nomination where negation is redoubled without achieving synthesis. This play remains endless to the extent that the God toward whom such naming is directed remains both all in all (giving way to affirmation) and nothing in anything (calling for a redoubled negation or hyper-negation). The radical futurity of Heideggerian thought would likewise imply a structure of significance that keeps language gaping. Precisely because the finite temporality of Dasein remains fundamentally open, Dasein's hermeneutic Being cannot reach closure. The openness of Dasein's finite Being and its essentially hermeneutic existence stand in contrast to the closure of Hegel's infinite Being and the absolute knowledge in which it would be realized.

How might one understand or account for these analogical formulations of expectation and openness? At a fundamental level, both concern the relation between, on the one hand, a finite, ecstatic being's use of and determination by language, and, on the other hand, that which essentially eludes such language even as language constantly points toward it. In both cases that pointing-toward takes the form of an insurmountable "as."

From a Heideggerian perspective, language surrounding death necessarily maintains a gap between itself and that to which it refers: as long as the significance of language remains operative, Dasein exists and so has not "reached" the death of which it nevertheless speaks. There where Dasein would have "reached" death (strictly speaking, an impossibility), the significance of language would have collapsed absolutely. Thus, the "as" that characterizes discourse surrounding death can never be surmounted, precisely because Dasein can never experience death *as such*. As Derrida comments, "the impossibility of existing or of *Dasein* that Heidegger speaks of under the name of 'death' is the disappearance, the end, the annihilation of the *as such*, of the possibility of the relation to

---

in terms of "the future" where alone my responses would bear witness to the call and thus bring it to appearance.

the phenomenon *as such* or to the phenomenon '*as such*'" (AP 75).[8] Because death "as such" ever eludes Dasein, or, I would say, because death has no "such" insofar as it remains singular or incomparable, the language of death can only ever speak according to the "as." The language of death (which in the end means all language) thus circles around death, alludes to it, imagines it, seeks it out, indeed desires it—but never attains it. The gap between language and death "itself" remains constant and unbridgeable, and for precisely this reason a commentator like Derrida can pose the question: "Who will guarantee that the name, the ability to name death (like that of the naming of the other, and it is the same) does not participate as much in the dissimulation of the 'as such' of death as in its revelation, and that language is not precisely the origin of the nontruth of death, and of the other?" (AP 76). To bring death—or the other—to language would be, precisely, to dissimulate the "thing itself" by contradicting its defining otherness and irreducibility to language—as well as to consciousness, experience, and their "truth." In this sense, the naming of death would echo the naming of God.

And this is precisely what I tried to show from the Dionysian perspective, where all language pertaining to God would have to speak of God in the mode of an "as" that constitutes, in Marion's terms, an "index of inadequation" between our language and the God to whom it would refer.[9] Now, while one might wonder with Derrida whether the Dionysian language surrounding God does not in fact, unavoidably, identify or determine that God within an effort to distinguish between more and less adequate modes of language, greater and lesser degrees of "truth" or "reality" in theological discourse, it remains the case also that such language seeks finally and explicitly to stress the absolute ineffability of that around or toward which it moves. This becomes especially clear in the theological language that pertains to the moment of mystical unknow-

8. For illuminating analysis of the paradoxes binding death and the "as such," and on the difficulties thus posed for Heidegger's distinction between the authentic and the inauthentic, see esp. AP 72–77.

9. Michael Sells's *Mystical Languages of Unsaying* (Chicago: University of Chicago Press, 1994) provides an insightful analysis of apophatic language's fundamental openness—which he sees as a function of its self-critical character: "Apophasis is a discourse in which any single proposition is acknowledged as falsifying, as reifying. It is a discourse of double propositions, in which meaning is generated through the tension between the saying and the unsaying" (p. 12). On the basis of his close textual analyses, Sells is able to develop a very helpful schematic and formal account of the principles of apophatic language (see esp. pp. 207–9).

ing: language simply cannot articulate that "place" or "moment" where God and soul would be unified, for "there" the subject of language would be undone.[10] There where God gives himself most fully or excessively, the created soul simply cannot find itself in the self-presence of its own thought or language—and thus the excess of God does finally exceed the distinction of presence and absence. Thought and language pertaining to the mystical unknowing of God, therefore, can only circle around that God in an endless proliferation that signals an insatiable—and unknowing—desire.

Toward a Mystical Thanatology: The Apophatic Analogy

Now, in attempting to establish, according to radical expectation and the irreducible openness of language, this analogy between Being-toward-death and the mystical unknowing of God, one should rightly ask: what significance might one attach to such an analogy? Does it attempt somehow to identify death and God? To reduce God to death or make of death a God? Does it involve some confusion between a negative language of the divine and a negative language of the human, between a theological mysticism and an anthropological thanatology? Not at all. Indeed, any such identification, reduction, or confusion would prove impossible for reasons inherent to the analogy itself: one could not identify two terms whose referents "in themselves" remain, strictly speaking, beyond the thought and language, beyond the knowledge and experience—in short, beyond the truth of the self-present subject. In both Being-toward-death and mystical unknowing, the final term of relation remains beyond identification and never becomes the content or object of a knowing experience. In this sense both God and death might prove to be, as Blanchot—or Dionysius—would put it, "without truth."

The type of analogy involved here, therefore, is, first, one of relation, not attribution: the being of Dasein in relation to the possibility of its impossible death is analogous to the created soul's naming of the unnameable God with whom it would be unified in mystical unknowing. One cannot say that Being-toward-death and mystical unknowing are "the same" relation because in each case the final term of relation is itself strictly unknown and unknowable. Indeed, the analogy holds precisely

10. Sells argues that the apophatic moment where language undoes itself functions as a "meaning event" that constitutes a "mimetic reenactment" of the moment of mystical union. On this, see Sells, *Mystical Languages of Unsaying*, pp. 6–10 and 213–17.

insofar as each relation contains such an unknown term—thus preventing any clear identification either of those terms or of the relations.

For this very same reason, however, an indiscretion creeps in, and one cannot securely or definitively say that the terms or relations remain wholly distinct. Because the analogy occurs between two relations to terms that are "in themselves" unknowable and indeterminate, one is prohibited from identifying those terms or relations. But insofar as the analogy indeed arises, one is compelled to ask how these two relations to two unknowns might come to illuminate one another—precisely *as* relations to unknowns. The analogy I have suggested between Dasein's relation to death and the created soul's unknowing relation to the unknowable God becomes fruitful in the measure that such a death and such a God might be thought together, indiscretely—as neither identical nor wholly distinct. Toward that end, the appropriate analogy is, second, itself apophatic: oscillating *between* distinction and identification, it would have constantly to unsay both whatever similarities and whatever differences it might assert.

One could still object here that such a project calls for some kind of further warrant and confirmation—since Dionysius does not fully or systematically elaborate mystical unknowing in terms of death and since Heidegger does not tie death to any God. Such confirmation can be found in two directions: in the history of mystical traditions, where the language of death and the language of unknowing union with God have in fact been used to illuminate one another; and in the genesis of Heideggerian thought, which may well prove indebted to precisely those historical traditions.

On the one hand, as Alois Haas substantially demonstrates in his study, "*Mors Mystica:* Thanatologie der Mystik, inbesondere der Deutschen Mystik,"[11] the uses of "death" language to articulate or describe the mystical moment have a rich, varied history within the Christian traditions.[12] Arguing that such a history could support, and indeed that it demands, a systematic "thanatology," Haas opposes the view that

11. Alois Haas, "*Mors Mystica:* Thanatologie der Mystik, inbesondere der Deutschen Mystik,"*Freiburger Zeitschrift für Philosophie und Theologie*, vol. 23, no. 3 (1976): 304–92 (reprinted in *Sermo Mysticus: Studien zu Theologie und Sprache der Deutschen Mystik* [Swiss Freiburg: Universitätsverlag, 1979]); hereafter cited parenthetically as MM. Translations are my own.

12. Such a history can be found also in Judaism. On this, see Michael Fishbane's recent work, *The Kiss of God: Spiritual and Mystical Death in Judaism* (Seattle: University of Washington Press, 1994).

mysticism has to do primarily "with a living experience of timeless being and therefore the consciousness of the unreality of death."[13] To the contrary, Haas will argue, "the mystical experience can (not must) be a death-experience (*Todeserfahrung*), either because death is the best and most adequate representational sphere (*Vorstellungsbereich*) for the event of the self's undoing (*Entselbstung*), or else because death *is* the reality of the mystical entrance into God" (MM 348).

As I myself have been indicating, so for Haas, from *this* side of mystical experience, that is, from within the thought and language where we might discuss, describe, or evoke that which finally eludes our thought and language, the "metaphor" of death always signals a gap between sign and referent. For Haas this gap is indicated by the *quasi:* "Never has a Christian mystic doubted that our dying in uniting with God is, here below, always encumbered with a *quasi*" (MM 351).

According to the thesis I have been pursuing, however, I would reverse the reasoning by which Haas accounts for this *quasi*. Haas maintains that "*without* translation, *without* the figuration (*Verbildlichung*) of death, this experience (of the power of death) would be impossible; and the experience is not definitive, because it rests on an image (*Bild*) and a comparison and is not yet completely the thing itself" (MM 351). Distinguishing between, on the one hand, the various tropes used in relation to death, and, on the other hand, the "thing itself" (death) to which they might refer, Haas argues that such tropes make the experience of death *possible*.

However, within the understanding of death I have developed here, one might well argue, term for term, the reverse: it is precisely because death remains a form of the *impossible*, because death "as such" or death "itself" can never actually give the object or content of an *experience*, that the language surrounding death remains irreducibly figurative, metaphorical, or translational. On this understanding, the term that might be thought to ground metaphor or secure translation is essentially inaccessible. The "not yet" of death, which Haas himself signals, remains from my perspective insurmountable; death never becomes the "thing itself" of an experience, and precisely for that reason the language surrounding death remains open—and comes indiscretely close to a language of the unnameable God.

When mystical discourse appeals to its "experience" in terms of "death," it would signal the sense in which, like death, the mystical mo-

---

13. R. C. Zaehner, quoted in MM, p. 348, n. 147.

ment can in fact *not* be articulated in the terms or categories of what we commonly know and express as experience.[14] The incommensurability of (at least certain) mystical moments with the structures and categories of common experience—that is, the proximity of the mystical to "the impossible"—can be precisely what leads to the openness, depth, and richness of language surrounding the mystical. Such language would proliferate endlessly precisely because it ever circles around a term that it never grasps "as such." On a certain reading, then, and in certain (not all) instances, the most negative movements of mystical language and logic might concern not an experience of absence but rather an absence of experience[15]—or even better, a point of indiscretion where this distinction would itself collapse.

14. On this point I am in a certain agreement with Sells, who, citing Wayne Proudfoot's *Religious Experience* (Berkeley: University of California Press, 1985), p. 192, argues that the nonintentional character of the mystical moment prohibits description of it in terms of "experience." On this, see Sells, *Mystical Languages of Unsaying*, p. 214: "The nonintentional aspect of apophasis runs up against the modern concept of experience: 'Religious experience is the experience of something. It is intentional in that it cannot be described without reference to a grammatical object. Just as fear is always fear of something, and a perceptual act can only be described by reference to its object, a religious experience must be identified under a certain description, and that description must include a reference to the object of experience' [Proudfoot, p. 192]. If the nonintentionality claims of apophatic mystics are taken seriously, and if experience is, by definition, intentional, it necessarily follows that mystical union is not an experience. All experience must have a grammatical object, but the prime motivation of apophatic language is to subvert or displace the grammatical object."

My main disagreement with Sells here concerns the contention that "all experience" requires an object. Some experience, such as the experience of *anxiety* (to cite perhaps the best known case—and one related with equal force to God or death), could in fact be defined, precisely, by its *lack* of object. This becomes clear in the analyses of Kierkegaard, Heidegger (see chap. 4 above), and even Freud, where, as distinct from fear, which is always fear *of* something and thus always has an object, anxiety has no object, or is occasioned by "nothing." In this sense, anxiety would "subvert or displace" the grammatical object in a manner similar to the apophatic moment in Sells, but it might remain nonetheless an experience.

15. This is the approach taken recently in a fine study by Denys Turner, who argues against the "positivism" involved in "the contemporary preoccupation with mysticism as 'experience,'" in *The Darkness of God: Negativity in Christian Mysticism* (Cambridge: Cambridge University Press, 1995), p. 262. For Turner's development of the distinction between the experience of absence and the absence of experience, see pp. 259–65. For a caution on Turner's possible overstatement of the case against experience in mystical traditions, see Bernard McGinn's review of *The Darkness of God* in *Journal of Religion* (Winter 1997). As my argument suggests, I believe that the indiscretion of apophatic analogy might eventually unsettle—while still exploiting—Turner's very powerful distinction. It might likewise unsettle a related distinction that appears (with very

Thus, following God's assertion in Exodus that "no one shall see me and live," the mystical—especially Dionysian—traditions themselves (e.g., from Bonaventure to Porete and Eckhart to Angelus Silesius) have at times articulated the most intimate relation to God in terms of a death or dispossession of the soul. Haas's work substantiates this, and future research will need further to draw out its significance—especially in relation to contemporary forms of negative anthropology (e.g., in figures from Nietzsche and Bataille to Levinas and Blanchot).[16]

On the other hand, a second confirmation arises from the direction of Heideggerian thought in its own genesis: it could well be that the Heideggerian analysis of death proves illuminating with respect to the mystical traditions because the Heideggerian understanding of finitude and temporality is already indebted to those traditions, as the work of Thomas Sheehan, John van Buren, and Theodore Kisiel very strongly suggests.[17] Again, future research will need further to elaborate this question.

---

different senses) in both Marion and Altizer: the distinction between a naming of absence and an absence of naming. See IED 232 and Altizer, *Total Presence*, p. 26.

16. For a preliminary attempt in this direction, see my essay, "The Poverty and Poetry of Indiscretion: Negative Theology and Negative Anthropology in Contemporary and Historical Perspective," *Christianity and Literature* 17, no. 2 (Winter 1998).

17. Theodore Kisiel and John van Buren, building on and expanding earlier studies by Thomas Sheehan, argue convincingly that the Heidegger who would explicate the character of finite existence in *Being and Time* had found during the decade just previous to that work a fundamental source both in Pauline eschatology and in medieval mysticism. In reading such Dionysian heirs as Bonaventure and Eckhart (in addition to other mystics such as Bernard of Clairvaux, Francis of Assisi, and Teresa of Avila), Heidegger found windows opening onto "primal" Christian themes that would become important to his analysis of finite existence. In the years just prior to the publication of *Being and Time*, then, Heidegger was reading and teaching mystics—and Dionysians—for whom the mystical moment is often most forcefully articulated as a form of "death."

In Kisiel's book, *The Genesis of Heidegger's "Being and Time"* (Berkeley: University of California Press, 1993), see esp. chap. 2, "Theo-logical Beginnings: Toward a Phenomenology of Christianity," and chap. 4, "The Religion Courses (1920–21)." In van Buren's *The Young Heidegger: Rumor of the Hidden King* (Bloomington: Indiana University Press, 1994), see esp. chaps. 6–8 and 14, which treat "Mysticism, Ontotheology, Antimodernism," "Demythologizing Metaphysics," "Primal Christianity," and "The Mystery of All Life." For crucial background see Sheehan's "Heidegger's 'Introduction to the Phenomenology of Religion,' 1920–21," in *The Personalist* 55 (1979–80): 312–24. Also helpful on Heidegger's early engagement with Christian thought is chap. 1 of John D. Caputo's *Heidegger and Aquinas: An Essay on Overcoming Metaphysics* (New York: Fordham University Press, 1982), "Heidegger's Beginnings and the Project of a Dialogue with Scholasticism." The pertinent early works of Heidegger on religion are now available

In Conclusion

One cannot ignore the existence and importance of traditions that bring together, on the one hand, deeply apophatic approaches to the mystical unknowing of God and, on the other hand, a thought concerning the finite being who, by definition, cannot be present in its death.

Consistent with the analogy of relation that I have signaled between Dionysius's apophatic unknowing and Heideggerian Being-toward-death, one would find in later Dionysian traditions both an intimate relation between the abandonment of beings and the dissolution or death of self, on the one hand, and, on the other, the enactment of such relation within a movement of love or desire whose endlessness is signaled through an openness of language that arises from the groundless "ground" of a radical apophaticism. Because the individual soul cannot be self-present there where the fullest union with God would occur, it cannot directly know, name, or represent the givenness of God within that union. As I have shown, language and representation surrounding the most intimate union with God or the most intense presence/absence of God, language that ever stands "this side" of that union or presence/absence, is constantly qualified by an "as"—and precisely that qualification keeps language open even as it marks language's failure or silence. Likewise according to the conception of death that I developed in the Heideggerian context, the constitutively finite being, Dasein, cannot be present, cannot itself *be* "there" where death would have occurred, for death marks the very collapse of the "there." Language surrounding the nonplace of death therefore remains an irreducibly open language, ever circling round a term that "in itself" or "as such" would mark language's utter collapse, for the structures of the "there" are the very structures of significance on which language and discourse would depend.

According to the indiscretion I have tried to signal through the apophatic analogy, objections that would insist here on a distinction between Dionysian presence and Heideggerian absence, or between super-plenitude and utter emptiness, could be answered by reemphasizing the radical *unknowing* that is operative both in Being-toward-death and in apophatic mysticism. When such unknowing is taken to its extreme, when it is pushed to the point of indiscretion, such distinctions may well be devastated. Where, then, would such an indiscretion leave us?

---

in vol. 60 of the *Gesamtausgabe: Phänomenologie des Religiösen Lebens* (Frankfurt am Main: Vittorio Klostermann, 1995).

If onto-theology in its modern, Hegelian consummation, finds a point of resistance in the Heideggerian conception of finitude according to which, in its death, finite existence cannot find itself in the self-presence of its thought or language; and if, in turn, mystical unknowing in the Dionysian framework likewise represents a point at which the subject of thought and language no longer finds itself in any self-presence; then, like the Heideggerian thought of finitude, a Dionysian conception of goodness, which grounds that mystical unknowing, might also be said to resist or elude the bounds of onto-theology. In this light, the destruction of the subject that reaches its completion in the modernity of Hegel's onto-theology could carry us beyond the Hegelian death of God to a thought of finitude in its possible relation to incomprehensible goodness.

This would require and invite further elaboration of the ties between negative theology and negative anthropology in both historical and contemporary terms. Clearly, the fascination today with negative languages of God in classical contexts is tied to the negative languages of self that dominate thinkers in the "post-" age. We need further to investigate both what negative languages concerning God might imply about the human subject in traditional contexts and, likewise, what negative languages concerning the human subject might imply about God in the contemporary world. Both traditionalists and postmoderns may be surprised by the indiscretions that eventually bind them each to the other. It will remain, then, from both historical and contemporary perspectives, to determine the boundaries and to exploit the ambiguities between the experience of absence and the absence of experience in both the theological and the thanatological spheres—and more broadly in all those aporetic instances toward which these might point, insofar as "death, as the possibility of the impossible *as such*, is a figure of the aporia in which 'death' and death can replace . . . all that is only possible as impossible, if there is such a thing: love, the gift, the other, testimony, and so forth" (AP 79). Insofar as religion may well concern what eludes experience at least as much as what fills it, the significance of religion for an exploration of such possibility and impossibility is, and will remain, incalculable. The "apophatic analogy," then, would promise to be indispensable for an articulation and elaboration of that significance—even as such analogy exceeds the religious sphere to touch others such as the ethical and the aesthetic.

I have tried to signal that promise here by posing the question of "experience" and its relation to "the gift" in theological and thanatological terms. As we saw, "experience" provided the central concept according to which Heidegger engaged Hegel in order to signal the insufficiency of Hegel's interpretation of finitude. In contrast to that insufficiency, I argued, stands the Heideggerian understanding of finitude according to which the absolute horizon of finitude, death, marks the "possibility of impossibility"—a possibility, in other words, that remains irreducible to the actuality of experience. When, inheriting a Heideggerian approach to the possibility of impossibility, both Derrida and Marion formulate the paradoxes of "gift" in terms of "the impossible," I take them to be indicating an essential incommensurability between, on the one hand, "gift" as "the impossible" and, on the other hand, experience as it pertains to an actuality that is (or becomes) present to a self-present subject. That incommensurability, however, does not indicate a mere separation or simple disjunction, since the gift that eludes experience at the same time *gives* experience, since "the impossible" opens and sustains the movement of the possible. The importance of the disagreement between Marion and Derrida over the precise limits of onto-theology seems finally to diminish in light of this more fundamental point of agreement concerning the relation of the gift to the impossible. On the reading that I myself attempted, which grows directly from that point of agreement, "the impossible" would signal a gift or giving of experience that itself remains beyond experience, and in this sense the question of gift and the question of experience prove inextricable. A phenomenology of the gift in terms of the impossible offers us the means for an account of possible experience in relation to its constitutive limits.

The realm of apophatic mysticism here proves crucial because it both demands such a phenomenology and at the same time offers the substantial terrain on which to develop one. Indeed, a paradigmatic instance of the relation between the "gift" and "the impossible" must be seen in that mystical moment where the subject of experience is undone by precisely the God, ineffable and incomprehensible, who gives all experience. The relation here works two ways: a phenomenology of the gift illuminates certain forms of mysticism even as those forms instruct that phenomenology and put it to the test. This interplay seems to me precisely what needs to be articulated and exploited in a contemporary philosophy of religion—that is, in a philosophy of religion where the philosophical and the religious might betray a common debt to that which exceeds them. The "philosophy of religion" in this context would have not to avoid or resolve but rather to explore and exploit the incalculable ambiguities that would mark the indiscrete interplay of two fields which, via the apophatic analogy, remain neither wholly distinct nor ever yet identical. The one could always prove both greater and smaller than the other.

If the end of metaphysics and the opening of all the various "post-" ages involve necessarily a critique of the modern (or at least Hegelian) subject and an encounter with its death of God, they involve equally, indissolubly, a questioning with regard to the category of experience—and that questioning can find a resource and testing ground in the paradoxical experience or nonexperience of the mystics. "Experience" itself has become problematic today. How to interpret experience, how to convey it, how to share it, indeed, how simply to have it, all remain questionable for more than a few. In light of my study, I would suggest that this problematic character of experience is in fact perfectly suitable to the category itself—in both contemporary and traditional contexts. If experience implies a trial or a test, if it is bound up essentially with the aporetics and apophatics of what goes unexperienced, then the category of experience ought rightly to remain problematic. This point is undoubtedly lost on those within the sphere of religious studies (and elsewhere) for whom an appeal to "experience" would serve as the primary and unshakable (because unquestioned) standard by which religious (or other "authentic") phenomena ought to be identified, approached, interpreted, and evaluated. Within such an appeal, "experience" is used to ground and settle interpretation when, in fact, it ought rightly to upset and provoke interpretation. With regard especially to mysticism, the appeal to experience can be all too automatic and all too secure. I have tried here to show, to the contrary, that at the very heart of mystical experience there can lie a certain "nonexperience," a certain "impossibility" of experience for the subject of experience. Likewise, at the very heart of life there can lie a "death" that would mark the impossible. It is precisely this nonexperience at the center of experience, this death at the center of life, that leads me to consider "experience" on the basis of the "gift" and its paradoxes. For in the end, I think, this nonexperience at the center of experience, this death at the center of life, does fundamentally *give*: it gives to our thinking and language their movement, to our desire its force, to our experience its possibility.

BIBLIOGRAPHY

Agamben, Giorgio. *Language and Death: The Place of Negativity.* Trans. Karen Pinkus and Michael Hardt. Minneapolis: University of Minnesota Press, 1991.

Altizer, Thomas J. J. *Genesis and Apocalypse.* Louisville: Westminster/John Knox, 1990.

———. *The Genesis of God.* Louisville: Westminster/John Knox, 1993.

———. *Radical Theology and the Death of God.* With William Hamilton. New York: Bobbs-Merrill, 1966.

———. *The Self-Embodiment of God.* New York: Harper and Row, 1977.

———. *Total Presence.* New York: Seabury Press, 1980.

Anderson, Delan S. *Hegel's Speculative Good Friday: The Death of God in Philosophical Perspective.* Atlanta: Scholars Press, 1996.

Aquinas, Thomas. *Summa Theologica.* Trans. Fathers of the English Dominican Province. New York: Benziger Brothers, 1947.

Aristotle. *The Complete Works.* Ed. Jonathan Barnes. Princeton, New Jersey: Princeton University Press, 1984.

Aubenque, Pierre. "La Question de l'onto-théologie chez Aristote et Hegel." In Koninck and Planty-Bonjour, pp. 259–83.

Augustine. *On Christian Doctrine.* Trans. D. W. Robertson Jr. New York: Macmillan Publishing Company, 1958.

Balthasar, Hans Urs von. *The Glory of the Lord.* New York: Crossroad, 1984.

Barth, Karl. *Protestant Thought: From Rousseau to Ritschl.* Salem, New Hampshire: Ayer Company, 1987.

Bataille, Georges. *Erotism: Death and Sensuality.* Trans. Mary Dalwood. San Francisco: City Lights Books, 1986.

———. *Inner Experience.* Trans. Leslie Anne Boldt. Albany: State University of New York Press, 1988.

———. *Theory of Religion.* Trans. Robert Hurley. New York: Zone Books, 1989.

Beaufret, Jean. *Dialogue avec Heidegger.* Paris: Editions de Minuit, 1973.

Beierwaltes, Werner. *Platonismus und Idealismus.* Frankfurt am Main: V. Klostermann, 1972.

Bernauer, James. *Michel Foucault's Force of Flight: Toward an Ethics for Thought.* Atlantic Highlands, New Jersey: Humanities Press International, 1990.

———. "The Prisons of Man: An Introduction to Foucault's Negative Theology." *International Philosophical Quarterly*, vol. 27, no. 4 (December 1987): 365–80.

Blanchot, Maurice. *L'Ecriture du désastre*. Paris: Gallimard, 1980.

———. *The Writing of the Disaster.* Trans. Ann Smock. Lincoln: University of Nebraska Press, 1986.

Bonaventure. *Itinerarium mentis in Deum*. In Henry Duméry, ed., *L'Itinéraire de l'esprit vers Dieu*. Paris: J. Vrin, 1960.

———. *The Soul's Journey into God*. In *Bonaventure*, trans. Ewert Cousins. New York: Paulist Press, 1978.

Brague, Rémi, and Jean-François Courtine, eds. *Herméneutique et ontologie*. Paris: Presses Universitaires de France, 1990.

Budick, Sanford, and Wolfgang Iser, eds. *Languages of the Unsayable: The Play of Negativity in Literature and Literary Theory*. New York: Columbia University Press, 1989.

Cadava, Eduardo, Peter Connor, and Jean-Luc Nancy. *Who Comes after the Subject?* New York: Routledge, 1991.

Caputo, John D. *Against Ethics: Contributions to a Poetics of Obligation with Constant Reference to Deconstruction*. Bloomington: Indiana University Press, 1993.

———. *Heidegger and Aquinas*. New York: Fordham University Press, 1982.

———. "Instants, Secrets, Singularities: Dealing Death in Kierkegaard and Derrida." In Martin Matuštík and Merold Westphal, eds., *Kierkegaard in Post/Modernity*. Bloomington: Indiana University Press, 1995.

———. *The Mystical Element in Heidegger's Thought*. Athens: Ohio University Press, 1978.

———. *The Prayers and Tears of Jacques Derrida: Religion without Religion*. Bloomington: Indiana University Press, 1997.

Certeau, Michel de. *La Fable mystique: XVIe–XVIIe siècle*. Paris: Gallimard, 1982.

———. *The Mystic Fable*. Volume 1: *The Sixteenth and Seventeenth Centuries*. Trans. Michael B. Smith. Chicago: University of Chicago Press, 1992.

Charles-Saget, Annick. "*Aphairesis* et *Gelassenheit*, Heidegger et Plotin." In Brague and Courtine, pp. 323–44.

Corbin, Michel. "Négation et transcendance dans l'oeuvre de Denys." *Revue des sciences philosophiques et théologiques* 69 (1985): 41–76.

Corrigan, Kevin. "Ecstasy and Ectasy in Some Early Pagan and Christian Mystical Writings." In William J. Carrol and John J. Furlong, eds., *Greek and Medieval Studies in Honor of Leo Sweeney, S.J.* New York: P. Lang, 1994.

Courtine, Jean-François, ed. *Phénoménologie et théologie*. Paris: Criterion, 1992.

Coward, Harold, and Toby Foshay, eds. *Derrida and Negative Theology*. New York: State University of New York Press, 1992.

Derrida, Jacques. *Aporias*. Trans. Thomas Dutoit. Stanford, California: Stanford University Press, 1993.

———. "Différance." In *Margins of Philosophy*, trans. Alan Bass. Chicago: University of Chicago Press, 1982.

———. *Donner la mort, l'éthique du don, Jacques Derrida et la pensée du don*. Paris: Métailié-Transition, 1992.

———. *L'Ecriture et la différence*. Paris: Editions du Seuil, 1967.

———. *The Gift of Death*. Trans. David Wills. Chicago: University of Chicago Press, 1995.

———. *Given Time: I. Counterfeit Money*. Trans. Peggy Kamuf. Chicago: University of Chicago Press, 1992.

———. *Glas*. Paris: Denoël/Gonthier, 1981.

———. *De la grammatologie*. Paris: Editions de Minuit, 1967.

———. "How to Avoid Speaking: Denials." In Coward and Foshay, pp. 73–142.

———. *Margins of Philosophy*. Trans. Alan Bass. Chicago: University of Chicago Press, 1982.

———. *Psyché*. Paris: Galilée, 1987.

———. "Post-Scriptum: Aporias, Ways and Voices." In Coward and Foshay, pp. 283–323.

Dupré, Louis. "Transitions and Tensions in Hegel's Treatment of Determinate Religion." In Kolb, pp. 81–92.

Eckhart, Meister. "Von Abgescheidenheit." In Josef Quint, ed., *Die Deutschen Werke*, vol. 5 Stuttgart: W. Kohlhammer Verlag, 1963.

———. *Meister Eckhart: The Essential Sermons, Commentaries, Treatises and Defense*. Ed. Edmund Colledge and Bernard McGinn. New York: Paulist Press, 1981.

———. *Meister Eckhart: Teacher and Preacher*. Ed. Bernard McGinn. New York: Paulist Press, 1986.

———. *Parisian Questions and Prologues*. Toronto: Pontifical Institute of Medieval Studies, 1974.

Fackenheim, Emil. *The Religious Dimension in Hegel's Thought*. Chicago: University of Chicago Press, 1967.

Feuerbach, Ludwig. *The Essence of Christianity*. Trans. George Eliot. Buffalo, New York: Prometheus Books, 1989.

———. *Principles of the Philosophy of the Future.* Trans. Manfred H. Vogel. Indianapolis: Hackett Publishing Company, 1986.

Fishbane, Michael. *The Kiss of God: Spiritual and Mystical Death in Judaism.* Seattle: University of Washington Press, 1994.

Gadamer, Hans-Georg. *Hegel's Dialectic.* Trans. P. Christopher Smith. New Haven, Connecticut: Yale University Press, 1976.

Garaudy, Roger. *Dieu est mort: Etude sur Hegel.* Paris: Presses Universitaires de France, 1962.

Gersh, Stephen. *From Iamblichus to Eriugena.* Leiden: Brill, 1978.

Gregory of Nyssa. *Commentary on the Song of Songs.* Trans. Casimir McCambley. Brookline, Massachusetts: Hellenic College Press, 1987.

———. *The Life of Moses.* Trans. Abraham J. Malherbe and Everett Ferguson. New York: Paulist Press, 1978.

Haas, Alois. "*Mors Mystica:* Thanatologie der Mystik, inbesondere der Deutschen Mystik." *Freiburger Zeitschrift für Philosophie und Theologie,* vol. 23, no. 3 (1976): 304–92.

Hadot, Pierre. "Heidegger et Plotin." *Critique* (June 1959).

Hart, Kevin. *Trespass of the Sign: Deconstruction, Philosophy and Theology.* Cambridge: Cambridge University Press, 1989.

Hegel, G. W. F. *Early Theological Writings.* Trans. T. M. Knox. Philadelphia: University of Pennsylvania Press, 1975.

———. *The Difference between Fichte's and Schelling's System of Philosophy.* Trans. Walter Cerf and H. S. Harris. Albany: State University of New York Press, 1977.

———. *Faith and Knowledge.* Trans. Walter Cerf and H. S. Harris. Albany: State University of New York Press, 1977.

———. *Hegel's Logic.* Trans. J. N. Findlay. Oxford: Clarendon Press, 1975.

———. *Lectures on the Philosophy of Religion.* Ed. Peter Hodgson. Berkeley: University of California Press, 1988.

———. *Phänomenologie des Geistes.* Ed. Wolfgang Bonsiepen and Reinhard Heede. In *Gesammelte Werke,* vol. 9. Hamburg: Felix Meiner Verlag, 1980.

———. *Phenomenology of Spirit.* Trans. A. V. Miller. Oxford: Oxford University Press, 1977.

———. *The Philosophical Propaedeutic.* Trans. A. V. Miller. Oxford: Basil Blackwell, 1986.

———. *Elements of the Philosophy of Right.* Ed. Allen Wood. Cambridge: Cambridge University Press, 1991.

———. *Science of Logic.* Trans. W. H. Johnston and L. G. Struthers. New York: Humanities Press, 1966.

———. *Vorlesungen über die Philosophie der Religion.* Ed. Walter Jaeschke. In

Vorlesungen: Ausgewählte Nachschriften und Manuskripte, vols. 3–5. Hamburg: Felix Meiner Verlag, 1983, 1984, 1985.

———. *Wissenschaft der Logik*. Zweiter Band: *Die Subjektive Logik*. Ed. Friedrich Hogemann and Walter Jaeschke. In *Gesammelte Werke*, vol. 12. Hamburg: Felix Meiner Verlag, 1981.

Heidegger, Martin. *The Basic Problems of Phenomenology*. Trans. Albert Hofstadter. Bloomington: Indiana University Press, 1982.

———. *Being and Time*. Trans. J. Macquarrie and E. Robinson. Oxford: Basil Blackwell.

———. "Hegels Begriff der Erfahrung." In *Holzwege*.

———. *Hegel's Concept of Experience*. New York: Harper and Row, 1970.

———. *Hegels Phänomenologie des Geistes*. In the *Gesamtausgabe*, vol. 32. Frankfurt am Main: Vittorio Klostermann, 1980.

———. *Hegel's Phenomenology of Spirit*. Trans. P. Emad and K. Maly. Bloomington: Indiana University Press, 1988.

———. *Holzwege*. In the *Gesamtausgabe*, vol. 5. Frankfurt am Main: Vittorio Klostermann, 1977.

———. *Identität und Differenz*. Pfullingen: Günther Neske, 1957.

———. *Identity and Difference*. Trans. Joan Stambaugh. New York: Harper and Row, 1969.

———. "Letter on Humanism." In Krell, pp. 193–242.

———. *On Time and Being*. Trans. J. Stambaugh. New York: Harper and Row, 1977.

———. "Phenomenology and Theology." In *The Piety of Thinking*, trans. James G. Hart and John C. Maraldo. Bloomington: Indiana University Press, 1976.

———. *Sein und Zeit*. 16th ed. Tübingen: Max Niemeyer, 1986.

———. "A Seminar on Hegel's *Differenzschrift*." *Southwestern Journal of Philosophy*, vol. 11, no. 3 (Fall 1980): 9–43.

———. "What Is Metaphysics?" With the 1943 postscript and 1949 introduction ("The Way Back into the Ground of Metaphysics"). In Kaufmann, pp. 242–79.

Henry, Michel. "Quatres principes de la phénoménologie." *Revue de métaphysique et de morale* (January–March 1991): 3–26.

Husserl, Edmund. *Cartesian Meditations*. Trans. Dorion Cairns. Dordrecht: Martinus Nijhoff, 1960.

———. *Ideas Pertaining to a Pure Phenomenology and a Phenomenological Philosophy*. Trans. F. Kersten. The Hague: Martinus Nijhoff, 1982.

———. *The Idea of Phenomenology*. Trans. William P. Alston and George Nakhnikian. Dordrecht: Kluwer, 1990.

Hyppolite, Jean. *Genesis and Structure of Hegel's Phenomenology of Spirit.* Trans. S. Cherniak and J. Heckman. Evanston, Illinois: Northwestern University Press, 1974.

———. *Logique et existence.* Paris: Presses Universitaires de France, 1953.

Jaeschke, Walter. "Philosophical Theology and Philosophy of Religion." In Kolb, pp. 1–18.

———. *Reason in Religion: The Foundations of Hegel's Philosophy of Religion.* Trans. J. M. Stewart and P. C. Hodgson. Berkeley: University of California Press, 1990.

Janicaud, Dominique. *Le Tournant théologique de la phénoménologie française.* Combas: Editions de L'Eclat, 1991.

Jonas, Hans. "Heidegger and Theology." In *The Phenomenon of Life.* Chicago: University of Chicago Press, 1982.

Jüngel, Eberhard. *God as the Mystery of the World.* Trans. Darrell L. Guder. Grand Rapids, Michigan: William B. Eerdmans Publishing Company, 1983.

Kant, Immanuel. *Critique of Practical Reason.* Trans. Lewis White Beck. New York: Macmillan, 1985.

———. *Critique of Pure Reason.* Trans. Norman Kemp Smith. New York: St. Martin's, 1965.

———. *Groundwork of the Metaphysic of Morals.* Trans. H. J. Paton. New York: Harper and Row, 1964.

———. *Lectures on Philosophical Theology.* Trans. Allen Wood and Gertrude Clark. Ithaca, New York: Cornell University Press, 1978.

———. *Prolegomena to Any Future Metaphysics.* Trans. Paul Carus. Rev. James W. Ellington. Indianapolis: Hackett Publishing Company, 1977.

———. *Religion within the Limits of Reason Alone.* Trans. Greene and Hudson. New York: Harper and Row, 1960.

Kaufmann, Walter. *Existentialism from Dostoyevsky to Sartre.* New York: Penguin, 1975.

———. "The Young Hegel and Religion." In MacIntyre, pp. 61–99.

Kierkegaard, Søren. *The Concept of Anxiety.* Trans. Reidar Thomte. Princeton, New Jersey: Princeton University Press, 1980.

Kisiel, Theodore. *The Genesis of Heidegger's Being and Time.* Berkeley: University of California Press, 1993.

Klemm, David. "Open Secrets: Derrida and Negative Theology." In Scharlemann, pp. 8–24.

Kojève, Alexandre. *Introduction à la lecture de Hegel.* Paris: Gallimard, 1947.

———. *Introduction to the Reading of Hegel.* Trans. J. Nichols. Ithaca, New York: Cornell University Press, 1969.

Kolb, David, ed. *New Perspectives on Hegel's Philosophy of Religion.* Albany: State University of New York Press, 1992.

Koninck, Thomas, and Guy Planty-Bonjour, eds. *La Question de Dieu selon Aristote et Hegel.* Paris: Presses Universitaires de France, 1991.

Krell, David Farrel. "Hegel, Heidegger, Heraclitus." In Sallis and Maly, eds., *Heraclitean Fragments,* pp. 22–42.

———, ed. *Martin Heidegger: Basic Writings.* New York: Harper and Row, 1977.

Küng, Hans. *The Incarnation of God: An Introduction to Hegel's Theological Thought as Prolegomena to a Future Christology.* Trans. J. R. Stephenson. New York: Crossroad, 1987.

Lauer, Quentin. *Essays in Hegelian Dialectic.* New York: Fordham University Press, 1977.

———. *Hegel's Concept of God.* Albany: State University of New York Press, 1982.

———. "Hegel's Negative Theology." *Dharma,* vol. 6, no. 1 (1981): 46–82.

Levinas, Emmanuel. *De Dieu qui vient à l'idée.* Paris: J. Vrin, 1986.

———. *En Découvrant l'existence avec Husserl et Heidegger.* Paris: Vrin, 1988.

———. *Entre nous: Essais sur le penser-à-l'autre.* Paris: Grasset, 1991.

———. *Otherwise Than Being or Beyond Essence.* Trans. Alphonso Lingis. Boston: Martinus Nijhoff, 1981.

———. *Totality and Infinity.* Trans. Alphonso Lingis. The Hague, 1979.

MacIntyre, Alisdair, ed. *Hegel: A Collection of Critical Essays.* New York: Doubleday, 1972.

Marion, Jean-Luc. *La Croisée du visible.* Paris: Presses Universitaires de France, 1996.

———. *Etant donné: Essai d'une phénoménologie de la donation.* Paris: Presses Universitaires de France, 1997.

———. *God without Being.* Trans. Thomas A. Carlson. Chicago: University of Chicago Press, 1991.

———. *L'Idole et la distance.* Paris: Grasset, 1977.

———. "L'Interloqué." Trans. E. Cadava and Anne Tomiche. In Cadava, Connor, and Nancy, pp. 236–45.

———. "Metaphysics and Phenomenology: A Relief for Theology." Trans. Thomas A. Carlson. *Critical Inquiry,* vol. 20, no. 4 (Summer 1994): 572–91.

———. "De la 'mort de dieu' aux noms divins: L'Itinéraire théologique de la métaphysique." In *Laval théologique et philosophique,* vol. 41, no. 1 (February 1985): 25–41.

———. "Le Phénomène saturé." In Courtine, ed., *Phénoménologie et théologie,* pp. 79–128.

———. *Le Prisme métaphysique.* Paris: Presses Universitaires de France, 1986.

———. *Questions Cartésiennes*. Paris: Presses Universitaires de France, 1991.

———. *Reduction and Givenness: Investigations of Husserl, Heidegger, and Phenomenology*. Trans. Thomas A. Carlson. Evanston, Ill.: Northwestern University Press, 1998.

———. "Le sujet en dernier appel." *Revue de métaphysique et de morale* (January–March 1991): 77–95.

McGinn, Bernard. *Foundations of Mysticism*. Vol. 1 of *The Presence of God: A History of Western Christian Mysticism*. New York: Crossroad, 1991.

———. "God as Eros: Metaphysical Foundations of Christian Mysticism." In *Historical Theology and the Unity of the Church: Essays in Honor of John Meyendorff*. Grand Rapids, Michigan: William B. Eerdmans Publishing Company, 1995.

———. *The Growth of Mysticism*. Vol. 2 of *The Presence of God: A History of Western Christian Mysticism*. New York: Crossroad, 1994.

———. "Pseudo-Dionysius and the Early Cistercians." In M. Basil Pennington, ed., *One Yet Two: Monastic Tradition East and West*. Kalamazoo, Michigan: Cistercian Publications, 1976, pp. 200–241.

———, ed. *Meister Eckhart: Teacher and Preacher*. New York: Paulist Press, 1986.

———, and Edmund Colledge, eds. *Meister Eckhart: The Essential Sermons, Commentaries, Treatises and Defense*. New York: Paulist Press, 1981.

———, and John Meyendorff, eds. *Christian Spirituality: Origins to the Twelfth Century*. New York: Crossroad, 1988.

Nancy, Jean-Luc. *The Birth to Presence*. Trans. Brian Holmes. Stanford, California: Stanford University Press, 1993.

———. *Des lieux divins*. Mauvezin: Trans-Europ-Repress, 1987.

Olson, Alan. *Hegel and the Spirit*. Princeton, New Jersey: Princeton University Press, 1992.

O'Meara, Dominic J., ed. *Neoplatonism and Christian Thought*. Albany: State University of New York Press, 1982.

O'Regan, Cyril. "Hegelian Philosophy of Religion and Eckhartian Mysticism." In Kolb, pp. 109– 29.

———. *The Heterodox Hegel*. Albany: State University of New York Press, 1994.

Origen. *On First Principles*. Trans. G. W. Butterworth. Gloucester, Massachusetts: Peter Smith, 1973.

Pippin, Robert B. *Hegel's Idealism: The Satisfactions of Consciousness*. Cambridge: Cambridge University Press, 1989.

———. *Modernism as a Philosophical Problem*. Oxford: Basil Blackwell, 1991.

Plato. *The Collected Dialogues*. Ed. E. Hamilton and H. Cairns. Princeton, New Jersey: Princeton University Press, 1982.

Plotinus. *Enneads*. Ed. A. H. Armstrong. Cambridge, Massachusetts: Harvard University Press, 1966–68.

Proclus. *Commentary on Plato's "Parmenides."* Trans. G. Morrow and J. Dillon. Princeton, New Jersey: Princeton University Press, 1987.

———. *The Elements of Theology*. Ed. and trans. E. R. Dodds. Oxford: Clarendon, 1963.

———. *Proclus: Alcibiades I. A Translation and Commentary*. William O'Neill. The Hague: Martinus Nijhoff, 1965.

———. *Théologie Platonicienne*. Ed. H. D. Saffrey and L. G. Westerink. Paris: Belles Lettres.

Pseudo-Dionysius. *The Complete Works*. Trans. Colm Luibheid. New York: Paulist Press, 1987.

———. *Corpus Dionysiacum*. Vols. 1 and 2. Ed. Beate Regina Suchla, Günter Heil, and Adolf Martin Ritter. Berlin: Walter De Gruyter, 1990, 1991.

———. *Opera Omnia*. In J. P. Migne, ed., *Patrologiae cursus completus. Series graeca*, vol. 3. Paris, 1857–66.

Puech, Henri-Charles. *En Quête de la gnose*. Vol. 1. Paris: Gallimard, 1978.

Ricoeur, Paul. "Hegel aujourd'hui." *Etudes Théologiques et Religieuses* 49 (1974): 335–55.

———. "The Status of *Vorstellung* in Hegel's Philosophy of Religion." In L. Rouner, ed., *Meaning, Truth, and God*. South Bend, Indiana: University of Notre Dame Press, 1982.

Roques, René. "De l'implication des méthodes théologiques chez le pseudo-Denys." *Revue d'ascétique et de mystique* 119 (1954): 267–74.

———. *L'Univers dionysien*. Paris: Editions du Cerf, 1983.

———, et al. "Denys l'Aréopagite." In *Dictionnaire de Spiritualité*, vol. 3, pp. 244–429.

Rorem, Paul. *Pseudo-Dionysius: A Commentary on the Texts and an Introduction to Their Influence*. Oxford: Oxford University Press, 1993.

———. "The Uplifting Spirituality of Pseudo-Dionysius." In McGinn and Meyendorff, eds., *Christian Spirituality: Origins to the Twelfth Century*. New York: Crossroad, 1988, pp. 132–51.

Rosen, Stanley. *G. W. F. Hegel: An Introduction to the Science of Wisdom*. New Haven, Connecticut: Yale University Press, 1974.

Saffrey, H.-D. "New Objective Links between the Pseudo-Dionysius and Proclus." In Dominic J. O'Meara, ed., *Neoplatonism and Christian Thought*. Albany: State University of New York Press, 1982.

Sallis, John, and Kenneth Maly, eds. *Heraclitean Fragments*. University: University of Alabama Press, 1980.

Scharlemann, Robert P., ed. *Negation and Theology.* Charlottesville: University Press of Virginia, 1992.

Schultz, Walter. "Hegel und das Problem der Aufhebung der Metaphysik." In Günther Neske, ed., *Martin Heidegger zum Siebzigsten Geburtstag.* Pfullingen: Neske Verlag, 1959.

Schürmann, Reiner. *Heidegger on Being and Acting: From Principles to Anarchy.* Bloomington: Indiana University Press, 1987.

———. *Meister Eckhart, Mystic and Philosopher.* Bloomington: Indiana University Press, 1978.

Sells, Michael A. *Mystical Languages of Unsaying.* Chicago: University of Chicago Press, 1994.

Sheehan, Thomas. "Heidegger's 'Introduction to the Phenomenology of Religion.'" *The Personalist* (July 1979): 312–24.

Sheldon-Williams, I. P. "The Pseudo-Dionysius." In A. H. Armstrong, ed., *The Cambridge History of Later Greek and Early Medieval Philosophy.* Cambridge: Cambridge University Press, 1967.

Sikka, Sonya. *Forms of Transcendence: Heidegger and Medieval Mystical Theology.* Albany: State University of New York Press, 1997.

Surber, Jere Paul. "Hegel's Speculative Sentence." *Hegel-Studien* 10 (1975): 211–30.

Taminiaux, Jacques. *Dialectic and Difference.* Ed. J. Decker and R. Crease. Atlantic Highlands, New Jersey: Humanities Press, 1985.

———. *Heidegger and the Project of Fundamental Ontology.* Trans. Michael Gendre. Albany: State University of New York Press, 1991.

———. *Le Regard et l'excédent.* The Hague: Martinus Nijhoff, 1977.

Taylor, Charles. *Hegel.* New York: Cambridge University Press, 1975.

Taylor, Mark C. *Altarity.* Chicago: University of Chicago Press, 1987.

———. *Disfiguring: Art, Architecture, Religion.* Chicago: University of Chicago Press, 1992.

———. *Erring: A Postmodern A/theology.* Chicago: University of Chicago Press, 1984.

———. *"Itinerarium mentis in Deum:* Hegel's Proofs of God's Existence." *Journal of Religion,* vol. 57, no. 3 (July 1977).

———. *Journeys to Selfhood: Hegel and Kierkegaard.* Berkeley: University of California Press, 1980.

———. *Tears.* Albany: State University of New York Press, 1990.

Tomasic, Thomas Michael. "The Logical Function of Metaphor and Oppositional Coincidence in the Pseudo-Dionysius and Johannes Scottus Eriugena." *Journal of Religion* 68 (1988): 361–77.

Tracy, David. *The Analogical Imagination.* New York: Crossroad, 1981.

———. "Mystics, Prophets, Rhetorics: Religion and Psychoanalysis." In Françoise Meltzer, ed., *The Trial(s) of Psychoanalysis.* Chicago: University of Chicago Press, 1988, pp. 259–72.

———. *Plurality and Ambiguity: Hermeneutics, Religion, Hope.* San Francisco: Harper and Row, 1987.

Turner, Denys. *The Darkness of God: Negativity in Christian Mysticism.* Cambridge: Cambridge University Press, 1995.

Van Buren, John. *The Young Heidegger: Rumor of the Hidden King.* Bloomington: Indiana University Press, 1994.

Vanneste, Jan. "Is the Mysticism of Pseudo-Dionysius Genuine?" *International Philosophical Quarterly*, vol. 3, no. 2 (May 1963).

Waelhens, Alphonse de. "Identité et différence: Heidegger et Hegel." *Revue Internationale de Philosophie* 52 (1960): 221–37.

Wahl, Jean. *Le Malheur de la conscience dans la philosophie de Hegel.* Paris: Les Editions Rieder, 1929.

Weber, Max. "Science as a Vocation." In H. H. Gerth and C. Wright Mills, eds., *From Max Weber: Essays in Sociology.* New York: Oxford University Press, 1946.

Winquist, Charles. "Body, Text, and Imagination." In *Deconstruction and Theology.* New York: Crossroad, 1982.

———. "Theology: Unsettled and Unsettling." *Journal of the American Academy of Religion*, vol. 62, no. 4 (Winter 1994): 1023–34.

Wittgenstein, Ludwig. *Tractatus Logico-Philosophicus.* Trans. D. F. Pears and B. F. McGuinness. London: Routledge and Kegan Paul, 1961.

Wyschogrod, Edith. *Saints and Postmodernism: Revisioning Moral Philosophy.* Chicago: University of Chicago Press, 1990.

———, David Crownfield, and Carl A. Raschke, eds. *Lacan and Theological Discourse.* Albany: State University of New York Press, 1989.

Yannaras, Christos. *De l'absence et de l'inconnaissance de Dieu d'après les écrits aréopagitiques et Martin Heidegger.* Trans. Jacques Touraille. Paris: Editions du Cerf, 1971.

Yerkes, James. *The Christology of Hegel.* Missoula, Montana: Scholars Press, 1978.

INDEX

General

soul carried beyond, 247; essentially finite, 251, 259; timeless, 256. *See also* being-given, the
Being-a-basis, 145
Being-at-an-end, 139
Being-a-whole, 147
being-given, the: par excellence, God as, 211, 212
Being-guilty, 147
Being-in-the-world, 10, 15, 117–21, 128, 132–33, 135, 139, 140
Beingness, 54, 71–73
Being-possible, 121, 124–25, 133. *See also* Possibility; Potentiality; Potentiality-for-Being
Being-toward-death, 4, 15–16, 119, 130, 133–34, 137, 140–44, 147–48, 150–52, 231–32, 236, 244–45, 251, 254, 259
Being-toward-God, 4, 134n, 231, 236
Being-toward-the-end, 139
Bernard of Clairvaux, 258n
Bernauer, James, 6n
Between: the, of birth and death, 152; thrownness and death, 251
Bewandtnisse, 117. *See also* Involvement(s)
Bewußtsein, 57, 70. *See also* Consciousness
Bezug-zum-Tode, 116
Bild, 256. *See also* Image; Representation
Birth: and death, 152; divine, 171–72; and surprise, 204, 234; fact of, 224n; through the call, 249
Blanchot, Maurice, 117, 227n, 228n, 246n, 254, 258
Bloom, Allan, 13n
Body: name as, 93; spiritualized, of Christ, 110n
Boehme, Jacob, 111n, 156
Bonaventure, 8n, 10n, 258
Boss, Medard, 116n

Cadava, Eduardo, 19n, 116n
Calculation: and disenchantment, 32n; resistance of death to, 141; and gift, 221, 224, 249. *See also* Economy
Call: of conscience, 144; and creation, 159, 251; beauty as, 180; and givenness, 191, 203, 204, 249; an-archy of, 198; performed in response, 205; as gift, 206; source of, 207; anonymity of, 208; indeterminacy of, 213; every mortal preceded by, 228; naming and renaming of, 229; bearing all names and no names, 231;

theological and phenomenological, 248; and the future, 252n. *See also* Claim
Calvin, John, 134n
Caputo, John D., 5, 6, 7, 16, 17, 222n, 239n, 240n, 246n, 258n
Care, 117, 130–31, 134–38, 145–47, 149–52
Carlson, Thomas A., 115n, 258n
Carpino, Joseph, 13n
Category: inversion of, 201; Kantian, saturation of, 209; of experience, 257
Causality: of the *causa sui*, 55; efficient, 122; intermediate, 164; and manifestation, 178; of no-thing, 180; and positive names, 181; of the Good, 182
Causa sui, 55, 194, 195
Causation, 55
Cause: immanent and transcendent, 16, 177, 178, 180; first cause(s), 51n, 55; highest being as, 84, 102, 194; of anxiety, 132; God, the divine as, in Dionysius, 159, 160, 176, 191; transcendent, 175; nothing as, 180, 185; final, 182; self-giving, 184; and kataphatic theology, 186; priority of, over thought and language, 187; ineffable and inconceivable, 188; and anonymity, 200; as Requisite, 201; efficient, and the gift, 225; of thought and language beyond thought and language, 247. *See also* Origin; Source
Cerf, Walter, 24n
Certainty, or certitude: of truth, 33, 82; of unity with God, 37; feeling of, in religion, 41; self-, of spirit, 58, 61, 63; self-, of self-consciousness, 64; self-, of knowing subject through representation, 68–69; immediate, of Being, 106; of death, 140; high, in poor phenomenon, 210. *See also* Sense-certainty
Certeau, Michel de, 6
Chalcedonian formula, 173n, 184n
Chance, and the gift, 222
Charity, 10, 191, 194, 196n–97, 213, 220. *See also* Agape; Gift; Giving; Love
Cherniak, S., 81n
Cherubim, 10n, 166
Christ: and the Good, 10n, 198; and revelation, 29, 171; determination of God in, 32; religious and philosophical meaning of, in Hegel, 33–35; death of humanity in, 38; death of, 32, 37, 39, 47–48, 110n, 173; history of, 47; sensuous, 105, 111; and death in Dionysius, 160; and hierar-

Dispossession: and death, 140, 142; of beings in desire, 182–83; christological, 184, 225, 227; and ecstasy, 185, 188; and mystical theology, 189; mystical, of the subject, 192; linguistic, 199, 213, 225, 227; originary, of the *adonné*, 204–5, 208, 213; of soul in relation to God, 258. *See also* Ecstasy

Dissemination, and the gift, 224, 225

Dissimilarity, and similarity, 162

Dissolution, of self, 259. *See also* Dispossession

Distance: of divine Goodness, 174; and language of the unthinkable, 198; and revelation/concealment, 199; received in prayer, 200; and essence of language, 202; prayer responds to, 205; Trinitarian play of, 206; and Christ, 208; of the Father, 221

Distinction: of divine and human threatened, 37–38n; between Being and beings, 116; between presence and absence, 168–69; and salvation, 172; between revelation and Revelation, 209; between essence and existence, 215n; and identification, oscillation between, 255. *See also* Difference

Dividing, original, of the concept, 95

Divine, the: absence of, 3; and the human, 5; abstraction of, 24; reconciled with humanity, 34; as content of Jesus story, 45; in onto-theology, 53; in first philosophy, 54; as universal, 91; *kenosis* of, 100; and the nature of language, 110–11; and interplay with cosmos, 157; erotic movement of, 159; procession of, 161, 177; hierarchical approximation to, 162, 166; modes of visibility of, 194, 208; reduction of, 196; self-negation of, 241; transcendence of, 245. *See also* God

Divinity, of soul, 165n

Divinization, 162, 164, 165n, 186

Division: self-, 27, 29; of consciousness, 48

Dominations, 165

Donation: and absence, of God, 212; and debt, 220; act of, 221. *See also* Gift; Givenness; Giving

Donation, 191

Donee, 222–23

Donor, 221–23, 225

Double bind, 226

Doxa, 72–73, 216n

Dupré, Louis, 42

Eckhart, Meister, 5, 6, 8n, 16, 111n, 156, 258

Economy: and gift, 14, 214, 220, 249; of Being, disrupted, 192, 248; of the call, 206; and circle, 221; of time, 223; of knowing, experiencing, living, 227; circular, and Hegel, 249. *See also* Circle; Exchange; Return

Ecstases, of temporality, 15, 134, 148–50

Ecstasy: of the divine and of the creature, 159; and hierarchy, 160; of created being, 161; and generosity, 163, 167; and unity, 167, 169; and theological method, 175; creative, of God, 177; and erotic circle of the Good, 183; and dispossession, 185, 188; and postmodernism, 246n. *See also* Dispossession

Ecstatic: temporality of Dasein, 15, 148; thinkers, 246n

Effect, of nothing, gift event as, 225

Ego: autonomy of, 10; and onto-theology, 56; modern, Cartesian, 64; constituting, 210. *See also* "I"; Self; Subject

Ego cogito, 83

Egology or ego-logy, and ego-logical: and onto-theology, 56, 57, 73; and infinity, 63, 64; and theology, 81; and certainty, 82; and speculative proposition, 83. *See also* Subjectivity

Eikon tou theou aoratou, 199

Emanation, 164. *See also* Procession

Embodiment: of consciousness, 59–60; of subject in predicates, 85. *See also* Incarnation

Emptiness: of language, 245; and plenitude, God beyond, 259

End: of Dasein, 138, 152; Being at and toward, 139; and freedom for possibilities, 144; and nullity, 147; endless, of desire, 168, 187; limit without, 180; and source of desire, 182, 183; transcendent, of desire, 185; of metaphysics 23, 262

Endlessness, of desire, 251

Enigma, of Dasein's "there," 119, 125

Enlightenment, 169; the Enlightenment, 24, 30, 99n

Ens supremum, 194. *See also* being(s)

Entselbstung, 256. *See also* Dispossession

God (*continued*)

cause, 16; without truth, 16, 254; as concept, 27–30, 86; triune, 29, 161, 170; known as spirit, 31; consciousness of, 33; *kenosis* of, 34; and negation, 35; use of, by man, 38; in religion, 40; in form of representation, 41, 46; as particular *this*, 47; present for consciousness, 48; and ontotheology, 53–55; and absolute subjectivity, 56; and negation, 62, 88; as a being, 85, 243; life of, 90; meaning of, in proposition, 92; name of fulfilled, 93; as subject in judgment, 94; as absolute, 111, 242; as object of reason, 96; concept of, and representation, 100; nature of, in Being, 102; absence of, 158; beyond Being, 159, 192; manifestation and concealment of, 162, 175; reflection of, 163; approximation or likeness to, 166–67; longing or desire for, 168, 171; turn from, 172; without Being, 172n; immanence of, to creation, 174; as cause, 176; hidden 178; distinct and indistinct, 179; positive names of, 181; transcendent, as a being, 184; as love and beloved, 185; mystical unknowing of, 186, 189; impossibility of thinking, 191, 197; of charity, 193n; distinguished from "God," 194; as *causa sui*, 195; and Being, 196; without Being, 198n; ineffable, 200n; distance of, 205; as source of call, 207; unconditional appearance of, 211; defined phenomenologically as "being-given" par excellence, 211–12; of phenomenology and theology, 213; without conditions, 213; absence and unknowability of, 214; truth of, 216; nomination and determination of, 218; and mystical union, 230; ineffable, Being-toward, 231; knowledge of, by creature in Aquinas, 235; ineffable goodness of, 236; and plenitude, 246n; as cause beyond thought and language, 247; desire for, 251; soul's union with, 254; unknowing relation to, 255, 259; death as entrance into, 256; and anxiety, 257n; and Exodus, 258; relation to, as death 258; union with, and death, 259–60. *See also* Death of God; Divine; Naming of God

Good: beyond or before Being, 9–11, 17–18, 158, 191, 193–94, 198; ineffable and/or inconceivable, 19, 229; generosity and call of, 159, 229; and the Beautiful, 166n,

180, 182–85; and Ezekiel, 169; desire for, 181; and mystical dispossession and death, 189; and destruction of ontotheology, 194; given in distance, 198; self-diffusive, 212; beyond Goodness, 218. *See also* Charity; Generosity; Gift; Giving; Love

Goodness: 10, 11, 14, 158, 159; inconceivable and/or ineffable, 18, 236; divine, 163, 169, 177; beyond all things, 174, 179; transcendent, 180; beguiling, 184; Good beyond, 218; as form of the impossible, 239; and finitude, 260. *See also* Charity; Generosity; Gift; Giving; Love

Grammar, of consciousness, 88

Gratitude, circle of, 222

Gratuity, of the gift, 225

Gregory of Nyssa, 39n, 159n, 241, 251

Ground: of death of God, christological and trinitarian, 23; of Christianity, in spirit, 31; and onto-theology, 55; of beings, 57; of consciousness in self-consciousness, 59, 63, 65; of appearance in representational subjectivity, 71; of metaphysics, ambiguity of, 84; of predicate in subject, 102; negative, of metaphysics, 106n; of experience and consciousness, 109–10; Dasein's lack of, 119; temporal, of care, 146; call of beauty as, 181; supreme being as, 194; of God, Being as, 195–96; of significant experience, and death, 244; groundless, 259. *See also* Basis; Foundation

Groundlessness: of Dasein, 124; of idle talk, 129, 130, 131

Guattari, Felix, 246n

Guder, Darrel L., 23n

Guilt, 144, 147

Haas, Alois, 192n, 255–56, 258

Hardt, Michael, 106n

Harris, H. S., 24n

Hart, Kevin, 8

Having-been: and ecstases of temporality, 146, 150; and thrownness, 148; in Hegel and Heidegger, 149

Heckman, J., 81n

Hegel, Georg Wilhelm Friedrich, 3, 8n, 10–15, 19, 23–33, 36–40, 42–44, 46–59, 61–64, 66–71, 73, 75–83, 85–94, 97–102, 103n, 104–7, 110–11, 115, 121, 124–25, 135–37, 146, 148, 152, 157, 160, 240–41, 243–45, 247, 251–52, 260–62